ARISTOTLE'S POLITICS

ARISTOTLE'S

POLITICS

WRITINGS FROM THE
COMPLETE WORKS

POLITICS • ECONOMICS • CONSTITUTION OF ATHENS

Edited by

JONATHAN BARNES

with an introduction by

MELISSA LANE

PRINCETON UNIVERSITY PRESS

Princeton and Oxford

Copyright © 2016 by Princeton University Press
Introduction, copyright © 2016 by Melissa Lane
Published by Princeton University Press, 41 William
Street, Princeton, New Jersey 08540
In the United Kingdom: Princeton University Press,
6 Oxford Street, Woodstock, Oxfordshire OX20 1TR

press.princeton.edu

ISBN 978-0-691-17345-0

Library of Congress Control Number: 2016952247

British Library Cataloging-in-Publication Data is available

This book has been composed in MVB Verdigris Pro,
Lydian MT, and Syntax LT Std.

Printed on acid-free paper ∞

Printed in the United States of America

1 3 5 7 9 10 8 6 4 2

CONTENTS

INTRODUCTION

Melissa Lane

This volume presents the reader with Aristotle's *Politics*, one of the most fecund and profound works of ancient Greek political philosophy. Written, or perhaps compiled as lecture notes, in the fourth century BCE (Aristotle lived from 384 to 322), it offers an account of politics as oriented toward the fulfillment and flourishing of human nature while also surveying the landscape of actual and possible political institutions and the dynamics of political conflict. Its vision of political community as ethically valuable has soared into political philosophy, while its attention to the sordid side of politics has been likewise influential. The work is remarkable in being a source for both the idealism of Thomas Aquinas and the realism of Niccolò Machiavelli.

The *Politics* is anticipated at the end of one of Aristotle's great ethical treatises, the *Nicomachean Ethics*, insofar as for most humans to become good, they need to be brought up under good laws, which requires study of the science of legislation and of politics and constitutions more generally. This volume takes the story from politics to the specifics of constitutional history and practice in Athens and on to a further exploration of an Aristotelian perspective on economics. It does so by including two works—the *Economics* and the *Constitution of Athens*—that are standardly included and translated as part of Aristotle's corpus of works, as in the Revised Oxford Translation volume from which the translations here are taken. However, the authenticity of the ascription of these two works to Aristotle is today "seriously doubted" and often denied outright, in the case of the *Economics*,[1] and not

---

[1] The *Economics* is marked by a single asterisk in the table of contents of *The Complete Works of Aristotle: The Revised Oxford Translation*, edited by

universally accepted by scholars, in the case of the *Constitution of Athens*.[2] The *Economics* most likely dates, in part or as a whole, from after Aristotle's death[3] (and its various books were probably penned by one or more members of his Peripatetic school, so called from the scholars' habit of walking as they talked); the *Constitution of Athens* was most likely com-

---

Jonathan Barnes, vol. 2 (Princeton: Princeton University Press, 1984), and on the title page of the work. This symbol is explained in its "Note to the Reader," p. vii: "The traditional *corpus aristotelicum* contains several works which were certainly or probably not written by Aristotle. A single asterisk against the title of a work indicates that its authenticity has been seriously doubted; a pair of asterisks indicates that its spuriousness has never been seriously contested." In a major recent edition of the text, the editor comments that it is "certamente spurio" (certainly spurious). See Marcello Valente, "Introduction," to [Aristotele], *Economici*, edited with introduction, revised text, translation and commentary by Marcello Valente (Alessandria: Edizioni dell'Orso, 2011), pp. 5–38, at p. 5.

[2] While the *Constitution of Athens* is not marked by any asterisk or pair of asterisks in *The Complete Works of Aristotle: The Revised Oxford Translation*, scholars disagree about whether it should be considered to have been written by Aristotle himself or by members of his Lyceum, perhaps under his direction. The author of the principal commentary on the work, P. J. Rhodes, concludes his introduction to that commentary thus: "On the evidence which we have, Aristotle could have written this work himself, but I do not believe he did. That does not diminish the interest and importance of [*Constitution of Athens*]." See P. J. Rhodes, "Introduction," in P. J. Rhodes, *A Commentary on the Aristotelian Athenaion Politeia* (Oxford: Clarendon Press, 1981), pp. 1–63, at p. 63. Some other studies of the work, however, defend it as authentic; see for example, John J. Keaney, *The Composition of Aristotle's Athenaion Politeia: Observation and Explanation* (New York: Oxford University Press, 1992).

[3] One attribution of the *Economics* in antiquity was to Aristotle's student Theophrastus. Many scholars, including Valente, *Economici*, consider its books likely to have been composed, perhaps by different authors, in the late fourth century or early third century BCE, though debate continues about the exact dating, especially of Book II. For example, a major edition of Book II in 1933 dated that book to 325–300 BCE, with its discussion of royal and satrapal economies referring to the Achaemenid Empire. See B. A. van Groningen, ed., *Le second livre de l'Économique* (Leiden: Société d'éditions A. W. Sijthoff, 1933). In contrast, one recent scholar has argued for a date of c.275 BCE for Book II, referring instead to the Seleucid Empire. See G. G. Aperghis, *The Seleukid Royal Economy: The Finances and Financial Administration of the Seleukid Empire* (Cambridge: Cambridge University Press, 2004), p. 175.

piled by a member or members of the Lyceum overseen by Aristotle, if not written by him.

In their close connections to Aristotle's circle in his lifetime and after his death, these two works help us respectively to understand important implications and extensions of his thought about politics for the management of households and estates—a topic introduced in Book I of the *Politics* and in the *Economics*—as well as the analysis of constitutional change and institutions, treated especially in Books IV–VI of the *Politics* and exhibited in the *Constitution of Athens*. The *Economics* (its second book in particular) extends the geographical and chronological range of the volume, for, unlike Aristotle's *Politics*, it does not focus its discussion of political forms on the Greek type of state known as the *polis*—the distinctive Greek political unit, composed of a single urban center surrounded by an agricultural hinterland, generally animated by a shared communal identity. Instead it reaches out beyond the *polis* to consider also the economic management of royal domains and satrapal provinces associated with some of the great empires that would consolidate their domination of the Greek world in the years following Aristotle's death—for he died less than a year after his erstwhile pupil Alexander the Great, whose empire was then carved up among his generals.

POLITICS

The *Politics* is advertised at the end of the *Nicomachean Ethics* as a necessary turn to "study the question of the constitution, in order to complete to the best of our ability the philosophy of human nature" (*EN* X.9, 1181b14–15). Indeed Aristotle there sets out a fuller program for the discussion that is needed to inform would-be legislators. It is to include a "review" of what previous thinkers on the subject have said well (done in Book II of the *Politics*); a study of "what sorts of influence preserve and destroy states, and what sorts preserve or destroy the particular kinds of constitution, and to what causes it is due that some are well and others ill administered" (done primarily in Books IV–VI of the *Politics*); and, building on these, seeing "which constitution is best, and how each must be ordered, and what laws and customs it must use" (done primarily in Books VII and VIII of the *Politics*, returning to an earlier question of "what form of government . . . is best suited to states in general," as opposed to "what is possible and what is easily attainable by all" [IV.1, 1288b33–39]).

This three-part program is undergirded, especially in Books I and III of the *Politics*, by an analysis of the nature of politics, the political community, humans as political animals, being a citizen, and a constitution. These books are perhaps the most original and influential of the whole work. Because they also provide relevant background for the other texts included in this volume (the *Economics* and *Constitution of Athens*, respectively), a selective overview of their arguments will serve here as an orientation to the *Politics* as a whole.

Book I begins by defining a *polis* as a kind of community or *koinonia*, a shared and mutually dependent way of life. Indeed the *polis* is defined as the highest kind of community, embracing all others, and as coming into being for the sake of mere life (physical survival) but maintaining its existence for the sake of the good life. The good here is to be understood as the happiness that consists principally or exclusively, depending on how Aristotle's ethical works are understood, in the actualization of one's rational capacities, both practical and theoretical. Humans are not the only "political" animals (ants, bees, and cranes are among those also considered "political" by Aristotle), but we are more so, by virtue of being the only ones endowed with the power of speech. Speech and the reasoning that it facilitates allow us not only to vocally signify pleasure or pain but also to articulate what is expedient and inexpedient, just and unjust.

Yet while humans naturally have the capacity and indeed the need to live in a political community, being not individually self-sufficient, this does not mean that we will always do so or that we will always act justly toward one another. Indeed, shortly after making his famous declaration that "it is evident that the state is a creation of nature, and that man

is by nature a political animal" (I.2, 1253a1–3), Aristotle ac-
knowledges that some men will choose to pursue "armed injustice" against one another (I.2, 1253a33–34). This is because
the capacity to make evaluative judgments about ethics and
politics does not ensure that this capacity will be exercised
correctly. We pursue what we judge to be expedient or just,
not necessarily what actually is so. Hence our political actions
are likely to differ profoundly, and sometimes violently, from
those of others, whether because our judgments are simply
mistaken, shaded by different upbringing and customs, or
systematically distorted by individual or group interests (all
mechanisms of disagreement that the *Politics* explores). Such
diverse perceptions, judgments, and orientations are among
the sources of the dizzying multiplicity of political forms that
arise on Aristotle's account notwithstanding his claim that
humans are political animals. Indeed they arise precisely because of what that claim means when properly understood.

At the beginning of Book III of the *Politics*, Aristotle ac-
knowledges just this diversity in making the very definition
of a citizen relative to a specific kind of state—for "[h]e who
is a citizen in a democracy will often not be a citizen in an oligarchy" (III.1, 1275a3–5). This example would have been especially significant for his contemporaries, for Greece in the
century or so before Aristotle wrote had been marked by an
ongoing struggle between emergent democracies, embodied
and led for most of the period by Athens (where Aristotle
studied and later taught, but of which he was never a citizen),
and oligarchies in which a relatively small and wealthy elite
group ruled and sometimes exploited a much larger group
of poorer people, embodied and led during the fifth-century
Peloponnesian War by Sparta. (At the same time, the Greeks
were contending with monarchies and tyrannies of various
kinds, both within Greece and in neighboring societies such
as Persia.) Each of these different political forms is a constitution or form of government, in Greek a *politeia*, a word
that can refer not just to a narrow set of legal rules but to the
whole set of practices that define the distinctive nature of a
given society.

For a constitution to be well ordered, it must both aim at the common good and also treat equal citizens equally—a citizen being understood as someone in a given constitution who is eligible to hold a magistracy or office. Aristotle identifies six principal kinds of constitutions. Three are good forms, in which the rulers aim at the common good of all the citizens: kingship, or the (good) rule of one; aristocracy, or the (good) rule of a few; and what Aristotle calls simply "constitution" or "constitutional government" to signify the (good) rule of the many. To each of these there corresponds a perverted counterpart, a form of government in which the ruling individual or group aims at their own good rather than the good of the whole: tyranny, oligarchy, and democracy (a word that Aristotle chooses to reserve here for the flawed constitutional form).

Unlike in the household, where natural capacities to rule and be ruled are (according to Aristotle) distributed in such a way as to enshrine ongoing hierarchical inequality, in the political domain, citizens who are equals are not naturally suited to be permanently ruled by others, nor is any one of them naturally suited permanently to rule. Kingship, on this account, would be suitable only where one person was in fact so superlative in excellence as to be uniquely suited to permanent rule. As this suggests, the question of who is to be counted as an equal is in practice one of the most central, and controversial, questions that any regime must confront. Are the common people to be counted as equals to the elite, as in polities and democracies, or are the elite able to insist that only those wealthy enough should count as full citizens who are eligible for office, as in the case of oligarchies? In Books IV–VI of the *Politics*, Aristotle details the rival understandings of equality, and therefore of justice, that partisans of oligarchy and democracy develop, and that animate both their own distribution of offices and their hostility toward one another. By contrast, the best constitution generally speaking, when Aristotle turns to discuss it in Books VII and VIII, will be one in which all citizens are equal in moral excellence or virtue and in their capacity to act as citizens.

THE *OIKOS* AND THE *POLIS*: BOOK I OF THE *POLITICS* AS THE BASIS FOR THE *ECONOMICS*

We must return now to another part of Book I of the *Politics*: its discussion of the origin of the *polis*, both chronologically and functionally, in the household, or *oikos*. The origin of the *polis* is in primordial relationships, the simplest forms of community, that meet two specific kinds of particular and reciprocal needs: the need that male and female have for each other in reproduction, and the need of what Aristotle calls "natural ruler and subject" for each other, "that both may be preserved" (I.2, 1252a30–31). Notice that, in Aristotle's view, each of these is rooted in nature (*phusis*), meaning the natural potential for growth and actualization of capacities belonging to a being, primarily by virtue of its belonging to a certain kind. Aristotle writes in Book III that "a state is not a mere society, having a common place, established for the prevention of mutual crime and for the sake of exchange"; rather, "to choose to live together is friendship," so that both the primordial relationships and the common life of the *polis* as a whole serve the end of the good life or living well (III.9, 1280b29–31, 1280b38–39). This remains the case even when that common life is structured according to principles of hierarchy that stem from differences in the developed natures of its members.

Natural ruler and natural subject are, according to Aristotle, found in principle in three sets of relationships within the household. He claims that a man with fully developed rational capacity is naturally able and suited to rule a woman whose rational faculty is less steady, a child whose rational faculty is undeveloped, and a slave whose rational faculty is stunted so as to be able only to serve as an instrument for the master's pursuit of the good life, not to determine or pursue virtuous ends alone. It should be noted that all these claims evince some tensions in Aristotle's own writing, such as whether these various fulfillments and limits in rational faculties are either internally consistent or typically manifested. It should also be noted that Aristotle's account of natural slavery was both unique in antiquity (so far as we know) and essentially irrelevant to the practices of Greek slavery at the time, which for the most part were viewed as originating simply in victory in war. Nevertheless, his claims about the value of subordination of those who are natural slaves, and of women to men, would have powerfully damaging effects in justifying many institutions and practices of domination in later centuries, for example in the early modern Spanish conquest of the Americas and in the rationalizations offered for slavery in the nineteenth-century United States.

ECONOMICS

To govern the household consisting of the relationships outlined here, together with the property needed to support them, is a skill, a form of knowledge or expertise named *oikonomia* or *oikonomikē*. In Book I of the *Politics*, Aristotle is emphatic that the expertise of governing an *oikos* is not the same as the expertise of governing a *polis* (contrary to the approach taken in Plato's *Statesman*, where the expertise possessed by the statesman, king, slavemaster, and household manager is said to be one and the same). He offers a discussion of the expertise of governing a household. This discussion famously distinguishes between the proper or natural aim of achieving a limited supply of money and property necessary to live the good life, and the unleashing of the arts of wealth-getting through commerce, usury, service, and exchange in an unlimited way that confuses money and property as means to the good life with their being ends in themselves.

Because for Aristotle *oikonomia* denotes the governance of the *oikos* for the sake of the good life, translations of it as "economics," while widespread, are potentially misleading. Modern "economics" is generally viewed as an autonomous science that includes the "economic" interactions of both households and whole societies and indeed the international order. By contrast, scholars continue to debate whether Aristotle's interests in the *Politics* (and in related discussions of money, wealth, and exchange in *Nicomachean Ethics* V.5) are so oriented by his ethical concerns that they cannot even be called properly "economic" in a modern sense.[4] And this debate is closely related to another, about whether the classical Greek economy itself can be considered "an economy" with recognizably modern institutions and dynamics based on prices, trade, and money, or whether the relevant classical Greek practices were so embedded in broader social practices that no autonomous economic analysis could make sense of them.[5]

Without seeking to resolve these controversies here, one way to approach just what Aristotle was doing in Book I of the *Politics*, and just what the anonymous Peripatetic author(s) of the *Economics* were doing in their turn, is to consider what it meant for Greeks at the time to compose works focusing on *oikonomia*. It has been noted that such works, known as *logoi oikonomikoi*, became an established fourth-century literary genre, generally accompanied by writings on marriage, an indication of their *oikos*-centered focus.[6] The "earliest extant Greek didactic work" to focus on the *oikos* is Xenophon's *Oikonomos*.[7] (In this Introduction, his work will be referred to by its common Latin title *Oeconomicus*, while the English title *Economics* is reserved here for the relevant pseudo-Aristotelian work that appears in the present volume.)

Xenophon's *Oeconomicus* clearly serves as a source and model for Books I and III of the *Economics*, even though the two works diverge in some important respects. In style, Xenophon uses the Socratic dialogue form, while the *Economics* does not. In substance, Xenophon argues that husband and

---

[4] For a useful overview that takes a distinct but intermediate position, see Scott Meikle, *Aristotle's Economic Thought* (Oxford: Clarendon Press, 1995).

[5] The debate pits "primitivists," such as Moses Finley and Karl Polanyi, against "modernists," such as Michael Rostovtzeff.

[6] Basileios A. Kyrkos and Christos P. Baloglou, eds., *[Aristotle's] Oikonomika* (Athēna: Hērodotos, 2013), p. 295.

[7] Sarah B. Pomeroy, *Xenophon, Oeconomicus: A Social and Historical Commentary, with a New English Translation* (Oxford: Clarendon Press, 1994), p. 41.

wife should equally govern children, for example, versus the gender hierarchy that the *Economics* posits as natural. But in understanding *oikonomia* to be focused on the increase of wealth without any limits, the *Economics* is much closer to Xenophon in treating the four functions of acquiring, guarding, ordering, and using wealth on a par than it is to Aristotle's insistence on natural limits to the acquisition of wealth in Book I of the *Politics*.

In contrast to the clear fourth-century BCE genre that can be established as background for Books I and III of the *Economics*, its Book II is sui generis (a point sometimes invoked in claims that it may have had a different author), for rather than contrasting the governing of an *oikos* with governing of a *polis* as do both Xenophon and Aristotle, Book II of the *Economics* extends the idea of *oikonomia* to include four kinds: of the royal domain, the gubernatorial domain (that of an imperial province), the *polis*, and the individual. This extends the idea of household management to the idea of the administration of the finances of a city more generally (an idea, it has been noted, for which there is some fourth-century BCE precedent, in a speech by the Athenian orator Dinarchus criticizing his rival Demosthenes for his uselessness in managing *oikonomia* involved in the city).[8]

Book II then goes on to a collection of notable historical stratagems for acquiring money, for the most part in the context of governing or administering a political community. Some involve self-denial, as in the case of the Lacedaemonians (Spartans) choosing to fast for a day in order to save money to give to the Samians for safe passage home after a war. Others involve clever ruses for exploitation, such as Timotheus the Athenian's decision to sell to the Samians he was besieging the very produce of their own lands, or Memnon the Rhodian's exploitation of his power in Lampsacus by first exacting tribute from the wealthy and then commandeering a forced loan of the very proceeds from the poor that the wealthy had collected to cover the original tribute. These

---

[8] Din. *In Dem.* [I] 96–97, a reference cited in Valente, *Economici*, p. 6.

stratagems often involve ruses, ranging from those practiced by a people or *demos* to those by tyrants, governors, or satraps. Most of the measures described are ad hoc ways for a ruler, or a people as a whole, to get hold of money or resources in times of immediate need. While some involve the establishment of institutions (such as a tax assessment by the Athenians in Potidaea), virtually none involve what we today would consider public macroeconomic interventions. "Economics" in Book II is not macroeconomic policy but rather, as befits the name, the clever management of a royal or public domain, or use of royal or public powers, for short-term financial gain. It treats the science of *oikonomia* as applying directly to political domains—a further indication that the work is not authentically by Aristotle, given that Book I of the *Politics* begins by denying that the forms of rule of statesman, king, householder, and master are the same.

CONSTITUTION OF ATHENS

Just as Aristotle's views about the naturalness of slavery did not blind him to the fact that many who were in fact legally enslaved should not have been so according to his theory, his views about the naturalness of the political life did not lead him to suppose that all human beings do in fact choose, or have the opportunity to choose, to live such a life. The *Politics* is as interested in tyrannies, which are perverted political orders (or, strictly, nonorders), and in the clashes between democrats and oligarchs, each of whom have in Aristotle's view a perverted understanding of the values of equality and justice that politics should instantiate, as it is in defining the kind of *polis* that one would wish and pray to live in. While "democracy" is used by Aristotle as the name of an inherently flawed regime, it commands considerable attention throughout the *Politics* as the constitution of Athens for most of its recent political history (and as a widespread form of constitution elsewhere in the Greek world in the fifth and fourth centuries BCE as well). And so one would expect that in the "collection of constitutions" that the *Nicomachean Ethics* mentions having been assembled as a source for the *Politics*—in which there were said in antiquity to be 158 individual constitutions (Diogenes Laertius V.27)—Athens would feature significantly.

And indeed the *Constitution of Athens* preserved in the Aristotelian corpus is a remarkable text, as much because of its textual history as because of the intrinsic interest of its subject matter for modern readers—for while fragments and ancient citations of many of the 158 constitutions survive, only that of Athens has been preserved in extensive (if still incomplete) textual form, recovered from two papyri in the late nineteenth century. It is difficult to know how typical this "constitution" may have been compared to the others in the collection, given the exceptionally extensive nature of the documentation of Athenian law and politics that existed even in antiquity. Nor was the Aristotelian collection of constitutions unique in being dubbed *"Constitution of [X]"* (where X is the people of a *polis*; the title here translated as *Constitution of Athens* is literally in Greek *Constitution of the Athenians*). Once again, Xenophon offers us useful points of comparison, in that he wrote a *Constitution of the Spartans* (discussions of the Spartan constitution having generally predated those of the constitutions of other cities), and in his corpus there is also preserved a *Constitution of the Athenians* that is now believed to have been written, probably in the late fifth century BCE, by an unknown author sometimes referred to as the Old Oligarch.[9] (While the titles of the ps.-Xenophontic and of the (pseudo?)-Aristotelian accounts of the constitution of the Athenians are identical in Greek, this Introduction distinguishes between them in English by using *Constitution of the Athenians* for the pseudo-Xenophontic work, while reserving *Constitution of Athens* for the Aristotelian or pseudo-Aristotelian work contained

---

[9]An accessible edition, with a helpful introduction to the questions of dating and authorship, is Robin Osborne, ed., *The Old Oligarch: Pseudo-Xenophon's Constitution of Athens* (London: London Association of Classical Teachers, 2004).

in the present volume.) These works serve as a useful context to pinpoint what is expected, and distinctive, in the Aristotelian text included in this volume.

Xenophon's *Constitution of the Spartans* was likely to have been fairly typical of the general classical Greek genre of "constitution of" works. While it discusses the Spartans' political institutions, it dwells far more on their customary practices, in particular their distinctive ways of organizing the activities of women, marriage, and the education of children, as all shaped to contribute to the austere military prowess needed to subordinate the helot serfs who provided the Spartan citizens with subsistence. By contrast, the *Constitution of the Athenians* found in Xenophon's corpus is a very different, and unusual, kind of work. It takes up a distinctive, argumentative point of view, that of a self-identified Athenian who is hostile to the contemporaneous democratic Athenian constitution for its assertion of popular power over the more wealthy and educated (and so, he takes it, worthier) elite, but who nevertheless devotes himself to explaining the mechanisms by which the Athenian poor majority successfully maintain their hegemony within the constitution.

In contrast to the explicitly partisan perspective adopted by pseudo-Xenophon in his *Constitution of the Athenians*, the Aristotelian *Constitution of Athens* in the present volume—whether written by Aristotle himself or by his students under his supervision—adopts a primarily analytical and historical approach (which is not to say that it betrays no political sympathies). Its account is summed up in the delineation of eleven distinct "constitutions" in that history, the institutions of the last of which (that current at the time of writing) are then described in depth. The innovations by Draco and Solon; the complex nature of the Pisistratid "tyranny," and its overthrow by a popular revolution giving legislative power to Cleisthenes to reorganize the tribes and demes, making the constitution "much more democratic"; the roles of Pericles and Ephialtes in redefining citizenship by birth and curtailing the traditional powers of the aristocratic Council of the Areopagus; the two attempted oligarchical coups that punctuated

Athens' waning fortunes during the Peloponnesian War with Sparta in 411 BCE and then its devastating loss in 404; the successful popular resistance to the Thirty who had led the most brutal of those coups and the eventual pioneering amnesty established by the restored democracy; and the bevy of complicated procedures for the offices of the "constitution of the present day" (including some chosen by election, some by lottery, many boards of collective responsibility, restrictions on repeating in office, procedures for scrutiny and accountability, and the complex voting procedures in the popular jury courts) all give a reader perhaps the best orientation to ancient Athenian politics and especially Athenian democracy one could hope to find.

This is to say that the *Constitution of Athens* furnishes much of its own historical context; it has been an enormously important historical source even where, and often because, it contradicts other ancient evidence. Indeed, on certain points of detail, it contradicts the *Politics*, something with which modern historians have coped in various ways (either by positing a sequence between the texts or sometimes by using this to support the claim that Aristotle could not have been the author). Yet other aspects of its composition seem to be Aristotelian in a deeper sense. One of the most interesting is its willingness to characterize as "democratic" constitutional reforms that took place long before the events generally taken by modern historians to have established democracy proper. Whereas the earliest Athenian constitutions are said to have given the people "no share in anything" (*AP* 2), the sixth-century lawgiver Solon is credited with having given the common people a share in the assembly and the juries, though no eligibility for holding the offices proper. The author does not hesitate to call that role of the people in the juries, together with the abolition of debts secured on a person's bodily services and the introduction of a right of prosecution on anyone's behalf, the "most democratic features" of Solon's constitution (*AP* 9). Doing so would seem anachronistic to a modern historian. Yet it fits into a typically Aristotelian teleological explanation of something's development in terms of its ultimate end or realization. In this sense, many aspects of the basic orientation of the *Constitution of Athens* are imbued with an Aristotelian approach and show us Aristotle's political theory put in motion to explain the history of Athens, whether or not the text was written by Aristotle himself.

Two of the most fundamental aspects of Aristotle's *Politics* are its treatment of the *oikos* as a building block of the *polis* and its analysis of constitutions as fundamental to the study of politics. The latter project is complemented by the *Constitution of Athens*, which brings its analysis to life in the vicissitudes of Athenian history, while the former is extended in the *Economics* both in terms of the *oikos* itself and in a novel extension of *oikonomia* to political domains both within and outside the *polis*. The texts collected in this volume can help to illuminate one another and to corroborate what this Introduction began by calling the extraordinary fecundity and profundity of Aristotle's *Politics*.[10]

NOTE ON THE TEXT

This note has been adapted in large part from notes in *The Complete Works of Aristotle*, edited by Jonathan Barnes (Princeton University Press, 1984), repeating those notes verbatim where relevant.

The texts contained in this volume are taken from the translations contained in *The Complete Works of Aristotle* published by Princeton University Press in 1984, which was in turn a revision, by Jonathan Barnes, of the eleven volumes of the Oxford Translation of Aristotle, which had been published between 1908 and 1954. The Oxford Translation was undertaken under the auspices of the Jowett Copyright Trustees, a body set up under the will of Benjamin Jowett, Master

[10] The research assistance for this Introduction provided by Emily Hulme and René de Nicolay, and funded by Princeton University, is gratefully acknowledged.

of Balliol College, Oxford, from 1870 to 1893. The original Oxford translation of the *Politics* was by Benjamin Jowett and for the 1984 edition was checked against the Greek text edited by A. Dreizehnter, published in Munich in 1970. The original Oxford translation of the *Economics* was by E. S. Forster; because the original Oxford translation did not include Book III of the *Economics*, the text of which is known only from Latin manuscripts rather than from any original Greek source, the 1984 edition, as here, included a translation of that book reprinted by permission of The Loeb Classical Library (William Heinemann and Harvard University Press). The Greek text used for checking the 1984 edition of the *Economics* was that by B. A. van Groningen and A. Wartelle, published in the Collection Budé series in Paris in 1968. The original Oxford translation of the *Constitution of Athens* was by F. G. Kenyon from the Greek text edited by Kenyon, published in the Oxford Classical Texts series in 1920, the same text used to check the 1984 edition. The Bollingen Foundation and the Benjamin Jowett Trust made the present paperback edition possible through their permission and support.

The numerals printed in the outer margins key the translation to Immanuel Bekker's standard edition of the Greek text of Aristotle of 1831. References consist of a page number, a column letter, and a line number. Thus "1343ᵃ" marks column one of page 1343 of Bekker's edition; and the following "5," "10," "15," etc., stand against lines 5, 10, 15, etc., of that column of text. Bekker references of this type are found in most editions of Aristotle's works, and they are used by all scholars who write about Aristotle (usually citing those in the Greek text, as is the case with the references given in the Introduction to this volume). The assistance of Merrick Anderson in checking the placement of the Bekker references in the present edition is gratefully acknowledged.

ARISTOTLE'S POLITICS

POLITICS

B. Jowett

BOOK I

1 • EVERY STATE IS A COMMUNITY OF SOME KIND, and every 1252ª1 community is established with a view to some good; for everyone always acts in order to obtain that which they think good. But, if all communities aim at some good, the state or political community, which is the highest of all, and which embraces all the rest, aims at good in a greater degree than any other, and at the highest good.

Some people think that the qualifications of a statesman, king, householder, and master are the same, and that they differ, not in kind, but only in the number of their subjects. For example, the ruler over a few is called a master; over more, the manager of a household; over a still larger number, a statesman or king, as if there were no difference between a great household and a small state. The distinction which is made between the king and the statesman is as follows: When the government is personal, the ruler is a king; when, according to the rules of the political science, the citizens rule and are ruled in turn, then he is called a statesman.

But all this is a mistake, as will be evident to any one who considers the matter according to the method which has hitherto guided us. As in other departments of science, so in politics, the compound should always be resolved into the simple elements or least parts of the whole. We must therefore look at the elements of which the state is composed, in order that we may see in what the different kinds of rule differ from one another, and whether any scientific result can be attained about each one of them.

TEXT: A. Dreizehnter, Munich, 1970

2 • He who thus considers things in their first growth and origin, whether a state or anything else, will obtain the clearest view of them. In the first place there must be a union of those who cannot exist without each other; namely, of male and female, that the race may continue (and this is a union which is formed, not of choice, but because, in common with other animals and with plants, mankind have a natural desire to leave behind them an image of themselves), and of natural ruler and subject, that both may be preserved. For that which can foresee by the exercise of mind is by nature lord and master, and that which can with its body give effect to such foresight is a subject, and by nature a slave; hence master and slave have the same interest. Now nature has distinguished between the female and the slave. For she is not niggardly, like the smith who fashions the Delphian knife for many uses; she makes each thing for a single use, and every instrument is best made when intended for one and not for many uses. But among barbarians no distinction is made between women and slaves, because there is no natural ruler among them: they are a community of slaves, male and female. That is why the poets say,—

It is meet that Hellenes should rule over barbarians;

as if they thought that the barbarian and the slave were by nature one.

Out of these two relationships the first thing to arise is the family, and Hesiod is right when he says,—

First house and wife and an ox for the plough,

for the ox is the poor man's slave. The family is the association established by nature for the supply of men's everyday wants, and the members of it are called by Charondas, 'companions of the cupboard', and by Epimenides the Cretan, 'companions of the manger'. But when several families are united, and the association aims at something more than the supply of daily needs, the first society to be formed is the village. And the most natural form of the village appears to be that of a colony from the family, composed of the children and grandchildren, who are said to be 'suckled with the same milk'. And this is the reason why Hellenic states were originally governed by kings; because the Hellenes were under royal rule before they came together, as the barbarians still are. Every family is ruled by the eldest, and therefore in the colonies of the family the kingly form of government prevailed because they were of the same blood. As Homer says:

> Each one gives law to his children and to his wives.

For they lived dispersedly, as was the manner in ancient times. That is why men say that the Gods have a king, because they themselves either are or were in ancient times under the rule of a king. For they imagine not only the forms of the Gods but their ways of life to be like their own.

When several villages are united in a single complete community, large enough to be nearly or quite self-sufficing, the state comes into existence, originating in the bare needs of life, and continuing in existence for the sake of a good life. And therefore, if the earlier forms of society are natural, so is the state, for it is the end of them, and the nature of a thing is its end. For what each thing is when fully developed, we call its nature, whether we are speaking of a man, a horse, or a family. Besides, the final cause and end of a thing is the best, and to be self-sufficing is the end and the best.

Hence it is evident that the state is a creation of nature, and that man is by nature a political animal. And he who by nature and not by mere accident is without a state, is either a bad man or above humanity; he is like the

> Tribeless, lawless, heartless one,

whom Homer denounces—the natural outcast is forthwith a lover of war; he may be compared to an isolated piece at draughts.

Now, that man is more of a political animal than bees or any other gregarious animals is evident. Nature, as we often say, makes nothing in vain, and man is the only animal who has the gift of speech. And whereas mere voice is but an indication

of pleasure or pain, and is therefore found in other animals (for their nature attains to the perception of pleasure and pain and the intimation of them to one another, and no further), the power of speech is intended to set forth the expe-
15 dient and inexpedient, and therefore likewise the just and the unjust. And it is a characteristic of man that he alone has any sense of good and evil, of just and unjust, and the like, and the association of living beings who have this sense makes a family and a state.

Further, the state is by nature clearly prior to the family
20 and to the individual, since the whole is of necessity prior to the part; for example, if the whole body be destroyed, there will be no foot or hand, except homonymously, as we might speak of a stone hand; for when destroyed the hand will be no better than that. But things are defined by their function and power; and we ought not to say that they are the same when they no longer have their proper quality, but only that they
25 are homonymous. The proof that the state is a creation of nature and prior to the individual is that the individual, when isolated, is not self-sufficing; and therefore he is like a part in relation to the whole. But he who is unable to live in society, or who has no need because he is sufficient for himself, must be either a beast or a god: he is no part of a state. A social in-
30 stinct is implanted in all men by nature, and yet he who first founded the state was the greatest of benefactors. For man, when perfected, is the best of animals, but, when separated from law and justice, he is the worst of all; since armed injustice is the more dangerous, and he is equipped at birth with arms, meant to be used by intelligence and excellence, which
35 he may use for the worst ends. That is why, if he has not excellence, he is the most unholy and the most savage of animals, and the most full of lust and gluttony. But justice is the bond of men in states; for the administration of justice, which is the determination of what is just, is the principle of order in political society.

1253ᵇ1   3 • Seeing then that the state is made up of households, before speaking of the state we must speak of the management of the household. The parts of household management correspond to the persons who compose the household, and a complete household consists of slaves and freemen. Now we should begin by examining everything in its fewest possible elements; and the first and fewest possible parts of a family are master and slave, husband and wife, father and children. We have therefore to consider what each of these three relations is and ought to be:—I mean the relation of master and servant, the marriage relation (the conjunction of man and wife has no name of its own), and thirdly, the paternal relation (this also has no proper name). And there is another element of a household, the so-called art of getting wealth, which, according to some, is identical with household management, according to others, a principal part of it; the nature of this art will also have to be considered by us.

Let us first speak of master and slave, looking to the needs of practical life and also seeking to attain some better theory of their relation than exists at present. For some are of the opinion that the rule of a master is a science, and that the management of a household, and the mastership of slaves, and the political and royal rule, as I was saying at the outset, are all the same. Others affirm that the rule of a master over slaves is contrary to nature, and that the distinction between slave and freeman exists by convention only, and not by nature; and being an interference with nature is therefore unjust.

4 · Property is a part of the household, and the art of acquiring property is a part of the art of managing the household; for no man can live well, or indeed live at all, unless he is provided with necessaries. And as in the arts which have a definite sphere the workers must have their own proper instruments for the accomplishment of their work, so it is in the management of a household. Now instruments are of various sorts; some are living, others lifeless; in the rudder, the pilot of a ship has a lifeless, in the look-out man, a living instrument; for in the arts the servant is a kind of instrument. Thus, too, a possession is an instrument for maintaining life.

And so, in the arrangement of the family, a slave is a living possession, and property a number of such instruments; and the servant is himself an instrument for instruments. For if every instrument could accomplish its own work, obeying or anticipating the will of others, like the statues of Daedalus, or the tripods of Hephaestus, which, says the poet,

> of their own accord entered the assembly of the Gods;

if, in like manner, the shuttle would weave and the plectrum touch the lyre, chief workmen would not want servants, nor masters slaves. Now the instruments commonly so called are instruments of production, whilst a possession is an instrument of action. From a shuttle we get something else besides the use of it, whereas of a garment or of a bed there is only the use. Further, as production and action are different in kind, and both require instruments, the instruments which they employ must likewise differ in kind. But life is action and not production, and therefore the slave is the minister of action. Again, a possession is spoken of as a part is spoken of; for the part is not only a part of something else, but wholly belongs to it; and this is also true of a possession. The master is only the master of the slave; he does not belong to him, whereas the slave is not only the slave of his master, but wholly belongs to him. Hence we see what is the nature and office of a slave; he who is by nature not his own but another's man, is by nature a slave; and he may be said to be another's man who, being a slave, is also a possession. And a possession may be defined as an instrument of action, separable from the possessor.

5 • But is there any one thus intended by nature to be a slave, and for whom such a condition is expedient and right, or rather is not all slavery a violation of nature?

There is no difficulty in answering this question, on grounds both of reason and of fact. For that some should rule and others be ruled is a thing not only necessary, but expedient; from the hour of their birth, some are marked out for subjection, others for rule.

And there are many kinds both of rulers and subjects (and that rule is the better which is exercised over better subjects—for example, to rule over men is better than to rule over wild beasts; for the work is better which is executed by better workmen, and where one man rules and another is ruled, they may be said to have a work); for in all things which form a composite whole and which are made up of parts, whether continuous or discrete, a distinction between the ruling and the subject element comes to light. Such a duality exists in living creatures, originating from nature as a whole; even in things which have no life there is a ruling principle, as in a musical mode. But perhaps this is matter for a more popular investigation. A living creature consists in the first place of soul and body, and of these two, the one is by nature the ruler and the other the subject. But then we must look for the intentions of nature in things which retain their nature, and not in things which are corrupted. And therefore we must study the man who is in the most perfect state both of body and soul, for in him we shall see the true relation of the two; although in bad or corrupted natures the body will often appear to rule over the soul, because they are in an evil and unnatural condition. At all events we may firstly observe in living creatures both a despotical and a constitutional rule; for the soul rules the body with a despotical rule, whereas the intellect rules the appetites with a constitutional and royal rule. And it is clear that the rule of the soul over the body, and of the mind and the rational element over the passionate, is natural and expedient; whereas the equality of the two or the rule of the inferior is always hurtful. The same holds good of animals in relation to men; for tame animals have a better nature than wild and all tame animals are better off when they are ruled by man; for then they are preserved. Again, the male is by nature superior, and the female inferior; and the one rules, and the other is ruled; this principle, of necessity, extends to all mankind. Where then there is such a difference as that between soul and body, or between men and animals (as in the case of those whose business is to use their body, and who can do nothing better), the

25

30

35

1254^{b}1

5

10

15

lower sort are by nature slaves, and it is better for them as for all inferiors that they should be under the rule of a master. For he who can be, and therefore is, another's, and he who participates in reason enough to apprehend, but not to have, is a slave by nature. Whereas the lower animals cannot even apprehend reason;[1] they obey their passions. And indeed the use made of slaves and of tame animals is not very different; for both with their bodies minister to the needs of life. Nature would like to distinguish between the bodies of freemen and slaves, making the one strong for servile labour, the other upright, and although useless for such services, useful for political life in the arts both of war and peace. But the opposite often happens—that some have the souls and others have the bodies of freemen. And doubtless if men differed from one another in the mere forms of their bodies as much as the statues of the Gods do from men, all would acknowledge that the inferior class should be slaves of the superior. And if this is true of the body, how much more just that a similar distinction should exist in the soul? But the beauty of the body is seen, whereas the beauty of the soul is not seen. It is clear, then, that some men are by nature free, and others slaves, and that for these latter slavery is both expedient and right.

6 • But that those who take the opposite view have in a certain way right on their side, may be easily seen. For the words slavery and slave are used in two senses. There is a slave or slavery by convention as well as by nature. The convention is a sort of agreement—the convention by which whatever is taken in war is supposed to belong to the victors. But this right many jurists impeach, as they would an orator who brought forward an unconstitutional measure: they detest the notion that, because one man has the power of doing violence and is superior in brute strength, another shall be his slave and subject. Even among philosophers there is a difference of opinion. The origin of the dispute, and what makes

[1] Reading λόγου.

the views invade each other's territory, is as follows: in some sense excellence, when furnished with means, has actually the greatest power of exercising force: and as superior power is only found where there is superior excellence of some kind, power seems to imply excellence, and the dispute to be simply one about justice (for it is due to one party identifying[2] justice with goodwill, while the other identifies it with the mere rule of the stronger). If these views are thus set out separately, the other views have no force or plausibility against the view that the superior in excellence ought to rule, or be master. Others, clinging, as they think, simply to a principle of justice (for convention is a sort of justice), assume that slavery in accordance with the custom of war is just, but at the same moment they deny this. For what if the cause of the war be unjust? And again, no one would ever say that he is a slave who is unworthy to be a slave. Were this the case, men of the highest rank would be slaves and the children of slaves if they or their parents chanced to have been taken captive and sold. That is why people do not like to call themselves slaves, but confine the term to foreigners. Yet, in using this language, they really mean the natural slave of whom we spoke at first; for it must be admitted that some are slaves everywhere, others nowhere. The same principle applies to nobility. People regard themselves as noble everywhere, and not only in their own country, but they deem foreigners noble only when at home, thereby implying that there are two sorts of nobility and freedom, the one absolute, the other relative. The Helen of Theodectes says:

> Who would presume to call me servant who am on both sides
> sprung from the stem of the Gods?

What does this mean but that they distinguish freedom and slavery, noble and humble birth, by the two principles of good and evil? They think that as men and animals beget men and animals, so from good men a good man springs. Nature intends to do this often but cannot.

---

[2] Reading τό... εὔνοιαν δοκεῖν.

We see then that there is some foundation for this difference of opinion, and that all are not either slaves by nature
or freemen by nature, and also that there is in some cases a
marked distinction between the two classes, rendering it expedient and right for the one to be slaves and the others to be
masters: the one practising obedience, the others exercising
the authority and lordship which nature intended them to
have. The abuse of this authority is injurious to both; for the
interests of part and whole, of body and soul, are the same,
and the slave is a part of the master, a living but separated
part of his bodily frame. Hence, where the relation of master
and slave between them is natural they are friends and have
a common interest, but where it rests merely on convention
and force the reverse is true.

7 • The previous remarks are quite enough to show that
the rule of a master is not a constitutional rule, and that
all the different kinds of rule are not, as some affirm, the
same as each other. For there is one rule exercised over subjects who are by nature free, another over subjects who are by
nature slaves. The rule of a household is a monarchy, for every
house is under one head: whereas constitutional rule is a
government of freemen and equals. The master is not called
a master because he has science, but because he is of a certain
character, and the same remark applies to the slave and the
freeman. Still there may be a science for the master and a science for the slave. The science of the slave would be such as
the man of Syracuse taught, who made money by instruct-
ing slaves in their ordinary duties. And such a knowledge
may be carried further, so as to include cookery and similar
menial arts. For some duties are of the more necessary, others of the more honourable sort; as the proverb says, 'slave
before slave, master before master'. But all such branches of
knowledge are servile. There is likewise a science of the master, which teaches the use of slaves; for the master as such
is concerned, not with the acquisition, but with the use of
them. Yet this science is not anything great or wonderful;
for the master need only know how to order that which the

slave must know how to execute. Hence those who are in a   35
position which places them above toil have stewards who attend to their households while they occupy themselves with
philosophy or with politics. But the art of acquiring slaves,
I mean of justly acquiring them, differs both from the art of
the master and the art of slave, being a species of hunting or
war. Enough of the distinction between master and slave.

8 · Let us now inquire into property generally, and into the   1256ª1
art of getting wealth, in accordance with our usual method,
for a slave has been shown to be a part of property. The first
question is whether the art of getting wealth is the same as
the art of managing a household or a part of it, or instru-   5
mental to it; and if the last, whether in the way that the art
of making shuttles is instrumental to the art of weaving, or
in the way that the casting of bronze is instrumental to the
art of the statuary, for they are not instrumental in the same
way, but the one provides tools and the other material; and
by material I mean the substratum out of which any work is
made; thus wool is the material of the weaver, bronze of the
statuary. Now it is easy to see that the art of household management is not identical with the art of getting wealth, for the   10
one uses the material which the other provides. For the art
which uses household stores can be no other than the art of
household management. There is, however, a doubt whether
the art of getting wealth is a part of household management
or a distinct art. If the getter of wealth has to consider whence   15
wealth and property can be procured, but there are many
sorts of property and riches, then are husbandry, and the care
and provision of food in general, parts of the art of household
management or distinct arts? Again, there are many sorts of
food, and therefore there are many kinds of lives both of animals and men; they must all have food, and the differences in   20
their food have made differences in their ways of life. For of
beasts, some are gregarious, others are solitary; they live in
the way which is best adapted to sustain them, accordingly
as they are carnivorous or herbivorous or omnivorous: and   25
their habits are determined for them by nature with regard

to their ease and choice of food. But the same things are not naturally pleasant to all of them; and therefore the lives of carnivorous or herbivorous animals further differ among 30 themselves. In the lives of men too there is a great difference. The laziest are shepherds, who lead an idle life, and get their subsistence without trouble from tame animals; their flocks having to wander from place to place in search of pasture, they are compelled to follow them, cultivating a sort of liv-35 ing farm. Others support themselves by hunting, which is of different kinds. Some, for example, are brigands, others, who dwell near lakes or marshes or rivers or a sea in which there are fish, are fishermen, and others live by the pursuit of birds or wild beasts. The greater number obtain a living from 40 the cultivated fruits of the soil. Such are the modes of subsistence which prevail among those whose industry springs up of itself, and whose food is not acquired by exchange and 1256ᵇ1 retail trade—there is the shepherd, the husbandman, the brigand, the fisherman, the hunter. Some gain a comfortable maintenance out of two employments, eking out the deficiencies of one of them by another: thus the life of a shepherd may 5 be combined with that of a brigand, the life of a farmer with that of a hunter. Other modes of life are similarly combined in any way which the needs of men may require. Property, in the sense of a bare livelihood, seems to be given by nature herself to all, both when they are first born, and when 10 they are grown up. For some animals bring forth, together with their offspring, so much food as will last until they are able to supply themselves; of this the vermiparous or oviparous animals are an instance; and the viviparous animals have up to a certain time a supply of food for their young in themselves, which is called milk. In like manner we may 15 infer that, after the birth of animals, plants exist for their sake, and that the other animals exist for the sake of man,[3] the tame for use and food, the wild, if not all, at least the greater part of them, for food, and for the provision of clothing 20 and various instruments. Now if nature makes nothing

[3] Retaining ζῷα τῶν ἀνθρώπων.

incomplete, and nothing in vain, the inference must be that she has made all animals for the sake of man. And so, from one point of view, the art of war is a natural art of acquisition, for the art of acquisition includes hunting, an art which we ought to practise against wild beasts, and against men who, though intended by nature to be governed, will not submit; for war of such a kind is naturally just. 25

Of the art of acquisition then there is one kind which by nature is a part of the management of a household, in so far as the art of household management must either find ready to hand, or itself provide, such things necessary to life, and useful for the community of the family or state, as can be 30 stored. They are the elements of true riches; for the amount of property which is needed for a good life is not unlimited, although Solon in one of his poems says that

No bound to riches has been fixed for man.

But there is a boundary fixed, just as there is in the other arts; for the instruments of any art are never unlimited, ei- 35 ther in number or size, and riches may be defined as a number of instruments to be used in a household or in a state. And so we see that there is a natural art of acquisition which is practised by managers of households and by statesmen, and the reason for this.

9 • There is another variety of the art of acquisition which 40 is commonly and rightly called an art of wealth-getting, and has in fact suggested the notion that riches and property 1257ᵃ1 have no limit. Being nearly connected with the preceding, it is often identified with it. But though they are not very different, neither are they the same. The kind already described is given by nature, the other is gained by experience and art. 5

Let us begin our discussion of the question with the following considerations. Of everything which we possess there are two uses: both belong to the thing as such, but not in the same manner, for one is the proper, and the other the improper use of it. For example, a shoe is used for wear, and is used for exchange; both are uses of the shoe. He who gives a 10

shoe in exchange for money or food to him who wants one, does indeed use the shoe as a shoe, but this is not its proper use, for a shoe is not made to be an object of barter. The same
15 may be said of all possessions, for the art of exchange extends to all of them, and it arises at first from what is natural, from the circumstance that some have too little, others too much. Hence we may infer that retail trade is not a natural part of the art of getting wealth; had it been so, men would have ceased to exchange when they had enough. In the first com-
20 munity, indeed, which is the family, this art is obviously of no use, but it begins to be useful when the society increases. For the members of the family originally had all things in common; later, when the family divided into parts, the parts shared in many things, and different parts in different things, which they had to give in exchange for what they wanted, a
25 kind of barter which is still practised among barbarous nations who exchange with one another the necessaries of life and nothing more; giving and receiving wine, for example, in exchange for corn, and the like. This sort of barter is not part of the wealth-getting art and is not contrary to nature, but is
30 needed for the satisfaction of men's natural wants. The other form of exchange grew, as might have been inferred, out of this one. When the inhabitants of one country became more dependent on those of another, and they imported what they needed, and exported what they had too much of, money necessarily came into use. For the various necessaries of life are not easily carried about, and hence men agreed to employ in their dealings with each other something which was in-
35 trinsically useful and easily applicable to the purposes of life, for example, iron, silver, and the like. Of this the value was at first measured simply by size and weight, but in process of time they put a stamp upon it, to save the trouble of weighing
40 and to mark the value.

    When the use of coin had once been discovered, out of
1257^b1 the barter of necessary articles arose the other art of wealth-getting, namely, retail trade; which was at first probably a simple matter, but became more complicated as soon as men learned by experience whence and by what exchanges the

greatest profit might be made. Originating in the use of coin, the art of getting wealth is generally thought to be chiefly concerned with it, and to be the art which produces riches and wealth, having to consider how they may be accumulated. Indeed, riches is assumed by many to be only a quantity of coin, because the arts of getting wealth and retail trade are concerned with coin. Others maintain that coined money is a mere sham, a thing not natural, but conventional only, because, if the users substitute another commodity for it, it is worthless, and because it is not useful as a means to any of the necessities of life, and, indeed, he who is rich in coin may often be in want of necessary food. But how can that be wealth of which a man may have a great abundance and yet perish with hunger, like Midas in the fable, whose insatiable prayer turned everything that was set before him into gold?

Hence men seek after a better notion of riches and of the art of getting wealth, and they are right. For natural riches and the natural art of wealth-getting are a different thing; in their true form they are part of the management of a household; whereas retail trade is the art of producing wealth, not in every way, but by exchange. And it is thought to be concerned with coin; for coin is the unit of exchange and the limit of it. And there is no bound to the riches which spring from this art of wealth-getting. As in the art of medicine there is no limit to the pursuit of health, and as in the other arts there is no limit to the pursuit of their several ends, for they aim at accomplishing their ends to the uttermost (but of the means there is a limit, for the end is always the limit), so, too, in this art of wealth-getting there is no limit of the end, which is riches of the spurious kind, and the acquisition of wealth. But the art of wealth-getting which consists in household management, on the other hand, has a limit;[4] the unlimited acquisition of wealth is not its business. And, therefore, from one point of view, all riches must have a limit; nevertheless, as a matter of fact, we find the opposite to be the case; for all getters of wealth increase their hoard of coin without limit. The

---

[4] Reading αὖ for οὐ.

35 source of the confusion is the near connexion between the
two kinds of wealth-getting; in both, the instrument is the
same, although the use is different, and so they pass into one
another; for each is a use of the same property, but with a difference: accumulation is the end in the one case, but there
is a further end in the other. Hence some persons are led to
believe that getting wealth is the object of household man-
40 agement, and the whole idea of their lives is that they ought
either to increase their money without limit, or at any rate
not to lose it. The origin of this disposition in men is that they
1258ᵃ1 are intent upon living only, and not upon living well; and, as
their desires are unlimited, they also desire that the means of
gratifying them should be without limit. Those who do aim at
5 a good life seek the means of obtaining bodily pleasures; and,
since the enjoyment of these appears to depend on property,
they are absorbed in getting wealth: and so there arises the
second species of wealth-getting. For, as their enjoyment is
in excess, they seek an art which produces the excess of enjoyment; and, if they are not able to supply their pleasures by
the art of getting wealth, they try other causes, using in turn
10 every faculty in a manner contrary to nature. The quality of
courage, for example, is not intended to make wealth, but
to inspire confidence; neither is this the aim of the general's
or of the physician's art; but the one aims at victory and the
other at health. Nevertheless, some men turn every quality
or art into a means of getting wealth; this they conceive to be
the end, and to the promotion of the end they think all things
must contribute.

15 Thus, then, we have considered the art of wealth-getting
which is unnecessary, and why men want it; and also the necessary art of wealth-getting, which we have seen to be different from the other, and to be a natural part of the art of managing a household, concerned with the provision of food, not,
however, like the former kind, unlimited, but having a limit.

10 • And we have found the answer to our original ques-
20 tion, Whether the art of getting wealth is the business of the
manager of a household and of the statesman or not their

business?—viz. that wealth is presupposed by them. For as political science does not make men, but takes them from nature and uses them, so too nature provides them with earth or sea or the like as a source of food. At this stage begins the duty of the manager of a household, who has to order the things which nature supplies—he may be compared to the weaver who has not to make but to use wool, and to know, too, what sort of wool is good and serviceable or bad and unserviceable. Were this otherwise, it would be difficult to see why the art of getting wealth is a part of the management of a household and the art of medicine not; for surely the members of a household must have health just as they must have life or any other necessity. The answer is that as from one point of view the master of the house and the ruler of the state have to consider about health, from another point of view not they but the physician has to; so in one way the art of household management, in another way the subordinate art, has to consider about wealth. But, strictly speaking, as I have already said, the means of life must be provided beforehand by nature; for the business of nature is to furnish food to that which is born, and the food of the offspring is always what remains over of that from which it is produced. That is why the art of getting wealth out of fruits and animals is always natural.

There are two sorts of wealth-getting, as I have said; one is a part of household management, the other is retail trade: the former is necessary and honourable, while that which consists in exchange is justly censured; for it is unnatural, and a mode by which men gain from one another. The most hated sort, and with the greatest reason, is usury, which makes a gain out of money itself, and not from the natural object of it. For money was intended to be used in exchange, but not to increase at interest. And this term interest, which means the birth of money from money, is applied to the breeding of money because the offspring resembles the parent. That is why of all modes of getting wealth this is the most unnatural.

11 • Enough has been said about the theory of wealth-getting; we will now proceed to the practical part. Such things

10 may be studied by a free man, but will only be practised from necessity. The useful parts of wealth-getting are, first, the knowledge of live-stock—which are most profitable, and where, and how—as for example, what sort of horses or sheep or oxen or any other animals are most likely to give a return. A man ought to know which of these pay better than others,

15 and which pay best in particular places, for some do better in one place and some in another. Secondly, husbandry, which may be either tillage or planting, and the keeping of bees and of fish, or fowl, or of any animals which may be useful to man.

20 These are the divisions of the true or proper art of wealth-getting and come first. Of the other, which consists in exchange, the first and most important division is commerce (of which there are three kinds—ship-owning, the conveyance of goods, exposure for sale—these again differing as they are safer or more profitable), the second is usury, the third, ser-

25 vice for hire—of this, one kind is employed in the mechanical arts, the other in unskilled and bodily labour. There is still a third sort of wealth-getting intermediate between this and the first or natural mode which is partly natural, but is also concerned with exchange, viz. the industries that make their profit from the earth, and from things growing from the earth

30 which, although they bear no fruit, are nevertheless profitable; for example, the cutting of timber and all mining. The art of mining itself has many branches, for there are various kinds of things dug out of the earth. Of the several divisions of wealth-getting I now speak generally; a minute consideration of them might be useful in practice, but it would be tiresome

35 to dwell upon them at greater length now.

Those occupations are most truly arts in which there is the least element of chance; they are the meanest in which the body is most maltreated, the most servile in which there is the greatest use of the body, and the most illiberal in which there is the least need of excellence.

Works have been written upon these subjects by various persons; for example, by Chares the Parian, and Apollodorus

1259ª1 the Lemnian, who have treated of Tillage and Planting, while others have treated of other branches; anyone who cares for such matters may refer to their writings. It would be well also to collect the scattered stories of the ways in which individuals have succeeded in amassing a fortune; for all this is useful to persons who value the art of getting wealth. There is the anecdote of Thales the Milesian and his financial scheme, which involves a principle of universal application, but is attributed to him on account of his reputation for wisdom. He was reproached for his poverty, which was supposed to show that philosophy was of no use. According to the story, he knew by his skill in the stars while it was yet winter that there would be a great harvest of olives in the coming year; so, having a little money, he gave deposits for the use of all the olive-presses in Chios and Miletus, which he hired at a low price because no one bid against him. When the harvest-time came, and many were wanted all at once and of a sudden, he let them out at any rate which he pleased, and made a quantity of money. Thus he showed the world that philosophers can easily be rich if they like, but that their ambition is of another sort. He is supposed to have given a striking proof of his wisdom, but, as I was saying, his scheme for getting wealth is of universal application, and is nothing but the creation of a monopoly. It is an art often practised by cities when they are in want of money; they make a monopoly of provisions.

There was a man of Sicily, who, having money deposited with him, bought up all the iron from the iron mines; afterwards, when the merchants from their various markets came to buy, he was the only seller, and without much increasing the price he gained 200 per cent. Which when Dionysius heard, he told him that he might take away his money, but that he must not remain at Syracuse, for he thought that the man had discovered a way of making money which was injurious to his own interests. He made the same discovery as Thales; they both contrived to create a monopoly for themselves. And statesmen as well ought to know these things; for a state is often as much in want of money and of such schemes for obtaining it as a household, or even more so; hence some public men devote themselves entirely to finance.

12 • Of household management we have seen that there are three parts—one is the rule of a master over slaves, which has been discussed already, another of a father, and the third of a husband. A husband and father, we saw, rules over wife and children, both free, but the rule differs, the rule over his children being a royal, over his wife a constitutional rule. For although there may be exceptions to the order of nature, the male is by nature fitter for command than the female, just as the elder and full-grown is superior to the younger and more immature. But in most constitutional states the citizens rule and are ruled by turns, for the idea of a constitutional state implies that the natures of the citizens are equal, and do not differ at all. Nevertheless, when one rules and the other is ruled we endeavour to create a difference of outward forms and names and titles of respect, which may be illustrated by the saying of Amasis about his foot-pan. The relation of the male to the female is always of this kind. The rule of a father over his children is royal, for he rules by virtue both of love and of the respect due to age, exercising a kind of royal power. And therefore Homer has appropriately called Zeus 'father of Gods and men', because he is the king of them all. For a king is the natural superior of his subjects, but he should be of the same kin or kind with them, and such is the relation of elder and younger, of father and son.

13 • Thus it is clear that household management attends more to men than to the acquisition of inanimate things, and to human excellence more than to the excellence of property which we call wealth, and to the excellence of freemen more than to the excellence of slaves. A question may indeed be raised, whether there is any excellence at all in a slave beyond those of an instrument and of a servant—whether he can have the excellences of temperance, courage, justice, and the like; or whether slaves possess only bodily services. And, whichever way we answer the question, a difficulty arises; for, if they have excellence, in what will they differ from freemen? On the other hand, since they are men and share in rational principle, it seems absurd to say that they have no excellence.

1259ᵇ1

A similar question may be raised about women and children, whether they too have excellences; ought a woman to be   30
temperate and brave and just, and is a child to be called temperate, and intemperate, or not? So in general we may ask about the natural ruler, and the natural subject, whether they have the same or different excellences. For if a noble nature is equally required in both, why should one of them always   35
rule, and the other always be ruled? Nor can we say that this is a question of degree, for the difference between ruler and subject is a difference of kind, which the difference of more and less never is. Yet how strange is the supposition that the one ought, and that the other ought not, to have excellence! For if the ruler is intemperate and unjust, how can he rule well? if the subject, how can he obey well? If he is licentious   1260ᵃ1
and cowardly, he will certainly not do what is fitting. It is evident, therefore, that both of them must have a share of excellence, but varying as natural subjects also vary among themselves. Here the very constitution of the soul has shown us the way; in it one part naturally rules, and the other is subject,   5
and the excellence of the ruler we maintain to be different from that of the subject—the one being the excellence of the rational, and the other of the irrational part. Now, it is obvious that the same principle applies generally, and therefore almost all things rule and are ruled according to nature. But the kind of rule differs—the freeman rules over the slave after another manner from that in which the male rules over the female, or the man over the child; although the parts of   10
the soul are present in all of them, they are present in different degrees. For the slave has no deliberative faculty at all; the woman has, but it is without authority, and the child has, but it is immature. So it must necessarily be supposed to be with the excellences of character also; all should partake of them,   15
but only in such manner and degree as is required by each for the fulfilment of his function. Hence the ruler ought to have excellence of character in perfection, for his function, taken absolutely, demands a master artificer, and reason is such an artificer; the subjects, on the other hand, require only that measure of excellence which is proper to each of them.

20 Clearly, then, excellence of character belongs to all of them;
but the temperance of a man and of a woman, or the courage and justice of a man and of a woman, are not, as Socrates
maintained, the same; the courage of a man is shown in commanding, of a woman in obeying. And this holds of all other
excellences, as will be more clearly seen if we look at them in
25 detail, for those who say generally that excellence consists in
a good disposition of the soul, or in doing rightly, or the like,
only deceive themselves. Far better than such definitions is
the mode of speaking of those who, like Gorgias, enumerate
the excellences. All classes must be deemed to have their special attributes; as the poet says of women,

30   Silence is a woman's glory,

but this is not equally the glory of man. The child is imperfect, and therefore obviously his excellence is not relative to
himself alone, but to the perfect man and to his teacher, and
in like manner the excellence of the slave is relative to a master. Now we determined that a slave is useful for the wants
35 of life, and therefore he will obviously require only so much
excellence as will prevent him from failing in his function
through cowardice or lack of self-control. Someone will ask
whether, if what we are saying is true, excellence will not be
required also in the artisans, for they often fail in their work
through the lack of self-control. But is there not a great dif-
40 ference in the two cases? For the slave shares in his master's
life; the artisan is less closely connected with him, and only
attains excellence in proportion as he becomes a slave. The
1260ᵇ1 meaner sort of mechanic has a special and separate slavery;
and whereas the slave exists by nature, not so the shoemaker
or other artisan. It is manifest, then, that the master ought to
be the source of such excellence in the slave, and not a mere
possessor of the art of mastership which trains the slave in
5 his functions. That is why they are mistaken who forbid us
to converse with slaves and say that we should employ command only, for slaves stand even more in need of admonition
than children.

So much for this subject; the relations of husband and
wife, father and child, their several excellences, what in their   10
intercourse with one another is good, and what is evil, and
how we may pursue the good and escape the evil, will have
to be discussed when we speak of the different forms of government. For, inasmuch as every family is a part of a state,
and these relationships are the parts of a family, and the excellence of the part must have regard to the excellence of the
whole, women and children must be trained by education   15
with an eye to the constitution, if the excellences of either of
them are supposed to make any difference in the excellences
of the state. And they must make a difference: for the children grow up to be citizens, and half the free persons in a   20
state are women.

Of these matters, enough has been said; of what remains,
let us speak at another time. Regarding, then, our present inquiry as complete, we will make a new beginning. And, first,
let us examine the various theories of a perfect state.

BOOK II

1 · Our purpose is to consider what form of political com-   25
munity is best of all for those who are most able to realize
their ideal of life. We must therefore examine not only this
but other constitutions, both such as actually exist in well-
governed states, and any theoretical forms which are held in   30
esteem, so that what is good and useful may be brought to
light. And let no one suppose that in seeking for something
beyond them we are anxious to make a sophistical display at
any cost; we only undertake this inquiry because all the con-   35
stitutions which now exist are faulty.

We will begin with the natural beginning of the subject.
The members of a state must either have all things or nothing in common, or some things in common and some not.
That they should have nothing in common is clearly impossible, for the constitution is a community, and must at any

1261ª1 rate have a common place—one city will be in one place, and the citizens are those who share in that one city. But should a well-ordered state have all things, as far as may be, in common, or some only and not others? For the citizens might

5 conceivably have wives and children and property in common, as Socrates proposes in the *Republic* of Plato. Which is better, our present condition, or one conforming to the law laid down in the *Republic*?

10 2 · There are many difficulties in the community of women. And the principle on which Socrates rests the necessity of such an institution evidently is not established by his arguments. Further, as a means to the end which he ascribes to the state, the scheme, taken literally, is impracticable, and how we are to interpret it is nowhere precisely stated. I am speaking of the supposition from which the argument of

15 Socrates proceeds, that it is best for the whole state to be as unified as possible. Is it not obvious that a state may at length attain such a degree of unity as to be no longer a state?— since the nature of a state is to be a plurality, and in tending to greater unity, from being a state, it becomes a family, and from being a family, an individual; for the family may be

20 said to be more one than the state, and the individual than the family. So that we ought not to attain this greatest unity even if we could, for it would be the destruction of the state. Again, a state is not made up only of so many men, but of different kinds of men; for similars do not constitute a state. It is not like a military alliance. The usefulness of the latter

25 depends upon its quantity even where there is no difference in quality (for mutual protection is the end aimed at), just as a greater weight depresses the scale more (in like manner, a state differs from a nation, when the nation has not its population organized in villages, but lives an Arcadian sort of life); but the elements out of which a unity is to be formed differ

30 in kind. That is why the principle of reciprocity, as I have already remarked in the *Ethics*, is the salvation of states. Even among freemen and equals this is a principle which must be maintained, for they cannot all rule together, but must

change at the end of a year or some other period of time or in some order of succession. The result is that upon this plan they all govern; just as if shoemakers and carpenters were to 35 exchange their occupations, and the same persons did not always continue shoemakers and carpenters. And since it is better that this should be so in politics as well, it is clear that while there should be continuance of the same persons in power where this is possible, yet where this is not possible by reason of the natural equality of the citizens, and at the same time it is just that all should share in the government 1261ᵇ1 (whether to govern be a good thing or a bad),—in these cases this is imitated.[1] Thus the one party rules and the others are ruled in turn, as if they were no longer the same persons. In like manner when they hold office there is a variety in the of- 5 fices held. Hence it is evident that a city is not by nature one in that sense which some persons affirm; and that what is said to be the greatest good of cities is in reality their destruction; but surely the good of things must be that which preserves them. Again, from another point of view, this extreme 10 unification of the state is clearly not good; for a family is more self-sufficing than an individual, and a city than a family, and a city only comes into being when the community is large enough to be self-sufficing. If then self-sufficiency is to be desired, the lesser degree of unity is more desirable than 15 the greater.

3 · But, even supposing that it were best for the community to have the greatest degree of unity, this unity is by no means proved to follow from the fact of all men saying 'mine' and 'not mine' at the same instant of time, which, according to Socrates, is the sign of perfect unity in a state. For the word 20 'all' is ambiguous. If the meaning be that every individual says 'mine' and 'not mine' at the same time, then perhaps the result at which Socrates aims may be in some degree accomplished; each man will call the same person his own son and the same person his own wife, and so of his property and of

---

[1] The text is uncertain.

25 all that falls to his lot. This, however, is not the way in which people would speak who had their wives and children in common; they would say 'all' but not 'each'. In like manner their property would be described as belonging to them, not severally but collectively. There is an obvious fallacy in the term 'all': like some other words, 'both', 'odd', 'even', it is am-

30 biguous, and even in abstract argument becomes a source of logical puzzles. That all persons call the same thing mine in the sense in which each does so may be a fine thing, but it is impracticable; or if the words are taken in the other sense, such a unity in no way conduces to harmony. And there is another objection to the proposal. For that which is common to the greatest number has the least care bestowed upon it. Everyone thinks chiefly of his own, hardly at all of the common

35 interest; and only when he is himself concerned as an individual. For besides other considerations, everybody is more inclined to neglect something which he expects another to fulfil; as in families many attendants are often less useful than a few. Each citizen will have a thousand sons who will not be his sons individually, but anybody will be equally the son of

1262ª1 anybody, and will therefore be neglected by all alike. Further, upon this principle, every one will use the word 'mine' of one who is prospering or the reverse, however small a fraction he may himself be of the whole number; the same boy will be my son, so and so's son, the son of each of the thousand, or what-

5 ever be the number of the citizens; and even about this he will not be positive; for it is impossible to know who chanced to have a child, or whether, if one came into existence, it has survived. But which is better—for each to say 'mine' in this way, making a man the same relation to two thousand or ten thousand citizens, or to use the word 'mine' as it is now used in states? For usually the same person is called by one man

10 his own son whom another calls his own brother or cousin or kinsman—blood relation or connexion by marriage—either of himself or of some relation of his, and yet another his clansman or tribesman; and how much better is it to be the real cousin of somebody than to be a son after Plato's fash-

15 ion! Nor is there any way of preventing brothers and children

and fathers and mothers from sometimes recognizing one another; for children are born like their parents, and they will necessarily be finding indications of their relationship to one another. Geographers declare such to be the fact; they say that in part of Upper Libya, where the women are common, nevertheless the children who are born are assigned to their respective fathers on the ground of their likeness. And some women, like the females of other animals—for example, mares and cows—have a strong tendency to produce offspring resembling their parents, as was the case with the Pharsalian mare called Honest Wife.

4 • Other difficulties, against which it is not easy for the authors of such a community to guard, will be assaults and homicides, voluntary as well as involuntary, quarrels and slanders, all of which are most unholy acts when committed against fathers and mothers and near relations, but not equally unholy when there is no relationship. Moreover, they are much more likely to occur if the relationship is unknown than if it is known and, when they have occurred, the customary expiations of them can be made if the relationship is known, but not otherwise. Again, how strange it is that Socrates, after having made the children common, should hinder lovers from carnal intercourse only, but should permit love and familiarities between father and son or between brother and brother, than which nothing can be more unseemly, since even without them love of this sort is improper. How strange, too, to forbid intercourse for no other reason than the violence of the pleasure, as though the relationship of father and son or of brothers with one another made no difference.

This community of wives and children seems better suited to the husbandmen than to the guardians, for if they have wives and children in common, they will be bound to one another by weaker ties, as a subject class should be, and they will remain obedient and not rebel. In a word, the result of such a law would be just the opposite of that which good laws ought to have, and the intention of Socrates in making

5 these regulations about women and children would defeat itself. For friendship we believe to be the greatest good of states and what best preserves them against revolutions; and Socrates particularly praises the unity of the state which seems and is said by him to be created by friendship. But the
10 unity which he commends would be like that of the lovers in the *Symposium*, who, as Aristophanes says, desire to grow together in the excess of their affection, and from being two to become one, in which case one or both would certainly perish. Whereas in a state having women and children common,
15 love will be diluted; and the father will certainly not say 'my son', or the son 'my father'. As a little sweet wine mingled with a great deal of water is imperceptible in the mixture, so, in this sort of community, the idea of relationship which is based upon these names will be lost; there is no reason why
20 the so-called father should care about the son, or the son about the father, or brothers about one another. Of the two qualities which chiefly inspire regard and affection—that a thing is your own and that it is precious—neither can exist in such a state as this.

Again, the transfer of children as soon as they are born
25 from the rank of husbandmen or of artisans to that of guardians, and from the rank of guardians into a lower rank, will be very difficult to arrange; the givers or transferrers cannot but know whom they are giving and transferring, and
30 to whom. And the previously mentioned assaults, unlawful loves, homicides, will happen more often among them; for they will no longer call the members of the class they have left brothers, and children, and fathers, and mothers, and will not, therefore, be afraid of committing any crimes by reason
35 of consanguinity. Touching the community of wives and children, let this be our conclusion.

5 • Next let us consider what should be our arrangements about property: should the citizens of the perfect state have their possessions in common or not?
40 This question may be discussed separately from the enactments about women and children. Even supposing that the

women and children belong to individuals, according to the custom which is at present universal, may there not be an advantage in having and using possessions in common? E.g. 1263ª1 (1) the soil may be appropriated, but the produce may be thrown for consumption into the common stock; and this is the practice of some nations. Or (2), the soil may be common, 5 and may be cultivated in common, but the produce divided among individuals for their private use; this is a form of common property which is said to exist among certain foreigners. Or (3), the soil and the produce may be alike common.

When the husbandmen are not the owners, the case will be different and easier to deal with; but when they till the ground 10 for themselves the question of ownership will give a world of trouble. If they do not share equally in enjoyments and toils, those who labour much and get little will necessarily complain of those who labour little and receive or consume much. 15 But indeed there is always a difficulty in men living together and having all human relations in common, but especially in their having common property. The partnerships of fellow-travellers are an example to the point; for they generally fall out over everyday matters and quarrel about any trifle which turns up. So with servants: we are most liable to take offence at those with whom we most frequently come into contact in 20 daily life.

These are only some of the disadvantages which attend the community of property; the present arrangement, if improved as it might be by good customs and laws, would be far better, and would have the advantages of both systems. Prop- 25 erty should be in a certain sense common, but, as a general rule, private; for, when everyone has a distinct interest, men will not complain of one another, and they will make more progress, because everyone will be attending to his own business. And yet by reason of goodness, and in respect of use, 30 'Friends', as the proverb says, 'will have all things common'. Even now there are traces of such a principle, showing that it is not impracticable, but, in well-ordered states, exists already to a certain extent and may be carried further. For, although every man has his own property, some things he will place at

the disposal of his friends, while of others he shares the use
35 with them. The Lacedaemonians, for example, use one another's slaves, and horses, and dogs, as if they were their own;
and when they lack provisions on a journey, they appropriate what they find in the fields throughout the country. It is
clearly better that property should be private, but the use of it
common; and the special business of the legislator is to create
in men this benevolent disposition. Again, how immeasurably greater is the pleasure, when a man feels a thing to be his
own; for surely the love of self is a feeling implanted by nature
1263ᵇ1 and not given in vain, although selfishness is rightly censured;
this, however, is not the mere love of self, but the love of self
in excess, like the miser's love of money; for all, or almost all,
men love money and other such objects in a measure. And
further, there is the greatest pleasure in doing a kindness or
5 service to friends or guests or companions, which can only be
rendered when a man has private property. These advantages
are lost by excessive unification of the state. The exhibition of
two excellences, besides, is visibly annihilated in such a state:
first, temperance towards women (for it is an honourable action to abstain from another's wife for temperance sake); sec-
10 ondly, liberality in the matter of property. No one, when men
have all things in common, will any longer set an example of
liberality or do any liberal action; for liberality consists in the
use which is made of property.
15 Such legislation may have a specious appearance of benevolence; men readily listen to it, and are easily induced to believe
that in some wonderful manner everybody will become everybody's friend—especially when someone is heard denouncing
the evils now existing in states, suits about contracts, convic-
tions for perjury, flatteries of rich men and the like, which are
20 said to arise out of the possession of private property. These
evils, however, are due not to the absence of communism but
to wickedness. Indeed, we see that there is much more quarrelling among those who have all things in common, though
25 there are not many of them when compared with the vast
numbers who have private property.

Again, we ought to reckon not only the evils from which the citizens will be saved, but also the advantages which they will lose. The life which they are to lead appears to be quite impracticable. The error of Socrates must be attributed to the false supposition from which he starts. Unity there should be, both of the family and of the state, but in some respects only. For there is a point at which a state may attain such a degree of unity as to be no longer a state, or at which, without actually ceasing to exist, it will become an inferior state, like harmony passing into unison, or rhythm which has been reduced to a single foot. The state, as I was saying, is a plurality, which should be united and made into a community by education; and it is strange that the author of a system of education which he thinks will make the state virtuous, should expect to improve his citizens by regulations of this sort, and not by philosophy or by customs and laws, like those which prevail at Sparta and Crete respecting common meals, whereby the legislator has made property common. Let us remember that we should not disregard the experience of ages; in the multitude of years these things, if they were good, would certainly not have been unknown; for almost everything has been found out, although sometimes they are not put together; in other cases men do not use the knowledge which they have. Great light would be thrown on this subject if we could see such a form of government in the actual process of construction; for the legislator could not form a state at all without distributing and dividing its constituents into associations for common meals, and into phratries and tribes. But all this legislation ends only in forbidding agriculture to the guardians, a prohibition which the Lacedaemonians try to enforce already.

But, indeed, Socrates has not said, nor is it easy to decide, what in such a community will be the general form of the state. The citizens who are not guardians are the majority, and about them nothing has been determined: are the husbandmen, too, to have their property in common? Or is each individual to have his own? and are their wives and children to be individual or common? If, like the guardians, they are to have all things in common, in what do they differ from them, or what will they gain by submitting to their government? Or upon what principle would they submit, unless

20 indeed the governing class adopt the ingenious policy of the Cretans, who give their slaves the same institutions as their own, but forbid them gymnastic exercises and the possession of arms. If, on the other hand, the inferior classes are to be like other cities in respect of marriage and property, what

25 will be the form of the community? Must it not contain two states in one, each hostile to the other? He makes the guardians into a mere occupying garrison, while the husbandmen and artisans and the rest are real citizens. But if so the suits and quarrels, and all the evils which Socrates affirms to exist in other states, will exist equally among them.

30 He says indeed that, having so good an education, the citizens will not need many laws, for example laws about the city or about the markets; but then he confines his education to the guardians. Again, he makes the husbandmen owners of the property upon condition of their paying a tribute.

35 But in that case they are likely to be much more unmanageable and conceited than the Helots, or Penestae, or slaves in general. And whether community of wives and property be necessary for the lower equally with the higher class or not, and the questions akin to this, what will be the education, form of government, laws of the lower class, Socrates has nowhere determined: neither is it easy to discover this, nor is their character of small importance if the common life of the guardians is to be maintained.

1264ᵇ1 Again, if Socrates makes the women common, and retains private property, the men will see to the fields, but who will see to the house? And who will do so if the agricultural class have both their property and their wives in common? Once more: it is absurd to argue, from the analogy of animals, that

5 men and women should follow the same pursuits, for animals have not to manage a household. The government, too, as constituted by Socrates, contains elements of danger; for he makes the same persons always rule. And if this is often

a cause of disturbance among the meaner sort, how much
more among high-spirited warriors? But that the persons 10
whom he makes rulers must be the same is evident; for the
gold which the God mingles in the souls of men is not at one
time given to one, at another time to another, but always to
the same: as he says, God mingles gold in some, and silver
in others, from their very birth; but brass and iron in those
who are meant to be artisans and husbandmen. Again, he de- 15
prives the guardians even of happiness, and says that the legislator ought to make the whole state happy. But the whole
cannot be happy unless most, or all, or some of its parts enjoy
happiness. In this respect happiness is not like the even prin- 20
ciple in numbers, which may exist only in the whole, but in
neither of the parts; not so happiness. And if the guardians
are not happy, who are? Surely not the artisans, or the common people. The Republic of which Socrates discourses has 25
all these difficulties, and others quite as great.

6 · The same, or nearly the same, objections apply to Plato's later work, the *Laws*, and therefore we had better examine briefly the constitution which is therein described. In the
Republic, Socrates has definitely settled in all a few questions
only; such as the community of women and children, the
community of property, and the constitution of the state. 30
The population is divided into two classes—one of husbandmen, and the other of warriors; from this latter is taken a
third class of counsellors and rulers of the state. But Socrates
has not determined whether the husbandmen and artisans
are to have a share in the government, and whether they, too, 35
are to carry arms and share in the military service, or not. He
certainly thinks that the women ought to share in the education of the guardians, and to fight by their side. The remainder of the work is filled up with digressions foreign to the
main subject, and with discussions about the education of
the guardians. In the *Laws* there is hardly anything but laws; 1265ª1
not much is said about the constitution.

This, which he had intended to make more of the ordinary
type, he gradually brings round to the other form. For with

the exception of the community of women and property, he supposes everything to be the same in both states; there is to be the same education; the citizens of both are to live free from servile occupations, and there are to be common meals in both. The only difference is that in the *Laws*, the common meals are extended to women, and the warriors number 5000, but in the *Republic* only 1000.

The discourses of Socrates are never commonplace; they always exhibit grace and originality and thought; but perfection in everything can hardly be expected. We must not overlook the fact that the number of 5000 citizens, just now mentioned, will require a territory as large as Babylon, or some other huge site, if so many persons are to be supported in idleness, together with their women and attendants, who will be a multitude many times as great. In framing an ideal we may assume what we wish, but should avoid impossibilities.

It is said that the legislator ought to have his eye directed to two points—the people and the country. But neighbouring countries also must not be forgotten by him, firstly because the state for which he legislates is to have a political and not an isolated life. For a state must have such a military force as will be serviceable against her neighbours, and not merely useful at home. Even if such a life is not accepted, either for individuals or states, still a city should be formidable to enemies, whether invading or retreating.

There is another point: Should not the amount of property be defined in some way which differs from this by being clearer? For Socrates says that a man should have so much property as will enable him to live temperately, which is only a way of saying to live well; this is too general a conception. Further, a man may live temperately and yet miserably. A better definition would be that a man must have so much property as will enable him to live not only temperately but liberally; if the two are parted, liberality will combine with luxury; temperance will be associated with toil. For liberality and temperance are the only eligible qualities which have to do with the use of property. A man cannot use property with mildness or courage, but temperately and liberally he may;

and therefore the practice of these excellences is inseparable
from property. There is an absurdity, too, in equalizing the
property and not regulating the number of citizens; the   40
population is to remain unlimited, and he thinks that it will
be sufficiently equalized by a certain number of marriages
being unfruitful, however many are born to others, because
he finds this to be the case in existing states. But greater care   1265ᵇ1
will be required than now; for among ourselves, whatever
may be the number of citizens, the property is always distributed among them, and therefore no one is in want; but, if the
property were incapable of division as in the *Laws,* the super-   5
numeraries, whether few or many, would get nothing. One
would have thought that it was even more necessary to limit
population than property; and that the limit should be fixed
by calculating the chances of mortality in the children, and
of sterility in married persons. The neglect of this subject,   10
which in existing states is so common, is a never-failing cause
of poverty among the citizens; and poverty is the parent of
revolution and crime. Pheidon the Corinthian, who was one
of the most ancient legislators, thought that the families and
the number of citizens ought to remain the same, although
originally all the lots may have been of different sizes; but in   15
the *Laws* the opposite principle is maintained. What in our
opinion is the right arrangement will have to be explained
hereafter.

There is another omission in the *Laws:* Socrates does not
tell us how the rulers differ from their subjects; he only says
that they should be related as the warp and the woof, which   20
are made out of different wools. He allows that a man's
whole property may be increased fivefold, but why should
not his land also increase to a certain extent? Again, will the
good management of a household be promoted by his arrangement of homesteads? for he assigns to each individual   25
two homesteads in separate places, and it is difficult to live in
two houses.

The whole system of government tends to be neither democracy nor oligarchy, but something in a mean between
them, which is usually called a polity, and is composed of the

heavy-armed soldiers. Now, if he intended to frame a constitution which would suit the greatest number of states, he was
very likely right, but not if he meant to say that this constitutional form came nearest to his first state; for many would
prefer the Lacedaemonian, or, possibly, some other more
aristocratic government. Some, indeed, say that the best constitution is a combination of all existing forms, and they
praise the Lacedaemonian because it is made up of oligarchy,
monarchy, and democracy, the king forming the monarchy,
and the council of elders the oligarchy, while the democratic
element is represented by the Ephors; for the Ephors are
selected from the people. Others, however, declare the Ephorate to be a tyranny, and find the element of democracy in the
common meals and in the habits of daily life. In the *Laws* it
is maintained that the best constitution is made up of democracy and tyranny, which are either not constitutions at all, or
are the worst of all. But they are nearer the truth who combine many forms; for the constitution is better which is made
up of more numerous elements. The constitution proposed
in the *Laws* has no element of monarchy at all; it is nothing
but oligarchy and democracy, leaning rather to oligarchy.
This is seen in the mode of appointing magistrates; for although the appointment of them by lot from among those
who have been already selected combines both elements, the
way in which the rich are compelled by law to attend the assembly and vote for magistrates or discharge other political
duties, while the rest may do as they like, and the endeavour
to have the greater number of the magistrates appointed out
of the richer classes and the highest officers selected from
those who have the greatest incomes, both these are oligarchical features. The oligarchical principle prevails also in the
choice of the council, for all are compelled to choose, but
the compulsion extends only to the choice out of the first
class, and of an equal number out of the second class and out
of the third class, but not in this latter case to all the voters
but to those from the third or fourth class; and the selection
of candidates out of the fourth class is only compulsory on
the first and second. Then, from the persons so chosen, he

says that there ought to be an equal number of each class selected. Thus a preponderance will be given to the better sort   20
of people, who have the larger incomes, because some of the
lower classes, not being compelled, will not vote. These considerations, and others which will be adduced when the time
comes for examining similar constitutions, tend to show that   25
states like Plato's should not be composed of democracy and
monarchy. There is also a danger in electing the magistrates
out of a body who are themselves elected; for, if but a small
number choose to combine, the elections will always go as
they desire. Such is the constitution which is described in the   30
Laws.

7 · Other constitutions have been proposed; some by private persons, others by philosophers and statesmen, which
all come nearer to established or existing ones than either of
Plato's. No one else has introduced such novelties as the community of women and children, or public tables for women: 35
other legislators begin with what is necessary. In the opinion of some, the regulation of property is the chief point of
all, that being the question upon which all revolutions turn.
This danger was recognized by Phaleas of Chalcedon, who
was the first to affirm that the citizens of a state ought to
have equal possessions. He thought that in a new colony the
equalization might be accomplished without difficulty, not   1266[b]1
so easily when a state was already established; and that then
the shortest way of compassing the desired end would be for
the rich to give and not to receive marriage portions, and
for the poor not to give but to receive them.

   Plato in the *Laws* was of the opinion that, to a certain extent, accumulation should be allowed, forbidding, as I have   5
already observed, any citizen to possess more than five times
the minimum qualification. But those who make such laws
should remember what they are apt to forget—that the legislator who fixes the amount of property should also fix the
number of children; for, if the children are too many for the   10
property, the law must be broken. And, besides the violation
of the law, it is a bad thing that many from being rich should

become poor; for men of ruined fortunes are sure to stir up revolutions. That the equalization of property exercises an influence on political society was clearly understood even by some of the old legislators. Laws were made by Solon and others prohibiting an individual from possessing as much land as he pleased; and there are other laws in states which forbid the sale of property: among the Locrians, for example, there is a law that a man is not to sell his property unless he can prove unmistakably that some misfortune has befallen him. Again, there have been laws which enjoin the preservation of the original lots. Such a law existed in the island of Leucas, and the abrogation of it made the constitution too democratic, for the rulers no longer had the prescribed qualification. Again, where there is equality of property, the amount may be either too large or too small, and the possessor may be living either in luxury or penury. Clearly, then, the legislator ought not only to aim at the equalization of properties, but at moderation in their amount. Further, if he prescribe this moderate amount equally to all, he will be no nearer the mark; for it is not the possessions but the desires of mankind which require to be equalized, and this is impossible, unless a sufficient education is provided by the laws. But Phaleas will probably reply that this is precisely what he means; and that, in his opinion, there ought to be in states, not only equal property, but equal education. Still he should tell us what will be the character of his education; there is no use in having one and the same for all, if it is of a sort that predisposes men to avarice, or ambition, or both. Moreover, civil troubles arise, not only out of the inequality of property, but out of the inequality of honour, though in opposite ways. For the common people quarrel about the inequality of property, the higher class about the equality of honour; as the poet says,

> The bad and good alike in honour share.

There are crimes for which the motive is want; and for these Phaleas expects to find a cure in the equalization of property, which will take away from a man the temptation to be a robber, because he is hungry or cold. But want is not the sole incentive to crime; men also wish to enjoy themselves and not to be in a state of desire—they wish to cure some desire, going beyond the necessities of life, which preys upon them; indeed this is not the only reason—they may desire to enjoy pleasures unaccompanied with pain, and therefore they commit crimes.

Now what is the cure of these three disorders? Of the first, moderate possessions and occupation; of the second, habits of temperance; as to the third, if any desire pleasures which depend on themselves, they will find the satisfaction of their desires nowhere but in philosophy; for all other pleasures we are dependent on others. The fact is, that the greatest crimes are caused by excess and not by necessity. Men do not become tyrants in order that they may not suffer cold; and hence great is the honour bestowed, not on him who kills a thief, but on him who kills a tyrant. Thus we see that the institutions of Phaleas avail only against petty crimes.

There is another objection to them. They are chiefly designed to promote the internal welfare of the state. But the legislator should consider also its relation to neighbouring nations, and to all who are outside of it. The government must be organized with a view to military strength; and of this he has said not a word. And so with respect to property: there should not only be enough to supply the internal wants of the state, but also to meet dangers coming from without. The property of the state should not be so large that more powerful neighbours may be tempted by it, while the owners are unable to repel the invaders; nor yet so small that the state is unable to maintain a war even against states of equal power, and of the same character. Phaleas has not laid down any rule; but we should bear in mind that abundance of wealth is an advantage. The best limit will probably be, that a more powerful neighbour must have no inducement to go to war with you by reason of the excess of your wealth, but only such as he would have had if you had possessed less. There is a story that Eubulus, when Autophradates was going to besiege Atarneus, told him to consider how long the operation would take, and then reckon up the cost which would be incurred in the time. 'For', said he, 'I am willing for a smaller sum than that to leave Atarneus at once'. These words of Eubulus made an impression on Autophradates, and he desisted from the siege.

The equalization of property is one of the things that tend to prevent the citizens from quarrelling. Not that the gain in this direction is very great. For the nobles will be dissatisfied because they think themselves worthy of more than an equal share of honours; and this is often found to be a cause of sedition and revolution. And the avarice of mankind is insatiable; at one time two obols was pay enough; but now, when this sum has become customary, men always want more and more without end; for it is of the nature of desire to be unlimited, and most men live only for the gratification of it. The beginning of reform is not so much to equalize property as to train the nobler sort of natures not to desire more, and to prevent the lower from getting more; that is to say, they must be kept down, but not ill-treated. Besides, the equalization proposed by Phaleas is imperfect; for he only equalizes land, whereas a man may be rich also in slaves, and cattle, and money, and in the abundance of what are called his movables. Now either all these things must be equalized, or some limit must be imposed on them, or they must all be let alone. It would appear that Phaleas is legislating for a small city only, if, as he supposes, all the artisans are to be public slaves and not to form a supplementary part of the body of citizens. But if there is a law that artisans are to be public slaves, it should only apply to those engaged on public works, as at Epidamnus, or at Athens on the plan which Diophantus once introduced.

From these observations any one may judge how far Phaleas was wrong or right in his ideas.

8 • Hippodamus, the son of Euryphon, a native of Miletus, the same who invented the art of planning cities, and who also laid out the Piraeus—a strange man, whose fondness for distinction led him into a general eccentricity of life, which made some think him affected (for he would wear

flowing hair and expensive ornaments; but these were worn
on a cheap but warm garment both in winter and summer);
he, besides aspiring to be an adept in the knowledge of nature, was the first person not a statesman who made inquiries about the best form of government.   30

The city of Hippodamus was composed of 10,000 citizens divided into three parts—one of artisans, one of husbandmen, and a third of armed defenders of the state. He
also divided the land into three parts, one sacred, one public, the third private:—the first was set apart to maintain the   35
customary worship of the gods, the second was to support
the warriors, the third was the property of the husbandmen.
He also divided laws into three classes, and no more, for he
maintained that there are three subjects of lawsuits—insult,
injury, and homicide. He likewise instituted a single final   40
court of appeal, to which all causes seeming to have been im-
properly decided might be referred; this court he formed of
elders chosen for the purpose. He was further of the opinion   1268ᵃ1
that the decisions of the courts ought not to be given by the
use of a voting pebble, but that everyone should have a tablet
on which he might not only write a simple condemnation, or
leave the tablet blank for a simple acquittal; but, if he partly
acquitted and partly condemned, he was to distinguish ac-   5
cordingly. To the existing law he objected that it obliged the
judges to be guilty of perjury, whichever way they voted. He
also enacted that those who discovered anything for the good
of the state should be honoured, and he provided that the
children of citizens who died in battle should be maintained
at public expense, as if such an enactment had never been   10
heard of before, yet it actually exists at Athens and in other
places. As to the magistrates, he would have them all elected
by the people, that is, by the three classes already mentioned,
and those who were elected were to watch over the interests
of the public, of strangers, and of orphans. These are the most
striking points in the constitution of Hippodamus. There is   15
not much else.

The first of these proposals to which objection may be
taken is the threefold division of the citizens. The artisans,

and the husbandmen, and the warriors, all have a share in the government. But the husbandmen have no arms, and the artisans neither arms nor land, and therefore they become all but slaves of the warrior class. That they should share in all the offices is an impossibility; for generals and guardians of the citizens, and nearly all the principal magistrates, must be taken from the class of those who carry arms. Yet, if the two other classes have no share in the government, how can they be loyal citizens? It may be said that those who have arms must necessarily be masters of both the other classes, but this is not so easily accomplished unless they are numerous; and if they are, why should the other classes share in the government at all, or have power to appoint magistrates?

Further, what use are farmers to the city? Artisans there must be, for these are wanted in every city, and they can live by their craft, as elsewhere; and the husbandmen, too, if they really provided the warriors with food, might fairly have a share in the government. But in the republic of Hippodamus they are supposed to have land of their own, which they cultivate for their private benefit. Again, as to this common land out of which the soldiers are maintained, if they are themselves to be the cultivators of it, the warrior class will be identical with the husbandmen, although the legislator intended to make a distinction between them. If, again, there are to be other cultivators distinct both from the husbandmen, who have land of their own, and from the warriors, they will make a fourth class, which has no place in the state and no share in anything. Or, if the same persons are to cultivate their own lands, and those of the public as well, they will have a difficulty in supplying the quantity of produce which will maintain two households:[2] and why, in this case, should there be any division, for they might find food themselves and give to the warriors from the same land and the same lots? There is surely a great confusion in all this.

Neither is the law to be commended which says that the judges, when a simple issue is laid before them, should make

²Reading οἰκίαιS.

a distinction in their judgement; for the judge is thus converted into an arbitrator. Now, in an arbitration, although the
arbitrators are many, they confer with one another about the
decision; but in courts of law this is impossible, and, indeed,
most legislators take pains to prevent the judges from hold-   10
ing any communication with one another. Again, will there
not be confusion if the judge thinks that damages should be
given, but not so much as the suitor demands? He asks, say,
for twenty minae, and the judge allows him ten minae (or in
general the suitor asks for more and the judge allows less),
while another judge allows five, another four minae. In this
way they will go on splitting up the damages, and some will   15
grant the whole and others nothing: how is the final reckoning to be taken? Again, no one contends that he who votes for
a simple acquittal or condemnation perjures himself, if the
indictment has been laid in an unqualified form; and this is
just, for the judge who acquits does not decide that the defendant owes nothing, but that he does not owe the twenty   20
minae. He only is guilty of perjury who thinks that the defendant ought not to pay twenty minae, and yet condemns him.

   To honour those who discover anything which is useful to
the state is a proposal which has a specious sound, but cannot
safely be enacted by law, for it may encourage informers, and
perhaps even lead to political commotions. This question
involves another. It has been doubted whether it is or is not   25
expedient to make any changes in the laws of a country, even
if another law be better. Now, if all changes are inexpedient,
we can hardly assent to the proposal of Hippodamus; for,
under pretence of doing a public service, a man may introduce measures which are really destructive to the laws or to   30
the constitution. But, since we have touched upon this subject, perhaps we had better go a little into detail, for, as I was
saying, there is a difference of opinion, and it may sometimes
seem desirable to make changes. Such changes in the other
arts and sciences have certainly been beneficial; medicine,
for example, and gymnastics, and every other art and craft
have departed from traditional usage. And, if politics be an   35
art, change must be necessary in this as in any other art. That

improvement has occurred is shown by the fact that old customs are exceedingly simple and barbarous. For the ancient
Hellenes went about armed and bought their brides from
each other. The remains of ancient laws which have come
down to us are quite absurd; for example, at Cumae there is
a law about murder, to the effect that if the accuser produce a
certain number of witnesses from among his own kinsmen,
the accused shall be held guilty. Again, men in general desire
the good, and not merely what their fathers had. But the primaeval inhabitants, whether they were born of the earth or
were the survivors of some destruction, may be supposed
to have been no better than ordinary or even foolish people
among ourselves (such is certainly the tradition concerning
the earth-born men); and it would be ridiculous to rest contented with their notions. Even when laws have been written
down, they ought not always to remain unaltered. As in other
sciences, so in politics, it is impossible that all things should
be precisely set down in writing; for enactments must be
universal, but actions are concerned with particulars. Hence
we infer that sometimes and in certain cases laws should be
changed; but when we look at the matter from another point
of view, great caution would seem to be required. For the
habit of lightly changing the laws is an evil, and, when the
advantage is small, some errors both of lawgivers and rulers
had better be left; the citizen will not gain so much by making
the change as he will lose by the habit of disobedience. The
analogy of the arts is false; a change in a law is a very different
thing from a change in an art. For the law has no power to
command obedience except that of habit, which can only be
given by time, so that a readiness to change from old to new
laws enfeebles the power of the law. Even if we admit that
the laws are to be changed, are they all to be changed, and in
every state? And are they to be changed by anybody who likes,
or only by certain persons? These are very important questions; and therefore we had better reserve the discussion of
them to a more suitable occasion.

9 • In the governments of Lacedaemon and Crete, and indeed in all governments, two points have to be considered:

first, whether any particular law is good or bad, when compared with the perfect state; secondly, whether it is or is not consistent with the idea and character which the lawgiver has set before his citizens. That in a well-ordered state the citizens should have leisure and not have to provide for their daily wants is generally acknowledged, but there is a difficulty in seeing how this leisure is to be attained. The Thessalian Penestae have often risen against their masters, and the Helots in like manner against the Lacedaemonians, for whose misfortunes they are always lying in wait. Nothing, however, of this kind has as yet happened to the Cretans; the reason probably is that the neighbouring cities, even when at war with one another, never form an alliance with rebellious serfs, rebellions not being for their interest, since they themselves have a dependent population. Whereas all the neighbours of the Lacedaemonians, whether Argives, Messenians, or Arcadians, were their enemies. In Thessaly, again, the original revolt of the slaves occurred because the Thessalians were still at war with the neighbouring Achaeans, Perrhaebians and Magnesians. Besides, if there were no other difficulty, the treatment or management of slaves is a troublesome affair; for, if not kept in hand, they are insolent, and think that they are as good as their masters, and, if harshly treated, they hate and conspire against them. Now it is clear that when these are the results the citizens of a state have not found out the secret of managing their subject population.

Again, the license of the Lacedaemonian women defeats the intention of the Spartan constitution, and is adverse to the happiness of the state. For, a husband and a wife being each a part of every family, the state may be considered as about equally divided into men and women; and, therefore, in those states in which the condition of the women is bad, half the city may be regarded as having no laws. And this is what has actually happened at Sparta; the legislator wanted to make the whole state hardy, and he has carried out his intention in the case of the men, but he has neglected the women, who live in every sort of intemperance and luxury. The consequence is that in such a state wealth is too highly valued, especially if the citizens fall under the dominion of

25   their wives, after the manner of most warlike races, except the Celts and a few others who openly approve of male homosexuality. The old mythologer would seem to have been right in uniting Ares and Aphrodite, for all warlike races

30   are prone to the love either of men or of women. This was exemplified among the Spartans in the days of their greatness; many things were managed by their women. But what difference does it make whether women rule, or the rulers are ruled by women? The result is the same. Even in regard

35   to boldness, which is of no use in daily life, and is needed only in war, the influence of the Lacedaemonian women has been most mischievous. The evil showed itself in the Theban invasion, when, unlike the women in other cities, they were utterly useless and caused more confusion than the enemy. This license of the Lacedaemonian women existed from the earliest times, and was only what might be expected. For, during the wars of the Lacedaemonians, first against the Ar-

1270ᵃ1   gives, and afterwards against the Arcadians and Messenians, the men were long away from home, and, on the return of peace, they gave themselves into the legislator's hand, already prepared by the discipline of a soldier's life (in which there

5   are many elements of excellence), to receive his enactments. But, when Lycurgus, as tradition says, wanted to bring the women under his laws, they resisted, and he gave up the attempt. These then are the causes of what then happened, and this defect in the constitution is clearly to be attributed

10   to them. We are not, however, considering what is or is not to be excused, but what is right or wrong, and the disorder of the women, as I have already said, not only gives an air of indecorum to the constitution considered in itself, but tends in a measure to foster avarice.

    The mention of avarice naturally suggests a criticism on

15   the inequality of property. While some of the Spartan citizens have quite small properties, others have very large ones: hence the land has passed into the hands of a few. And this is due also to faulty laws; for, although the legislator rightly

20   holds up to shame the sale or purchase of an inheritance, he allows anybody who likes to give or bequeath it.

Yet both practices lead to the same result. And nearly two-fifths of the whole country are held by women; this is owing to the number of heiresses and to the large dowries which are customary. It would surely have been better to have given no dowries at all, or, if any, but small or moderate ones. As the law now stands, a man may bestow his heiress on any one whom he pleases, and, if he die intestate, the privilege of giving her away descends to his heir. Hence, although the country is able to maintain 1500 cavalry and 30,000 hoplites, the whole number of Spartan citizens fell below 1000. The result proves the faulty nature of their laws respecting property; for the city sank under a single defeat; the want of men was their ruin. There is a tradition that, in the days of their ancient kings, they were in the habit of giving the rights of citizenship to strangers, and therefore, in spite of their long wars, no lack of population was experienced by them; indeed, at one time Sparta is said to have numbered not less than 10,000 citizens. Whether this statement is true or not, it would certainly have been better to have maintained their numbers by the equalization of property. Again, the law which relates to the procreation of children is adverse to the correction of this inequality. For the legislator, wanting to have as many Spartans as he could, encouraged the citizens to have large families; and there is a law at Sparta that the father of three sons shall be exempt from military service, and he who has four from all the burdens of the state. Yet it is obvious that, if there were many children, the land being distributed as it is, many of them must necessarily fall into poverty.

The Lacedaemonian constitution is defective also in respect of the Ephorate. This magistracy has authority in the highest matters, but the Ephors are chosen from the whole people, and so the office is apt to fall into the hands of very poor men, who, being badly off, are open to bribes. There have been many examples at Sparta of this evil in former times; and quite recently, in the matter of the Andrians, certain of the Ephors who were bribed did their best to ruin the state. And so great and tyrannical is their power, that even the kings have been compelled to court them, so that,

in this way as well, together with the royal office the whole constitution has deteriorated, and from being an aristocracy has turned into a democracy. The Ephorate certainly does keep the state together; for the people are contented when they have a share in the highest office, and the result,
20 whether due to the legislator or to chance, has been advantageous. For if a constitution is to be permanent, all the parts of the state must wish that it should exist and these arrangements be maintained. This is the case at Sparta, where the kings desire its permanence because they have due honour in
25 their own persons; the nobles because they are represented in the council of elders (for the office of elder is a reward of excellence); and the people, because all are eligible for the Ephorate. The election of Ephors out of the whole people is perfectly right, but ought not to be carried on in the present fashion, which is too childish. Again, they have the decision of great causes, although they are quite ordinary men,
30 and therefore they should not determine them merely on their own judgement, but according to written rules, and to the laws. Their way of life, too, is not in accordance with the spirit of the constitution—they have a deal too much license; whereas, in the case of the other citizens, the excess of strictness is so intolerable that they run away from the law into the
35 secret indulgence of sensual pleasures.

Again, the council of elders is not free from defects. It may be said that the elders are good men and well trained in manly virtue; and that, therefore, there is an advantage to the state in having them. But that judges of important causes should hold office for life is a disputable thing, for the mind grows old as well as the body.
1271ᵃ1 And when men have been educated in such a manner that even the legislator himself cannot trust them, there is real danger. Many of the elders are well known to have taken bribes and to have been guilty of partiality in public affairs.
5 And therefore they ought not to be non-accountable; yet at Sparta they are so. All magistracies are accountable to the Ephors. But this prerogative is too great for them, and we maintain that the control should be exercised in some other

manner. Further, the mode in which the Spartans elect their elders is childish; and it is improper that the person to be elected should canvass for the office; the worthiest should be appointed, whether he chooses or not. And here the legislator clearly indicates the same intention which appears in other parts of his constitution; he would have his citizens ambitious, and he has reckoned upon this quality in the election of the elders; for no one would ask to be elected if he were not. Yet ambition and avarice, almost more than any other passions, are the motives of voluntary injustices.

Whether kings are or are not an advantage to states, I will consider at another time; they should at any rate be chosen, not as they are now, but with regard to their personal life and conduct. The legislator himself obviously did not suppose that he could make them really good men; at least he shows a great distrust of their virtue. For this reason the Spartans used to join enemies with them in the same embassy, and the quarrels between the kings were held to preserve the state.

Neither did the first introducer of the common meals, called 'phiditia', regulate them well. The entertainment ought to have been provided at public cost, as in Crete; but among the Lacedaemonians everyone is expected to contribute, and some of them are too poor to afford the expense; thus the intention of the legislator is frustrated. The common meals were meant to be a democratic institution, but the existing manner of regulating them is the reverse of democratic. For the very poor can scarcely take part in them; and, according to ancient custom, those who cannot contribute are not allowed to retain their rights of citizenship.

The law about the Spartan admirals has often been censured, and with justice; it is a source of dissension, for the kings are perpetual generals, and this office of admiral is but the setting up of another king.

The charge which Plato brings, in the *Laws*, against the intention of the legislator, is likewise justified; the whole constitution has regard to one part of excellence only—the excellence of the soldier, which gives victory in war. So long as they were at war, therefore, their power was preserved,

but when they had attained empire they fell, for of the arts
of peace they knew nothing, and have never engaged in any
employment higher than war. There is another error, equally
great, into which they have fallen. Although they truly think
that the goods for which men contend are to be acquired by
excellence rather than by vice, they err in supposing that
these goods are to be preferred to the excellence which gains
them.

Again, the revenues of the state are ill-managed; there
is no money in the treasury, although they are obliged to
carry on great wars, and they are unwilling to pay taxes. The
greater part of the land being in the hands of Spartans, they
do not look closely into one another's contributions. The result which the legislator has produced is the reverse of beneficial; for he has made his city poor, and his citizens greedy.

Enough respecting the Spartan constitution, of which
these are the principal defects.

10 • The Cretan constitution nearly resembles the Spartan, and in some few points is quite as good; but for the most
part less perfect in form. The older constitutions are generally less elaborate than the later, and the Lacedaemonian is
said to be, and probably is, in a very great measure, a copy
of the Cretan. According to tradition, Lycurgus, when he
ceased to be the guardian of King Charillus, went abroad and
spent most of his time in Crete. For the two countries are
nearly connected; the Lyctians are a colony of the Lacedaemonians, and the colonists, when they came to Crete, adopted
the constitution which they found existing among the inhabitants. Even to this day the Perioeci are governed by the
original laws which Minos is supposed to have enacted. The
island seems to be intended by nature for dominion in Hellas, and to be well situated; it extends right across the sea,
around which nearly all the Hellenes are settled; and while
one end is not far from the Peloponnese, the other almost
reaches to the region of Asia about Triopium and Rhodes.
Hence Minos acquired the empire of the sea, subduing some

of the islands and colonizing others; at last he invaded Sicily, 40
where he died near Camicus.

The Cretan institutions resemble the Lacedaemonian.
The Helots are the husbandmen of the one, the Perioeci of the 1272ᵃ1
other, and both Cretans and Lacedaemonians have common
meals, which were anciently called by the Lacedaemonians
not 'phiditia' but 'andria'; and the Cretans have the same
word, the use of which proves that the common meals originally came from Crete. Further, the two constitutions are
similar; for the office of the Ephors is the same as that of the 5
Cretan Cosmi, the only difference being that whereas the
Ephors are five, the Cosmi are ten in number. The elders, too,
answer to the elders in Crete, who are termed by the Cretans
the council. And the kingly office once existed in Crete, but
was abolished, and the Cosmi have now the duty of leading 10
them in war. All classes share in the ecclesia, but it can only
ratify the decrees of the elders and the Cosmi.

The common meals of Crete are certainly better managed
than the Lacedaemonian; for in Lacedaemon every one pays
so much per head, or, if he fails, the law, as I have already ex- 15
plained, forbids him to exercise the rights of citizenship. But
in Crete they are of a more popular character. There, of all
the fruits of the earth the cattle raised on the public lands,
and of the tribute which is paid by the Perioeci, one portion
is assigned to the gods and to the service of the state, and an- 20
other to the common meals, so that men, women, and children are all supported out of a common stock. The legislator
has many ingenious ways of securing moderation in eating,
which he conceives to be a gain; he likewise encourages the
separation of men from women, lest they should have too
many children, and the companionship of men with one 25
another—whether this is a good or bad thing I shall have an
opportunity of considering at another time. Thus that the
Cretan common meals are better ordered than the Lacedaemonian there can be no doubt.

On the other hand, the Cosmi are even a worse institution
than the Ephors, of which they have all the evils without the

30   good. Like the Ephors, they are any chance persons, but in
Crete this is not counterbalanced by a corresponding political advantage. At Sparta everyone is eligible, and the body of
the people, having a share in the highest office, want the constitution to be permanent. But in Crete the Cosmi are elected
out of certain families, and not out of the whole people, and
35   the elders out of those who have been Cosmi.

The same criticism may be made about the Cretan, which
has been already made about the Lacedaemonian affairs.
Their unaccountability and life tenure is too great a privilege,
and their arbitrary power of acting upon their own judgement, and dispensing with written law, is dangerous. It is
no proof of the goodness of the institution that the people
40   are not discontented at being excluded from it. For there is
no profit to be made out of the office as out of the Ephorate,
since, unlike the Ephors, the Cosmi, being in an island, are
1272ᵇ1   removed from temptation.

The remedy by which they correct the evil of this institution is an extraordinary one, suited rather to a dynasty than
to a constitutional state. For the Cosmi are often expelled by
a conspiracy of their own colleagues, or of private individuals; and they are allowed also to resign before their term of
5   office has expired. Surely all matters of this kind are better
regulated by law than by the will of man, which is a very un-
safe rule. Worst of all is the suspension of the office of Cosmi,
a device to which the nobles often have recourse when they
will not submit to justice. This shows that the Cretan govern-
10   ment, although possessing some of the characteristics of a
constitutional state, is really a dynasty.

The nobles have a habit, too, of setting up a chief; they get
together a party among the common people and their own
friends and then quarrel and fight with one another. What is
this but the temporary destruction of the state and dissolu-
15   tion of society? A city is in a dangerous condition when those
who are willing are also able to attack her. But, as I have already said, the island of Crete is saved by her situation; distance has the same effect as the prohibition of strangers. This
is the reason why the Perioeci are contented in Crete, whereas

the Helots are perpetually revolting. For the Cretans have no foreign dominions and, when lately foreign invaders found their way into the island, the weakness of the Cretan constitution was revealed. Enough of the government of Crete. 20

11 • The Carthaginians are also considered to have an excellent form of government, which differs from that of any other state in several respects, though it is in some very like the Lacedaemonian. Indeed, all three states—the Lacedaemonian, the Cretan, and the Carthaginian—nearly resemble one another, and are very different from any others. Many of the Carthaginian institutions are excellent. The superiority of their constitution is proved by the fact that the common people remains loyal to the constitution; the Carthaginians have never had any rebellion worth speaking of, and have never been under the rule of a tyrant. 25

Among the points in which the Carthaginian constitution resembles the Lacedaemonian are the following:—The common tables of the clubs answer to the Spartan phiditia, and their magistracy of the 104 to the Ephors; but, whereas the Ephors are any chance persons, the magistrates of the Carthaginians are elected according to merit—this is an improvement. They have also their kings and their council of elders, who correspond to the kings and elders of Sparta. Their kings, unlike the Spartan, are not always of the same family, nor that an ordinary one, but if there is some distinguished family they are selected out of it and not appointed by seniority—this is far better. Such officers have great power, and therefore, if they are persons of little worth, do a great deal of harm, and they have already done harm at Lacedaemon. 35

1273ª1

Most of the defects or deviations from the perfect state, for which the Carthaginian constitution would be censured, apply equally to all the forms of government which we have mentioned. But of the deflections from aristocracy and constitutional government, some incline more to democracy and some to oligarchy. The kings and elders, if unanimous, may determine whether they will or will not bring a matter before the people, but when they are not unanimous, the 5

people decide on such matters as well. And whatever the
kings and elders bring before the people is not only heard
but also determined by them, and anyone who likes may oppose it; now this is not permitted in Sparta and Crete. That
the magistracies of five who have under them many important matters should be co-opted, that they should choose the
supreme council of 100, and should hold office longer than
other magistrates (for they are virtually rulers both before
and after they hold office)—these are oligarchical features;
their being without salary and not elected by lot, and any
similar points, such as the practice of having all suits tried
by the magistrates, and not some by one class and some by
another, as at Lacedaemon, are characteristic of aristocracy.
The Carthaginian constitution deviates from aristocracy and
inclines to oligarchy, chiefly on a point where popular opinion is on their side. For men in general think that magistrates should be chosen not only for their merit, but for their
wealth: a man, they say, who is poor cannot rule well—he
has not the leisure. If, then, election of magistrates for their
wealth be characteristic of oligarchy, and election for merit
of aristocracy, there will be a third form under which the constitution of Carthage is comprehended; for the Carthaginians choose their magistrates, and particularly the highest of
them—their kings and generals—with an eye both to merit
and to wealth.

But we must acknowledge that, in thus deviating from
aristocracy, the legislator has committed an error. Nothing
is more absolutely necessary than to provide that the highest class, not only when in office, but when out of office,
should have leisure and not disgrace themselves in any way;
and to this his attention should be first directed. Even if you
must have regard to wealth, in order to secure leisure, yet it
is surely a bad thing that the greatest offices, such as those of
kings and generals, should be bought. The law which allows
this abuse makes wealth of more account than excellence,
and the whole state becomes avaricious. For, whenever the
chiefs of the state deem anything honourable, the other citizens are sure to follow their example; and, where excellence

has not the first place, there aristocracy cannot be firmly es-   1273^b1
tablished. Those who have been at the expense of purchasing
their places will be in the habit of repaying themselves; and
it is absurd to suppose that a poor and honest man will be
wanting to make gains, and that a lower stamp of man who   5
has incurred a great expense will not. That is why they should
rule who are able to rule best. And even if the legislator does
not care to protect the good from poverty, he should at any
rate secure leisure for them when in office.

It would seem also to be a bad principle that the same person should hold many offices, which is a favourite practice
among the Carthaginians, for one business is better done by
one man. The legislator should see to this and should not appoint the same person to be a flute-player and a shoemaker.   10
Hence, where the state is large, it is more in accordance both
with constitutional and with democratic principles that the
offices of state should be distributed among many persons.
For, as I said, this arrangement is fairer to all, and any action
familiarized by repetition is better and sooner performed. We   15
have a proof in military and naval matters; the duties of command and of obedience in both these services extend to all.

The government of the Carthaginians is oligarchical, but
they successfully escape the evils of oligarchy by being wealthy,
sending out one portion of the people after another to the
cities. This is their panacea and the means by which they give
stability to the state. This is the result of chance but it is the   20
legislator who should be able to provide against revolution.
As things are, if any misfortune occurred, and the bulk of the
subjects revolted, there would be no way of restoring peace by
legal methods.

Such is the character of the Lacedaemonian, Cretan, and
Carthaginian constitutions, which are justly celebrated.   25

12 · Of those who have treated of governments, some have
never taken any part at all in public affairs, but have passed
their lives in a private station; about most of them, what was
worth telling has been already told. Others have been lawgiv-   30
ers, either in their own or in foreign cities, whose affairs they

have administered; and of these some have only made laws, others have framed constitutions; for example, Lycurgus and Solon did both. Of the Lacedaemonian constitution I have already spoken. As to Solon, he is thought by some to have been a good legislator, who put an end to the exclusiveness of the oligarchy, emancipated the people, established the ancient Athenian democracy, and harmonized the different elements of the state. According to their view, the council of Areopagus was an oligarchical element, the elected magistracy, aristocratic, and the courts of law, democratic. The truth seems to be that the council and the elected magistracy existed before the time of Solon, and were retained by him, but that he formed the courts of law out of all the citizens, thus creating the democracy, which is the very reason why he is sometimes blamed. For in giving the supreme power to the law courts, which are elected by lot, he is thought to have destroyed the non-democratic element. When the law courts grew powerful, to please the people who were now playing the tyrant the old constitution was changed into the existing democracy. Ephialtes and Pericles curtailed the power of the Areopagus; Pericles also instituted the payment of the juries, and thus every demagogue in turn increased the power of the democracy until it became what we now see. All this seems, however, to be the result of circumstances, and not to have been intended by Solon. For the people, having been instrumental in gaining the empire of the sea in the Persian War, began to get a notion of itself, and followed worthless demagogues, whom the better class opposed. Solon, himself, appears to have given the Athenians only that power of electing to offices and calling to account the magistrates which was absolutely necessary; for without it they would have been in a state of slavery and enmity to the government. All the magistrates he appointed from the notables and the men of wealth, that is to say, from the pentacosiomedimni, or from the class called zeugitae, or from a third class of so-called knights. The fourth class were labourers who had no share in any magistracy.

Mere legislators were Zaleucus, who gave laws to the Epizephyrian Locrians, and Charondas, who legislated for

his own city of Catana, and for the other Chalcidian cities in   25
Italy and Sicily. Some people attempt to make out that Ono-
macritus was the first person who had any special skill in legislation, and that he, although a Locrian by birth, was trained
in Crete, where he lived in the exercise of his prophetic art;
that Thales was his companion, and that Lycurgus and Za-   30
leucus were disciples of Thales, as Charondas was of Zaleucus. But their account is quite inconsistent with chronology.

There was also Philolaus, the Corinthian, who gave laws
to the Thebans. This Philolaus was one of the family of the
Bacchiadae, and a lover of Diocles, the Olympic victor, who
left Corinth in horror of the incestuous passion which his
mother Halcyone had conceived for him, and retired to The-   35
bes, where the two friends together ended their days. The
inhabitants still point out their tombs, which are in full view
of one another, but one is visible from the Corinthian territory, the other not. Tradition says the two friends arranged
them thus, Diocles out of horror at his misfortunes, so that   40
the land of Corinth might not be visible from his tomb;
Philolaus that it might. This is the reason why they settled   1274ᵇ1
at Thebes, and so Philolaus legislated for the Thebans, and,
besides some other enactments, gave them laws about the
procreation of children, which they call the 'Laws of Adop-
tion'. These laws were peculiar to him, and were intended to   5
preserve the number of the lots.

In the legislation of Charondas there is nothing distinctive, except the suits against false witnesses. He is the first
who instituted denunciation for perjury. His laws are more
exact and more precisely expressed than even those of our
modern legislators.

(Characteristic of Phaleas is the equalization of property;   10
of Plato, the community of women, children, and property,
the common meals of women, and the law about drinking,
that the sober shall be masters of the feast; also the training
of soldiers to acquire by practice equal skill with both hands,
so that one should be as useful as the other.)

Draco has left laws, but he adapted them to a constitution   15
which already existed, and there is no peculiarity in them

which is worth mentioning, except the greatness and severity of the punishments.

Pittacus, too, was only a lawgiver, and not the author of a constitution; he has a law which is peculiar to him, that, if a drunken man do something wrong, he shall be more heavily punished than if he were sober; he looked not to the excuse which might be offered for the drunkard, but only to expediency, for drunken more often than sober people commit acts of violence.

Androdamas of Rhegium gave laws to the Chalcidians of Thrace. Some of them relate to homicide, and to heiresses; but there is nothing distinctive in them.

And here let us conclude our inquiry into the various constitutions which either actually exist, or have been devised by theorists.

BOOK III

1 • He who would inquire into the essence and attributes of various kinds of government must first of all determine what a state is. At present this is a disputed question. Some say that the state has done a certain act; others, not the state, but the oligarchy or the tyrant. And the legislator or statesman is concerned entirely with the state, a government being an arrangement of the inhabitants of a state. But a state is composite, like any other whole made up of many parts—these are the citizens, who compose it. It is evident, therefore, that we must begin by asking, Who is the citizen, and what is the meaning of the term? For here again there may be a difference of opinion. He who is a citizen in a democracy will often not be a citizen in an oligarchy. Leaving out of consideration those who have been made citizens, or who have obtained the name of citizen in any other accidental manner, we may say, first, that a citizen is not a citizen because he lives in a certain place, for resident aliens and slaves share in the place; nor is he a citizen who has legal rights to the extent of suing and being sued; for this right may be enjoyed under the pro-

visions of a treaty. Resident aliens in many places do not 10
possess even such rights completely, for they are obliged to
have a patron, so that they do but imperfectly participate in
the community, and we call them citizens only in a qualified
sense, as we might apply the term to children who are too
young to be on the register, or to old men who have been re- 15
lieved from state duties. Of these we do not say quite simply
that they are citizens, but add in the one case that they are not
of age, and in the other, that they are past the age, or something of that sort; the precise expression is immaterial, for
our meaning is clear. Similar difficulties to those which I have
mentioned may be raised and answered about disfranchised
citizens and about exiles. But the citizen whom we are seeking to define is a citizen in the strictest sense, against whom 20
no such exception can be taken, and his special characteristic
is that he shares in the administration of justice, and in offices. Now of offices some are discontinuous, and the same
persons are not allowed to hold them twice, or can only hold 25
them after a fixed interval; others have no limit of time—for
example, the office of juryman or member of the assembly. It
may, indeed, be argued that these are not magistrates at all,
and that their functions give them no share in the government. But surely it is ridiculous to say that those who have
the supreme power do not govern. Let us not dwell further
upon this, which is a purely verbal question; what we want is 30
a common term including both juryman and member of the
assembly. Let us, for the sake of distinction, call it 'indefinite
office', and we will assume that those who share in such office
are citizens. This is the most comprehensive definition of a
citizen, and best suits all those who are generally so called.

But we must not forget that things of which the underly- 35
ing principles differ in kind, one of them being first, another
second, another third, have, when regarded in this relation,
nothing, or hardly anything, worth mentioning in common. Now we see that governments differ in kind, and that
some of them are prior and that others are posterior; those 1275ᵇ1
which are faulty or perverted are necessarily posterior to
those which are perfect. (What we mean by perversion will

be hereafter explained.) The citizen then of necessity differs
under each form of government; and our definition is best
adapted to the citizen of a democracy; but not necessarily to
other states. For in some states the people are not acknowledged, nor have they any regular assembly, but only extraordinary ones; and law-suits are distributed by sections among
the magistrates. At Lacedaemon, for instance, the Ephors determine suits about contracts, which they distribute
among themselves, while the elders are judges of homicide,
and other causes are decided by other magistrates. A similar
principle prevails at Carthage; there certain magistrates decide all causes. We may, indeed, modify our definition of the
citizen so as to include these states. In them it is the holder
of a definite, not an indefinite office, who is juryman and
member of the assembly, and to some or all such holders of
definite offices is reserved the right of deliberating or judging
about some things or about all things. The conception of the
citizen now begins to clear up.

He who has the power to take part in the deliberative or
judicial administration of any state is said by us to be a citizen of that state; and, speaking generally, a state is a body of
citizens sufficing for the purposes of life.

2 • But in practice a citizen is defined to be one of whom
both the parents are citizens (and not just one, i.e. father or
mother); others insist on going further back; say to two or
three or more ancestors. This is a short and practical definition; but there are some who raise the further question of
how this third or fourth ancestor came to be a citizen. Gorgias of Leontini, partly because he was in a difficulty, partly
in irony, said that mortars are what is made by the mortar-
makers, and the citizens of Larissa are those who are made
by the magistrates; for it is their trade to 'make Larissaeans'.
Yet the question is really simple, for, if according to the definition just given they shared in the government, they were
citizens. This is a better definition than the other. For the
words, 'born of a father or mother who is a citizen', cannot
possibly apply to the first inhabitants or founders of a state.

There is a greater difficulty in the case of those who have been made citizens after a revolution, as by Cleisthenes at Athens after the expulsion of the tyrants, for he enrolled in tribes many metics, both strangers and slaves. The doubt in these cases is, not who is, but whether he who is ought to be a citizen; and there will still be a further doubt, whether he who ought not to be a citizen, is one in fact, for what ought not to be is what is false. Now, there are some who hold office, and yet ought not to hold office, whom we describe as ruling, but ruling unjustly. And the citizen was defined by the fact of his holding some kind of rule or office—he who holds a certain sort of office fulfils our definition of a citizen. It is evident, therefore, that the citizens about whom the doubt has arisen must be called citizens.

3 • Whether they ought to be so or not is a question which is bound up with the previous inquiry. For a parallel question is raised respecting the state, whether a certain act is or is not an act of the state; for example, in the transition from an oligarchy or a tyranny to a democracy. In such cases persons refuse to fulfil their contracts or any other obligations, on the ground that the tyrant and not the state, contracted them; they argue that some constitutions are established by force, and not for the sake of the common good. But this would apply equally to democracies, and then the acts of the democracy will be neither more nor less acts of the state in question than those of an oligarchy or of a tyranny. This question runs up into another:—on what principle shall we ever say that the state is the same, or different? It would be a very superficial view which considered only the place and the inhabitants (for the soil and the population may be separated, and some of the inhabitants may live in one place and some in another). This, however, is not a very serious difficulty; we need only remark that the word 'state' is ambiguous.

It is further asked: When are men, living in the same place, to be regarded as a single city—what is the limit? Certainly not the wall of the city, for you might surround all Peloponnesus with a wall. Babylon, we may say, is like this, and every

city that has the compass of a nation rather than a city; Babylon, they say, had been taken for three days before some part
of the inhabitants became aware of the fact.

30   This difficulty may, however, with advantage be deferred
to another occasion; the statesman has to consider the size
of the state, and whether it should consist of more than one
race or not.

    Again, shall we say that while the race of inhabitants re-
35   mains the same, the city is also the same, although the citizens are always dying and being born, as we call rivers and
fountains the same, although the water is always flowing away
and more coming? Or shall we say that the generations of
men, like the rivers, are the same, but that the state changes?
1276ᵇ1   For, since the state is a partnership, and is a partnership of
citizens in a constitution, when the form of the government
changes, and becomes different, then it may be supposed that
the state is no longer the same, just as a tragic differs from a
5   comic chorus, although the members of both may be identical. And in this manner we speak of every union or composition of elements as different when the form of their composition alters; for example, a scale containing the same sounds
is said to be different, accordingly as the Dorian or the Phrygian mode is employed. And if this is true it is evident that
10   the sameness of the state consists chiefly in the sameness
of the constitution, and it may be called or not called by the
same name, whether the inhabitants are the same or entirely
different. It is quite another question, whether a state ought
or ought not to fulfil engagements when the form of govern-
15   ment changes.

    4 • There is a point nearly allied to the preceding: whether
the excellence of a good man and a good citizen is the same
or not. But before entering on this discussion, we must certainly first obtain some general notion of the excellence of
20   the citizen. Like the sailor, the citizen is a member of a community. Now, sailors have different functions, for one of
them is a rower, another a pilot, and a third a look-out man, a
fourth is described by some similar term; and while the pre-

cise definition of each individual's excellence applies exclu-   25
sively to him, there is, at the same time, a common definition
applicable to them all. For they have all of them a common
object, which is safety in navigation. Similarly, one citizen
differs from another, but the salvation of the community is
the common business of them all.

This community is the constitution; the excellence of the   30
citizen must therefore be relative to the constitution of
which he is a member. If, then, there are many forms of government, it is evident that there is not one single excellence
of the good citizen which is perfect excellence. But we say
that the good man is he who has one single excellence which
is perfect excellence. Hence it is evident that the good citizen
need not of necessity possess the excellence which makes a   35
good man.

The same question may also be approached by another
road, from a consideration of the best constitution. If the
state cannot be entirely composed of good men, and yet each
citizen is expected to do his own business well, and must
therefore have excellence, still, inasmuch as all the citizens
cannot be alike, the excellence of the citizen and of the good   1277ª1
man cannot coincide. All must have the excellence of the
good citizen—thus, and thus only, can the state be perfect;
but they will not have the excellence of a good man, unless we
assume that in the good state all the citizens must be good.

Again, the state, as composed of unlikes, may be com-   5
pared to the living being: as the first elements into which a
living being is resolved are soul and body, as soul is made up
of rational principle and appetite, the family of husband and
wife, property of master and slave, so of all these, as well as
other dissimilar elements, the state is composed; and there-   10
fore the excellence of all the citizens cannot possibly be the
same, any more than the excellence of the leader of a chorus
is the same as that of the performer who stands by his side.
I have said enough to show why the two kinds of excellence
cannot be absolutely the same.

But will there then be no case in which the excellence of
the good citizen and the excellence of the good man coincide?

15 To this we answer that the good *ruler* is a good and wise man, but the citizen need not be wise. And some persons say that even the education of the ruler should be of a special kind; for are not the children of kings instructed in riding and military exercises? As Euripides says:

No subtle arts for me, but what the state requires.

20 As though there were a special education needed for a ruler. If the excellence of a good ruler is the same as that of a good man, and we assume further that the subject is a citizen as well as the ruler, the excellence of the good citizen and the excellence of the good man cannot be absolutely the same, although in some cases they may; for the excellence of a ruler differs from that of a citizen. It was the sense of this difference which made Jason say that 'he felt hungry when he was 25 not a tyrant', meaning that he could not endure to live in a private station. But, on the other hand, it may be argued that men are praised for knowing both how to rule and how to obey, and he is said to be a citizen of excellence who is able to do both well. Now if we suppose the excellence of a good man to be that which rules, and the excellence of the citizen to include ruling and obeying, it cannot be said that they are equally worthy of praise. Since, then, it is sometimes thought that the ruler and the ruled must learn different things and 30 not the same, but that the citizen must know and share in them both, the inference is obvious. There is, indeed, the rule of a master, which is concerned with menial offices—the master need not know how to perform these, but may employ others in the execution of them: the other would be degrad-35 ing; and by the other I mean the power actually to do menial duties, which vary much in character and are executed by various classes of slaves, such, for example, as handicrafts-men, who, as their name signifies, live by the labour of their hands—under these the mechanic is included. Hence in an-1277ᵇ1 cient times, and among some nations, the working classes had no share in the government—a privilege which they only acquired under extreme democracy. Certainly the good man and the statesman and the good citizen ought not to learn 5 the crafts of inferiors except for their own occasional use; if

they habitually practise them, there will cease to be a distinction between master and slave.

But there is a rule of another kind, which is exercised over freemen and equals by birth—a constitutional rule, which the ruler must learn by obeying, as he would learn the duties of a general of cavalry by being under the orders of a general of cavalry, or the duties of a general of infantry by being under the orders of a general of infantry, and by having had the command of a regiment and of a company. It has been well said that he who has never learned to obey cannot be a good commander. The excellence of the two is not the same, but the good citizen ought to be capable of both; he should know how to govern like a freeman, and how to obey like a freeman—these are the excellences of a citizen. And, although the temperance and justice of a ruler are distinct from those of a subject, the excellence of a good man will include both; for the excellence of the good man who is free and also a subject, e.g. his justice, will not be one but will comprise distinct kinds, the one qualifying him to rule, the other to obey, and differing as the temperance and courage of men and women differ. For a man would be thought a coward if he had no more courage than a courageous woman, and a woman would be thought loquacious if she imposed no more restraint on her conversation than the good man; and indeed their part in the management of the household is different, for the duty of the one is to acquire, and of the other to preserve. Practical wisdom is the only excellence peculiar to the ruler: it would seem that all other excellences must equally belong to ruler and subject. The excellence of the subject is certainly not wisdom, but only true opinion; he may be compared to the maker of the flute, while his master is like the flute-player or user of the flute.

From these considerations may be gathered the answer to the question, whether the excellence of the good man is the same as that of the good citizen, or different, and how far the same, and how far different.

5 • There still remains one more question about the citizen: Is he only a true citizen who has a share of office, or is

35 the mechanic to be included? If they who hold no office are to be deemed citizens, not every citizen can have this excellence; for this man is a citizen. And if none of the lower class are citizens, in which part of the state are they to be placed? For they are not resident aliens, and they are not foreigners.

1278ª1 May we not reply, that as far as this objection goes there is no more absurdity in excluding them than in excluding slaves and freedmen from any of the above-mentioned classes? It must be admitted that we cannot consider all those to be citizens who are necessary to the existence of the state; for example, children are not citizens equally with grown-up men,

5 who are citizens absolutely, but children, not being grown up, are only citizens on a certain assumption. In ancient times, and among some nations, the artisan class *were* slaves or foreigners, and therefore the majority of them are so now. The best form of state will not admit them to citizenship; but if they are admitted, then our definition of the excellence of a citizen will not apply to every citizen, nor to every free

10 man as such, but only to those who are freed from necessary services. The necessary people are either slaves who minister to the wants of individuals, or mechanics and labourers who are the servants of the community. These reflections carried a little further will explain their position; and indeed what has been said already is of itself, when understood, explanation enough.

15 Since there are many forms of government there must be many varieties of citizens, and especially of citizens who are subjects; so that under some governments the mechanic and the labourer will be citizens, but not in others, as, for example, in so-called aristocracies, if there are any, in which

20 honours are given according to excellence and merit; for no man can practise excellence who is living the life of a mechanic or labourer. In oligarchies the qualification for office is high, and therefore no labourer can ever be a citizen; but a mechanic may, for an actual majority of them are rich. At

25 Thebes there was a law that no man could hold office who had not retired from business for ten years. But in many states the law goes to the length of admitting aliens; for in some de-

mocracies a man is a citizen though his mother only be a citizen; and a similar principle is applied to illegitimate children among many. Nevertheless they make such people citizens because of the dearth of legitimate citizens (for they introduce this sort of legislation owing to lack of population); so when the number of citizens increases, first the children of a male or a female slave are excluded; then those whose mothers only are citizens; and at last the right of citizenship is confined to those whose fathers and mothers are both citizens.

30

Hence, as is evident, there are different kinds of citizens; and he is a citizen in the fullest sense who shares in the honours of the state. Compare Homer's words 'like some dishonoured stranger';[1] he who is excluded from the honours of the state is no better than an alien. But when this exclusion is concealed, then its object is to deceive their fellow inhabitants.

35

As to the question whether the excellence of the good man is the same as that of the good citizen, the considerations already adduced prove that in some states the good man and the good citizen are the same, and in others different. When they are the same it is not every citizen who is a good man, but only the statesman and those who have or may have, alone or in conjunction with others, the conduct of public affairs.

1278ᵇ1

5

6 • Having determined these questions, we have next to consider whether there is only one form of government or many, and if many, what they are, and how many, and what are the differences between them.

A constitution is the arrangement of magistracies in a state, especially of the highest of all. The government is everywhere sovereign in the state, and the constitution is in fact the government. For example, in democracies the people are supreme, but in oligarchies, the few; and, therefore, we say that these two constitutions also are different: and so in other cases.

10

[1] *Iliad* IX 648.

15 First, let us consider what is the purpose of a state, and how many forms of rule there are by which human society is regulated. We have already said, in the first part of this treatise, when discussing household management and the rule of a master, that man is by nature a political animal. And therefore, men, even when they do not require one another's help, 20 desire to live together; not but that they are also brought together by their common interests in so far as they each attain to any measure of well-being. This is certainly the chief end, both of individuals and of states. And mankind meet 25 together and maintain the political community also for the sake of mere life (in which there is possibly some noble element so long as the evils of existence do not greatly overbalance the good). And we all see that men cling to life even at the cost of enduring great misfortune, seeming to find in life 30 a natural sweetness and happiness.

There is no difficulty in distinguishing the various kinds of rule; they have been often defined already in our popular discussions. The rule of a master, although the slave by nature and the master by nature have in reality the same interests, is nevertheless exercised primarily with a view to the interest of 35 the master, but accidentally considers the slave, since, if the slave perish, the rule of the master perishes with him. On the other hand, the government of a wife and children and of a household, which we have called household management, is exercised in the first instance for the good of the governed or for the common good of both parties, but essentially for the good of the governed, as we see to be the case in medicine, 1279ᵃ1 gymnastics, and the arts in general, which are only accidentally concerned with the good of the artists themselves. For there is no reason why the trainer may not sometimes practise gymnastics, and the helmsman is always one of the crew. The trainer or the helmsman considers the good of those 5 committed to his care. But, when he is one of the persons taken care of, he accidentally participates in the advantage, for the helmsman is also a sailor, and the trainer becomes one of those in training. And so in politics: when the state is framed upon the principle of equality and likeness, the citi-

zens think that they ought to hold office by turns. Formerly,   10
as is natural, everyone would take his turn of service; and
then again, somebody else would look after his interest, just
as he, while in office, had looked after theirs. But nowadays,
for the sake of the advantage which is to be gained from the
public revenues and from office, men want to be always in
office. One might imagine that the rulers, being sickly, were   15
only kept in health while they continued in office; in that case
we may be sure that they would be hunting after places. The
conclusion is evident: that governments which have a regard
to the common interest are constituted in accordance with
strict principles of justice, and are therefore true forms; but
those which regard only the interest of the rulers are all de-   20
fective and perverted forms, for they are despotic, whereas a
state is a community of freemen.

7 • Having determined these points, we have next to consider how many forms of government there are, and what
they are; and in the first place what are the true forms, for
when they are determined the perversions of them will at   25
once be apparent. The words constitution and government
have the same meaning, and the government, which is the
supreme authority in states, must be in the hands of one,
or of a few, or of the many. The true forms of government,
therefore, are those in which the one, or the few, or the many,
govern with a view to the common interest; but governments
which rule with a view to the private interest, whether of the
one, or of the few, or of the many, are perversions. For the   30
members of a state, if they are truly citizens, ought to participate in its advantages. Of forms of government in which
one rules, we call that which regards the common interest,
kingship; that in which more than one, but not many, rule,   35
aristocracy; and it is so called, either because the rulers are
the best men, or because they have at heart the best interests
of the state and of the citizens. But when the many administer the state for the common interest, the government is
called by the generic name—a constitution. And there is a
reason for this use of language. One man or a few may excel

in excellence; but as the number increases it becomes more
difficult for them to attain perfection in every kind of excellence, though they may in military excellence, for this is
found in the masses. Hence in a constitutional government
the fighting-men have the supreme power, and those who
possess arms are the citizens.

Of the above-mentioned forms, the perversions are as follows:—of kingship, tyranny; of aristocracy, oligarchy; of
constitutional government, democracy. For tyranny is a kind
of monarchy which has in view the interest of the monarch
only; oligarchy has in view the interest of the wealthy; democracy, of the needy: none of them the common good of all.

8 • But there are difficulties about these forms of government, and it will therefore be necessary to state a little more
at length the nature of each of them. For he who would make
a philosophical study of the various sciences, and is not only
concerned with practice, ought not to overlook or omit anything, but to set forth the truth in every particular. Tyranny,
as I was saying, is monarchy exercising the rule of a master
over the political society; oligarchy is when men of property
have the government in their hands; democracy, the opposite, when the indigent, and not the men of property, are
the rulers. And here arises the first of our difficulties, and it
relates to the distinction just drawn. For democracy is said
to be the government of the many. But what if the many are
men of property and have the power in their hands? In like
manner oligarchy is said to be the government of the few; but
what if the poor are fewer than the rich, and have the power
in their hands because they are stronger? In these cases the
distinction which we have drawn between these different
forms of government would no longer hold good.

Suppose, once more, that we add wealth to the few and
poverty to the many, and name the governments accordingly—an oligarchy is said to be that in which the few and
the wealthy, and a democracy that in which the many and the
poor are the rulers—there will still be a difficulty. For, if the
only forms of government are the ones already mentioned,

1279ᵇ1

5

10

15

20

25

30

how shall we describe those other governments also just mentioned by us, in which the rich are the more numerous and the poor are the fewer, and both govern in their respective states?

The argument seems to show that, whether in oligarchies or in democracies, the number of the governing body, whether the greater number, as in a democracy, or the smaller number, as in an oligarchy, is an accident due to the fact that the rich everywhere are few, and the poor numerous. But if so, there is a misapprehension of the causes of the difference between them. For the real difference between democracy and oligarchy is poverty and wealth. Wherever men rule by reason of their wealth, whether they be few or many, that is an oligarchy, and where the poor rule, that is a democracy. But in fact the rich are few and the poor many; for few are well-to-do, whereas freedom is enjoyed by all, and wealth and freedom are the grounds on which the two parties claim power in the state.

9 • Let us begin by considering the common definitions of oligarchy and democracy, and what is oligarchical and democratic justice. For all men cling to justice of some kind, but their conceptions are imperfect and they do not express the whole idea. For example, justice is thought by them to be, and is, equality—not, however, for all, but only for equals. And inequality is thought to be, and is, justice; neither is this for all, but only for unequals. When the persons are omitted, then men judge erroneously. The reason is that they are passing judgement on themselves, and most people are bad judges in their own case. And whereas justice implies a relation to persons as well as to things, and a just distribution, as I have already said in the *Ethics*, implies the same ratio between the persons and between the things, they agree about the equality of the things, but dispute about the equality of the persons, chiefly for the reason which I have just given—because they are bad judges in their own affairs; and secondly, because both the parties to the argument are speaking of a limited and partial justice, but imagine

35

1280ᵃ1

5

10

15

20

themselves to be speaking of absolute justice. For the one party, if they are unequal in one respect, for example wealth, consider themselves to be unequal in all; and the other party, if they are equal in one respect, for example free birth, consider themselves to be equal in all. But they leave out the
25 capital point. For if men met and associated out of regard to wealth only, their share in the state would be proportioned to their property, and the oligarchical doctrine would then seem to carry the day. It would not be just that he who paid one mina should have the same share of a hundred minae,
30 whether of the principal or of the profits, as he who paid the remaining ninety-nine. But a state exists for the sake of a good life, and not for the sake of life only: if life only were the object, slaves and brute animals might form a state, but they cannot, for they have no share in happiness or in a life based
35 on choice. Nor does a state exist for the sake of alliance and security from injustice, nor yet for the sake of exchange and mutual intercourse; for then the Tyrrhenians and the Carthaginians, and all who have commercial treaties with one another, would be the citizens of one state. True, they have agreements about imports, and engagements that they will do no wrong to one another, and written articles of alliance. But there are no magistracies common to the contracting
1280ᵇ1 parties; different states have each their own magistracies. Nor does one state take care that the citizens of the other are such as they ought to be, nor see that those who come under the terms of the treaty do no wrong or wickedness at all, but only that they do no injustice to one another. Whereas, those
5 who care for good government take into consideration political excellence and defect. Whence it may be further inferred that excellence must be the care of a state which is truly so called, and not merely enjoys the name: for without this end the community becomes a mere alliance which differs only
10 in place from alliances of which the members live apart; and law is only a convention, 'a surety to one another of justice', as the sophist Lycophron says, and has no real power to make the citizens good and just.

This is obvious; for suppose distinct places, such as Corinth 15
and Megara, to be brought together so that their walls
touched, still they would not be one city, not even if the citizens had the right to intermarry, which is one of the rights
peculiarly characteristic of states. Again, if men dwelt at a
distance from one another, but not so far off as to have no intercourse, and there were laws among them that they should
not wrong each other in their exchanges, neither would this
be a state. Let us suppose that one man is a carpenter, an- 20
other a farmer, another a shoemaker, and so on, and that
their number is ten thousand: nevertheless, if they have
nothing in common but exchange, alliance, and the like, that
would not constitute a state. Why is this? Surely not because
they are at a distance from one another; for even supposing 25
that such a community were to meet in one place, but that
each man had a house of his own, which was in a manner his
state, and that they made alliance with one another, but only
against evil-doers; still an accurate thinker would not deem
this to be a state, if their intercourse with one another was of
the same character after as before their union. It is clear then
that a state is not a mere society, having a common place, es- 30
tablished for the prevention of mutual crime and for the sake
of exchange. These are conditions without which a state cannot exist; but all of them together do not constitute a state,
which is a community of families and aggregations of families in well-being, for the sake of a perfect and self-sufficing
life. Such a community can only be established among those 35
who live in the same place and intermarry. Hence there arise
in cities family connexions, brotherhoods, common sacrifices, amusements which draw men together. But these are
created by friendship, for to choose to live together is friendship. The end of the state is the good life, and these are the 1281ᵃ1
means towards it. And the state is the union of families and
villages in a perfect and self-sufficing life, by which we mean
a happy and honourable life.

Our conclusion, then, is that political society exists for the
sake of noble actions, and not of living together. Hence they

who contribute most to such a society have a greater share in
it than those who have the same or a greater freedom or nobility of birth but are inferior to them in political excellence;
or than those who exceed them in wealth but are surpassed
by them in excellence.

From what has been said it will be clearly seen that all the
partisans of different forms of government speak of a part of
justice only.

10 • There is also a doubt as to what is to be the supreme
power in the state:—Is it the multitude? Or the wealthy? Or
the good? Or the one best man? Or a tyrant? Any of these al-
ternatives seems to involve disagreeable consequences. If the
poor, for example, because they are more in number, divide
among themselves the property of the rich—is not this unjust? No, by heaven (will be the reply), for the supreme authority justly willed it. But if this is not extreme injustice,
what is? Again, when in the first division all has been taken,
and the majority divide anew the property of the minority,
is it not evident, if this goes on, that they will ruin the state?
Yet surely, excellence is not the ruin of those who possess it,
nor is justice destructive of a state; and therefore this law of
confiscation clearly cannot be just. If it were, all the acts of
a tyrant must of necessity be just; for he only coerces other
men by superior power, just as the multitude coerce the rich.
But is it just then that the few and the wealthy should be the
rulers? And what if they, in like manner, rob and plunder the
people—is this just? If so, the other case will likewise be just.
But there can be no doubt that all these things are wrong
and unjust.

Then ought the good to rule and have supreme power? But
in that case everybody else, being excluded from power, will
be dishonoured. For the offices of a state are posts of honour; and if one set of men always hold them, the rest must be
deprived of them. Then will it be well that the one best man
should rule? That is still more oligarchical, for the number of
those who are dishonoured is thereby increased. Someone
may say that it is bad in any case for a man, subject as he is

to all the accidents of human passion, to have the supreme   35
power, rather than the law. But what if the law itself be democratic or oligarchical, how will that help us out of our difficulties? Not at all; the same consequences will follow.

11 · Most of these questions may be reserved for another
occasion. The principle that the multitude ought to be in   40
power rather than the few best might seem to be solved and
to contain some difficulty and perhaps even truth.[2] For the
many, of whom each individual is not a good man, when they
meet together may be better than the few good, if regarded   1281ᵇ1
not individually but collectively, just as a feast to which many
contribute is better than a dinner provided out of a single
purse. For each individual among the many has a share of excellence and practical wisdom, and when they meet together,
just as they become in a manner one man, who has many feet,   5
and hands, and senses, so too with regard to their character
and thought. Hence the many are better judges than a single
man of music and poetry; for some understand one part, and
some another, and among them they understand the whole.   10
There is a similar combination of qualities in good men, who
differ from any individual of the many, as the beautiful are
said to differ from those who are not beautiful, and works of
art from realities, because in them the scattered elements are
combined, although, if taken separately, the eye of one person or some other feature in another person would be fairer   15
than in the picture. Whether this principle can apply to every
democracy, and to all bodies of men, is not clear. Or rather,
by heaven, in some cases it is impossible to apply; for the
argument would equally hold about brutes; and wherein, it
will be asked, do some men differ from brutes? But there may   20
be bodies of men about whom our statement is nevertheless
true. And if so, the difficulty which has been already raised,
and also another which is akin to it—viz. what power should
be assigned to the mass of freemen and citizens, who are not   25
rich and have no personal merit—are both solved. There is

---

[2] The text of this sentence is corrupt.

still a danger in allowing them to share the great offices of
state, for their folly will lead them into error, and their dis-
honesty into crime. But there is a danger also in not letting
them share, for a state in which many poor men are excluded
30   from office will necessarily be full of enemies. The only way
of escape is to assign to them some deliberative and judicial
functions. For this reason Solon and certain other legislators
give them the power of electing to offices, and of calling the
magistrates to account, but they do not allow them to hold
35   office singly. When they meet together their perceptions are
quite good enough, and combined with the better class they
are useful to the state (just as impure food when mixed with
what is pure sometimes makes the entire mass more whole-
some than a small quantity of the pure would be), but each individual, left to himself, forms an imperfect judgement. On
the other hand, the popular form of government involves cer-
40   tain difficulties. In the first place, it might be objected that he
who can judge of the healing of a sick man would be one who
could himself heal his disease, and make him whole—that is,
1282ª1   in other words, the physician; and so in all professions and
arts. As, then, the physician ought to be called to account by
physicians, so ought men in general to be called to account
by their peers. But physicians are of three kinds:—there is
the ordinary practitioner, and there is the master physician,
5   and thirdly the man educated in the art: in all arts there is
such a class; and we attribute the power of judging to them
quite as much as to professors of the art. Secondly, does not
the same principle apply to elections? For a right election can
only be made by those who have knowledge; those who know
geometry, for example, will choose a geometrician rightly,
10   and those who know how to steer, a pilot; and, even if there
be some occupations and arts in which private persons share
in the ability to choose, they certainly cannot choose better
than those who know. So that, according to this argument,
neither the election of magistrates, nor the calling of them to
account, should be entrusted to the many. Yet possibly these
15   objections are to a great extent met by our old answer, that
if the people are not utterly degraded, although individually

they may be worse judges than those who have special knowledge, as a body they are as good or better. Moreover, there are
some arts whose products are not judged of solely, or best,
by the artists themselves, namely those arts whose products
are recognized even by those who do not possess the art; for
example, the knowledge of the house is not limited to the   20
builder only; the user, or, in other words, the master, of the
house will actually be a better judge than the builder, just as
the pilot will judge better of a rudder than the carpenter, and
the guest will judge better of a feast than the cook.

  This difficulty seems now to be sufficiently answered, but
there is another akin to it. That inferior persons should have
authority in greater matters than the good would appear to   25
be a strange thing, yet the election and calling to account of
the magistrates is the greatest of all. And these, as I was saying, are functions which in some states are assigned to the
people, for the assembly is supreme in all such matters. Yet
persons of any age, and having but a small property qualification, sit in the assembly and deliberate and judge, although   30
for the great officers of state, such as treasurers and generals,
a high qualification is required. This difficulty may be solved
in the same manner as the preceding, and the present practice of democracies may be really defensible. For the power
does not reside in the juryman, or counsellor, or member of
the assembly, but in the court, and the council, and the as-   35
sembly, of which the aforesaid individuals—counsellor, as-
semblyman, juryman—are only parts or members. And for
this reason the many may claim to have a higher authority
than the few; for the people, and the council, and the courts
consist of many persons, and their property collectively is
greater than the property of one or of a few individuals hold-   40
ing great offices. But enough of this.

  The discussion of the first question shows nothing so   1282ᵇ1
clearly as that laws, when good, should be supreme; and that
the magistrate or magistrates should regulate those matters
only on which the laws are unable to speak with precision
owing to the difficulty of any general principle embracing all   5
particulars. But what are good laws has not yet been clearly

explained; the old difficulty remains. The goodness or badness, justice or injustice, of laws varies of necessity with the
constitutions of states. This, however, is clear, that the laws
must be adapted to the constitutions.

10   But, if so, true forms of government will of necessity have
just laws, and perverted forms of government will have unjust laws.

12 · In all sciences and arts the end is a good, and the
greatest good and in the highest degree a good in the most
15   authoritative of all—this is the political science of which the
good is justice, in other words, the common interest. All
men think justice to be a sort of equality; and to a certain
extent they agree with what we have said in our philosophi-
20   cal works about ethics. For they say that what is just is just
for someone and that it should be equal for equals. But there
still remains a question: equality or inequality of what? Here
is a difficulty which calls for political speculation. For very
likely some persons will say that offices of state ought to be
unequally distributed according to superior excellence, in
whatever respect, of the citizen, although there is no other
25   difference between him and the rest of the community; for
those who differ in any one respect have different rights and
claims. But, surely, if this is true, the complexion or height of
a man, or any other advantage, will be a reason for his obtaining a greater share of political rights. The error here lies upon
30   the surface, and may be illustrated from the other arts and
sciences. When a number of flute-players are equal in their
art, there is no reason why those of them who are better born
should have better flutes given to them; for they will not play
any better on the flute, and the superior instrument should
35   be reserved for him who is the superior artist. If what I am
saying is still obscure, it will be made clearer as we proceed.
For if there were a superior flute-player who was far inferior
in birth and beauty, although either of these may be a greater
40   good than the art of flute-playing and may excel flute-playing
in a greater ratio than he excels the others in his art, still he
1283ᵃ1   ought to have the best flutes given to him, unless the advan-

tages of wealth and birth contribute to excellence in flute-playing, which they do not. Moreover, upon this principle any good may be compared with any other.

For if a given height[3] may be measured against wealth and against freedom, height in general may be so measured. Thus if A excels in height more than B in excellence, even if excellence in general excels height still more, all goods will be comparable; for if a certain amount is better than some other, it is clear that some other will be equal. But since no such comparison can be made, it is evident that there is good reason why in politics men do not ground their claim to office on every sort of inequality. For if some be slow, and others swift, that is no reason why the one should have little and the others much; it is in gymnastic contests that such excellence is rewarded. Whereas the rival claims of candidates for office can only be based on the possession of elements which enter into the composition of a state. And therefore the well-born, or free-born, or rich, may with good reason claim office; for holders of offices must be freemen and tax-payers: a state can be no more composed entirely of poor men than entirely of slaves. But if wealth and freedom are necessary elements, justice and valour are equally so; for without the former qualities a state cannot exist at all, without the latter not well.

13 · If the existence of the state is alone to be considered, then it would seem that all, or some at least, of these claims are just; but, if we take into account a good life, then, as I have already said, education and excellence have superior claims. As, however, those who are equal in one thing ought not to have an equal share in all, nor those who are unequal in one thing to have an unequal share in all, it is certain that all forms of government which rest on either of these principles are perversions.

All men have a claim in a certain sense, as I have already admitted, but not all have an absolute claim. The rich claim

---

[3]Omitting συμβάλλοιτο.

because they have a greater share in the land, and land is the common element of the state; also they are generally more trustworthy in contracts. The free claim under the same title as the well-born; for they are nearly akin. For the well-born

35 are citizens in a truer sense than the low-born, and good birth is always valued in a man's own home. Another reason is, that those who are sprung from better ancestors are likely to be better men, for good birth is excellence of race. Excellence, too, may be truly said to have a claim, for justice has been acknowledged by us to be a social excellence, and it im-

40 plies all others. Again, the many may urge their claim against the few; for, when taken collectively, and compared with the few, they are stronger and richer and better. But, what if the good, the rich, the well-born, and the other classes who

1283ᵇ1 make up a state, are all living together in the same city, will there, or will there not, be any doubt who shall rule?—No doubt at all in determining who ought to rule in each of the

5 above-mentioned forms of government. For states are characterized by differences in their governing bodies—one of them has a government of the rich, another of the good, and so on. But a difficulty arises when all these elements coexist. How are we to decide? Suppose the good to be very few in

10 number: may we consider their numbers in relation to their duties, and ask whether they are enough to administer the state, or so many as will make up a state? Objections may be urged against all the aspirants to political power. For those who found their claims on wealth or family might be thought

15 to have no basis of justice; on this principle, if any one person were richer than all the rest, it is clear that he ought to be ruler of them. In like manner he who is very distinguished by his birth ought to have the superiority over all those who claim on the ground that they are free-born. In an aristocracy

20 a like difficulty occurs about excellence; for if one citizen is better than the other members of the government, however good they may be, he too, upon the same principle of justice, should rule over them. And if the people are to be supreme because they are stronger than the few, then if one man, or

more than one, but not a majority, is stronger than the many, 25
they ought to rule, and not the many.

All these considerations appear to show that none of the
principles on which men claim to rule and to hold all other
men in subjection to them are right. To those who claim to
be masters of the government on the ground of their excellence or their wealth, the many might fairly answer that 30
they themselves are often better and richer than the few—I
do not say individually, but collectively. And another problem which is sometimes put forward may be met in a simi- 35
lar manner. Some persons doubt whether the legislator who
desires to make the justest laws ought to legislate with a
view to the good of the better or of the many, when the case
which we have mentioned occurs. Now what is right must be
construed as equally right, and what is equally right is to be 40
considered with reference to the advantage of the state, and
the common good of the citizens. And a citizen is one who
shares in governing and being governed. He differs under
different forms of government, but in the best state he is one 1284ª1
who is able and chooses to be governed and to govern with a
view to the life of excellence.

If, however, there be some one person, or more than one,
although not enough to make up the full complement of a
state, whose excellence is so pre-eminent that the excellence
or the political capacity of all the rest admit of no comparison with his or theirs, he or they can be no longer regarded 5
as part of a state; for justice will not be done to the superior,
if he is reckoned only as the equal of those who are so far
inferior to him in excellence and in political capacity. Such
a man may truly be deemed a God among men. Hence we 10
see that legislation is necessarily concerned only with those
who are equal in birth and in capacity; and that for men of
pre-eminent excellence there is no law—they are themselves
a law. Anyone would be ridiculous who attempted to make
laws for them: they would probably retort what, in the fable 15
of Antisthenes, the lions said to the hares, when in the council of the beasts the latter began haranguing and claiming

equality for all. And for this reason democratic states have instituted ostracism; equality is above all things their aim, and therefore they ostracized and banished from the city for a time those who seemed to predominate too much through their wealth, or the number of their friends, or through any other political influence. Mythology tells us that the Argonauts left Heracles behind for a similar reason; the ship Argo would not take him because she feared that he would have been too much for the rest of the crew. That is why those who denounce tyranny and blame the counsel which Periander gave to Thrasybulus cannot be held altogether just in their censure. The story is that Periander, when the herald was sent to ask counsel of him, said nothing, but only cut off the tallest ears of corn till he had brought the field to a level. The herald did not know the meaning of the action, but came and reported what he had seen to Thrasybulus, who understood that he was to cut off the principal men in the state; and this is a policy not only expedient for tyrants or in practice confined to them, but equally necessary in oligarchies and democracies. Ostracism is a measure of the same kind, which acts by disabling and banishing the most prominent citizens. Great powers do the same to whole cities and nations, as the Athenians did to the Samians, Chians, and Lesbians; no sooner had they obtained a firm grasp of the empire, than they humbled their allies contrary to treaty; and the Persian king has repeatedly crushed the Medes, Babylonians, and other nations, when their spirit has been stirred by the recollection of their former greatness.

The problem is a universal one, and equally concerns all forms of government, true as well as false; for, although perverted forms with a view to their own interests may adopt this policy, those which seek the common interest do so likewise. The same thing may be observed in the arts and sciences; for the painter will not allow the figure to have a foot which, however beautiful, is not in proportion, nor will the ship-builder allow the stern or any other part of the vessel to be unduly large, any more than the chorus-master will allow anyone who sings louder or better than all the rest to sing in the choir. Monarchs, too, may practise compulsion and still live in harmony with their cities, if their own government is for the interest of the state. Hence where there is an acknowledged superiority the argument in favour of ostracism is based upon a kind of political justice. It would certainly be better that the legislator should from the first so order his state as to have no need of such a remedy. But if the need arises, the next best thing is that he should endeavour to correct the evil by this or some similar measure. The principle, however, has not been fairly applied in states; for, instead of looking to the good of their own constitution, they have used ostracism for factious purposes. It is true that under perverted forms of government, and from their special point of view, such a measure is just and expedient, but it is also clear that it is not absolutely just. In the perfect state there would be great doubts about the use of it, not when applied to excess in strength, wealth, popularity, or the like, but when used against someone who is pre-eminent in excellence—what is to be done with him? People will not say that such a man is to be expelled and exiled; on the other hand, he ought not to be a subject—that would be as if mankind should claim to rule over Zeus, dividing his offices among them. The only alternative is that all should happily obey such a ruler, according to what seems to be the order of nature, and that men like him should be kings in their state for life.

14 · The preceding discussion, by a natural transition, leads to the consideration of kingship, which we say is one of the true forms of government. Let us see whether in order to be well governed a state or country should be under the rule of a king or under some other form of government; and whether monarchy, although good for some, may not be bad for others. But first we must determine whether there is one species of kingship or many. It is easy to see that there are many, and that the manner of government is not the same in all of them.

Of kingships according to law, the Lacedaemonian is thought to be the best example; but there the royal power is not absolute, except when the kings go on an expedition, and then they take the command. Matters of religion are likewise committed to them. The kingly office is in truth a kind of generalship, sovereign and perpetual. The king has not the power of life and death, except in certain cases, as for instance, in ancient times, he had it when upon a campaign, by right of force. This custom is described in Homer. For Agamemnon puts up with it when he is attacked in the assembly, but when the army goes out to battle he has the power even of life and death. Does he not say: 'When I find a man skulking apart from the battle, nothing shall save him from the dogs and vultures, for in my hands is death'?[4]

This, then, is one form of kingship—a generalship for life; and of such kingships some are hereditary and others elective.

There is another sort of monarchy not uncommon among foreigners, which nearly resembles tyranny. But this is both legal and hereditary. For foreigners, being more servile in character than Hellenes, and Asiatics than Europeans, do not rebel against a despotic government. Such kingships have the nature of tyrannies because the people are by nature slaves; but there is no danger of their being overthrown, for they are hereditary and legal. For the same reason, their guards are such as a king and not such as a tyrant would employ, that is to say, they are composed of citizens, whereas the guards of tyrants are mercenaries. For kings rule according to law over voluntary subjects, but tyrants over involuntary; and the one are guarded by their fellow-citizens, the others are guarded against them.

These are two forms of monarchy, and there was a third which existed in ancient Hellas, called an Aesymnetia. This may be defined generally as an elective tyranny, which, like foreign monarchy, is legal, but differs from it in not being hereditary. Sometimes the office was held for life, sometimes for a term of years, or until certain duties had been performed. For example, the Mytilenaeans once elected Pittacus leader against the exiles, who were headed by Antimenides

[4] *Iliad* II 391–393.

and Alcaeus the poet. And Alcaeus himself shows in one of his banquet odes that they chose Pittacus tyrant, for he reproaches his fellow-citizens for 'having made the low-born Pittacus tyrant of the spiritless and ill-fated city, with one voice shouting his praises'.

1285ᵇ1

These forms of government have always had the character of tyrannies, because they possess despotic power; but inasmuch as they are elective and acquiesced in by their subjects, they are kingly.

There is a fourth species of kingly monarchy—that of the heroic times—which was hereditary and legal, and was exercised over willing subjects. For the first chiefs were benefactors of the people in arts or arms; they either gathered them into a community, or procured land for them; and thus they became kings of voluntary subjects, and their power was inherited by their descendants. They took the command in war and presided over the sacrifices, except those which required a priest. They also decided law-suits either with or without an oath; and when they swore, the form of the oath was the stretching out of their sceptre. In ancient times their power extended continuously to all things in city and country and across the border; but at a later date they relinquished several of these privileges, and others the people took from them, until in some states nothing was left to them but the sacrifices; and where they retained more of the reality they had only the right of leadership in war beyond the border.

5

10

15

These, then, are the four kinds of kingship. First the monarchy of the heroic ages; this was exercised over voluntary subjects, but limited to certain functions; the king was a general and a judge, and had the control of religion. The second is that of foreigners, which is an hereditary despotic government in accordance with law. A third is the power of the so-called Aesymnete; this is an elective tyranny. The fourth is the Lacedaemonian, which is in fact a generalship, hereditary and perpetual. These four forms differ from one another in the manner which I have described.

20

25

There is a fifth form of kingly rule in which one man has the disposal of all, just as each nation or each state has the

30

disposal of public matters; this form corresponds to the control of a household. For as household management is the kingly rule of a house, so kingly rule is the household management of a city, or of a nation, or of many nations.

15 • Of these forms we need only consider two, the Lace-
35 daemonian and the absolute royalty; for most of the others lie in a region between them, having less power than the last, and more than the first. Thus the inquiry is reduced to two points: first, is it advantageous to the state that there should be a perpetual general, and if so, should the office be confined to one family, or open to the citizens in turn?
1286ª1 Secondly, is it well that a single man should have the supreme power in all things? The first question falls under the head of laws rather than of constitutions; for perpetual generalship might equally exist under any form of government,
5 so that this matter may be dismissed for the present. The other kind of kingship is a sort of constitution; this we have now to consider, and to run over the difficulties involved in it. We will begin by inquiring whether it is more advantageous to be ruled by the best man or by the best laws.

The advocates of kingship maintain that the laws speak
10 only in general terms, and cannot provide for circumstances; and that for any science to abide by written rules is absurd. In Egypt the physician is allowed to alter his treatment after the fourth day, but if sooner, he takes the risk. Hence it is clear that a government acting according to written laws is
15 plainly not the best. Yet surely the ruler cannot dispense with the general principle which exists in law; and that is a better ruler which is free from passion than that in which it is innate. Whereas the law is passionless, passion must always
20 sway the heart of man. Yes, it may be replied, but then on the other hand an individual will be better able to deliberate in particular cases.

The best man, then, must legislate, and laws must be passed, but these laws will have no authority when they miss the mark, though in all other cases retaining their authority. But when the law cannot determine a point at all, or not

well, should the one best man or should all decide? Accord- 25
ing to our present practice assemblies meet, sit in judgement, deliberate, and decide, and their judgements all relate
to individual cases. Now any member of the assembly, taken
separately, is certainly inferior to the wise man. But the state
is made up of many individuals. And as a feast to which all
the guests contribute is better than a banquet furnished by
a single man, so a multitude is a better judge of many things 30
than any individual.

Again, the many are more incorruptible than the few; they
are like the greater quantity of water which is less easily corrupted than a little. The individual is liable to be overcome by
anger or by some other passion, and then his judgement is
necessarily perverted; but it is hardly to be supposed that a
great number of persons would all get into a passion and go
wrong at the same moment. Let us assume that they are the 35
freemen, and that they never act in violation of the law, but
fill up the gaps which the law is obliged to leave. Or, if such
virtue is scarcely attainable by the multitude, we need only
suppose that the majority are good men and good citizens,
and ask which will be the more incorruptible, the one good
ruler, or the many who are all good? Will not the many? But,
you will say, there may be factions among them, whereas the 1286ᵇ1
one man is not divided against himself. To which we may answer that their character is as good as his. If we call the rule
of many men, who are all of them good, aristocracy, and the
rule of one man kingship, then aristocracy will be better for 5
states than kingship, whether the government is supported
by force or not, provided only that a number of men equal in
excellence can be found.

The first governments were kingships, probably for this
reason, because of old, when cities were small, men of eminent excellence were few. Further, they were made kings 10
because they were benefactors, and benefits can only be bestowed by good men. But when many persons equal in merit
arose, no longer enduring the pre-eminence of one, they desired to have a commonwealth, and set up a constitution. The
ruling class soon deteriorated and enriched themselves out

of the public treasury; riches became the path to honour, and
so oligarchies naturally grew up. These passed into tyrannies
and tyrannies into democracies; for love of gain in the ruling
classes was always tending to diminish their number, and so
to strengthen the masses, who in the end set upon their masters and established democracies.

Since cities have increased in size, no other form of government appears to be any longer even easy to establish.

Even supposing the principle to be maintained that kingly
power is the best thing for states, how about the family of the
king? Are his children to succeed him?

If they are no better than anybody else, that will be mischievous. But perhaps the king, though he might, will not
hand on his power to his children? That, however, is hardly
to be expected, and is too much to ask of human nature.
There is also a difficulty about the force which he is to employ; should a king have guards about him by whose aid he
may be able to coerce the refractory? If not, how will he administer his kingdom? Even if he is the lawful sovereign who
does nothing arbitrarily or contrary to law, still he must have
some force wherewith to maintain the law. In the case of a
limited monarchy there is not much difficulty in answering
this question; the king must have such force as will be more
than a match for one or more individuals, but not so great as
that of the people. The ancients observed this principle when
they gave guards to anyone whom they appointed Aesymnete or tyrant. Thus, when Dionysius asked the Syracusans
to allow him guards, somebody advised that they should give
him only such a number.

16 • At this place in the discussion there impends the inquiry respecting the king who acts solely according to his
own will; he has now to be considered. The so-called kingship
according to law, as I have already remarked, is not a form of
government, for under all governments, as, for example, in
a democracy or aristocracy, there may be a general holding
office for life, and one person is often made supreme over the
administration of a state. A magistracy of this kind exists at

Epidamnus, and also at Opus, but in the latter city has a more limited power. Now, absolute monarchy, or the arbitrary rule of a sovereign over all the citizens, in a city which consists of   10
equals, is thought by some to be quite contrary to nature; it is argued that those who are by nature equals must have the same natural right and worth, and that for unequals to have an equal share, or for equals to have an unequal share, in the offices of state, is as bad as for different bodily constitutions   15
to have the same food and clothing. That is why it is thought to be just that among equals everyone be ruled as well as rule, and therefore that all should have their turn. We thus arrive at law; for an order of succession implies law. And the rule of the law, it is argued, is preferable to that of any individual. On   20
the same principle, even if it be better for certain individuals to govern, they should be made only guardians and ministers of the law. For magistrates there must be—this is admitted; but then men say that to give authority to any one man when all are equal is unjust. There may indeed be cases which the law seems unable to determine, but such cases a man could   25
not determine either. But the law trains officers for this express purpose, and appoints them to determine matters which are left undecided by it, to the best of their judgement. Further, it permits them to make any amendment of the existing laws which experience suggests. Therefore he who bids the law rule may be deemed to bid God and Reason alone rule, but he who bids man rule adds an element of the beast;   30
for desire is a wild beast, and passion perverts the minds of rulers, even when they are the best of men. The law is reason unaffected by desire. We are told that a patient should call in a physician; he will not get better if he is doctored out of a book. But the parallel of the arts is clearly not in point; for the physician does nothing contrary to rule from motives of friendship; he only cures a patient and takes a fee; whereas   35
magistrates do many things from spite and partiality. And, indeed, if a man suspected the physician of being in league with his enemies to destroy him for a bribe, he would rather have recourse to the book. But certainly physicians, when they are sick, call in other physicians, and training-masters,   1287ᵇ1

when they are in training, other training-masters, as if they could not judge truly about their own case and might be influenced by their feelings. Hence it is evident that in seeking for justice men seek for the mean, for the law is the mean. Again, customary laws have more weight, and relate to more important matters, than written laws, and a man may be a safer ruler than the written law, but not safer than the customary law. Again, it is by no means easy for one man to superintend many things; he will have to appoint a number of subordinates, and what difference does it make whether these subordinates always existed or were appointed by him because he needed them? If, as I said before, the good man has a right to rule because he is better, still two good men are better than one: this is the old saying,

two going together,

and the prayer of Agamemnon,

would that I had ten such counsellors!

And even now there are magistrates, for example judges, who have authority to decide some matters which the law is unable to determine, since no one doubts that the law would command and decide in the best manner whatever it could. But some things can, and other things cannot, be comprehended under the law, and this is the origin of the vexed question whether the best law or the best man should rule. For matters of detail about which men deliberate cannot be included in legislation. Nor does anyone deny that the decision of such matters must be left to man, but it is argued that there should be many judges, and not one only. For every ruler who has been trained by the law judges well; and it would surely seem strange that a person should see better with two eyes, or hear better with two ears, or act better with two hands or feet, than many with many; indeed, it is already the practice of kings to make to themselves many eyes and ears and hands and feet. For they make colleagues of those who are the friends of themselves and their governments. They must be friends of the monarch and of his government; if not his

friends, they will not do what he wants; but friendship implies likeness and equality; and, therefore, if he thinks that
his friends ought to rule, he must think that those who
are equal to himself and like himself ought to rule equally
with himself. These are the principal controversies relating   35
to monarchy.

17 • But may not all this be true in some cases and not in
others? for there is by nature both a justice and an advantage
appropriate to the rule of a master, another to kingly rule,
another to constitutional rule; but there is none naturally ap-   40
propriate to tyranny, or to any other perverted form of government; for these come into being contrary to nature. Now,
to judge at least from what has been said, it is manifest that,   1288ª1
where men are alike and equal, it is neither expedient nor just
that one man should be lord of all, whether there are laws,
or whether there are no laws, but he himself is in the place of
law. Neither should a good man be lord over good men, nor a
bad man over bad; nor, even if he excels in excellence, should
he have a right to rule, unless in a particular case, at which I   5
have already hinted, and to which I will once more recur. But
first of all, I must determine what natures are suited for government by a king, and what for an aristocracy, and what for
a constitutional government.

A people who are by nature capable of producing a race
superior in the excellence needed for political rule are fitted
for kingly government; and a people submitting to be ruled   10
as freemen by men whose excellence renders them capable of
political command are adapted for an aristocracy: while the
people who are suited for constitutional freedom are those
among whom there naturally exists a warlike multitude. In
the former case the multitude is capable of being ruled by
men whose excellence is appropriate to political command;
in the latter case the multitude is able to rule and to obey in
turn by a law which gives office to the well-to-do according
to their desert. But when a whole family, or some individual,   15
happens to be so pre-eminent in excellence as to surpass
all others, then it is just that they should be the royal family

and supreme over all, or that this one citizen should be king.
For, as I said before, to give them authority is not only agree-
20 able to that notion of justice which the founders of all states,
whether aristocratic, or oligarchical, or again democratic, are
accustomed to put forward (for these all recognize the claim
of superiority, although not the same superiority), but ac-
cords with the principle already laid down. For surely it
25 would not be right to kill, or ostracize, or exile such a person,
or require that he should take his turn in being governed.
The whole is naturally superior to the part, and he who has
this pre-eminence is in the relation of a whole to a part. But
if so, the only alternative is that he should have the supreme
power, and that mankind should obey him, not in turn, but
30 always. These are the conclusions at which we arrive respecting kingship and its various forms, and this is the answer to
the question, whether it is or is not advantageous to states,
and to which, and how.

18 • We maintain that the true forms of government are
three, and that the best must be that which is administered by
35 the best, and in which there is one man, or a whole family, or
many persons, excelling all the others together in excellence,
and both rulers and subjects are fitted, the one to rule, the
others to be ruled, in such a manner as to attain the most desirable life. We showed at the commencement of our inquiry
that the excellence of the good man is necessarily the same as
the excellence of the citizen of the perfect state. Clearly then
in the same manner, and by the same means through which
1288ᵇ1 a man becomes truly good, he will frame a state that is to be
ruled by an aristocracy or by a king, and the same education
and the same habits will be found to make a good man and a
man fit to be a statesman or king.

Having arrived at these conclusions, we must proceed to
speak of the perfect state, and describe how it comes into being and is established.
5 So if we are to inquire in the appropriate way about it, we
must. . . .

BOOK IV

1 · In all arts and sciences which embrace the whole of any   10
subject, and do not come into being in a fragmentary way, it
is the province of a single art or science to consider all that ap-
pertains to a single subject. For example, the art of gymnastics considers not only the suitableness of different modes of
training to different bodies, but what sort is the best (for the
best must suit that which is by nature best and best furnished   15
with the means of life), and also what common form of training is adapted to the great majority of men. And if a man does
not desire the best habit of body, or the greatest skill in gymnastics, which might be attained by him, still the trainer or
the teacher of gymnastics should be able to impart any lower
degree of either. The same principle equally holds in medicine and ship-building, and the making of clothes, and in the   20
arts generally.

Hence it is obvious that government too is the subject of
a single science, which has to consider what government is
best and of what sort it must be, to be most in accordance
with our aspirations, if there were no external impediment,
and also what kind of government is adapted to particular
states. For the best is often unattainable, and therefore the
true legislator and statesman ought to be acquainted, not   25
only with that which is best in the abstract, but also with
that which is best relatively to circumstances. We should be
able further to say how a state may be constituted under any
given conditions; both how it is originally formed and, when
formed, how it may be longest preserved; the supposed state
neither having the best constitution nor being provided even   30
with the conditions necessary for the best, nor being the best
under the circumstances, but of an inferior type.

We ought, moreover, to know the form of government
which is best suited to states in general; for political writers,
although they have excellent ideas, are often unpractical. We   35
should consider, not only what form of government is best,
but also what is possible and what is easily attainable by all.

There are some who would have none but the most perfect; for this many natural advantages are required. Others, again, speak of a more attainable form, and, although they reject the constitution under which they are living, they extol some one in particular, for example the Lacedaemonian. Any change of government which has to be introduced should be one which men, starting from their existing constitutions, will be both willing and able to adopt, since there is quite as much trouble in the reformation of an old constitution as in the establishment of a new one, just as to unlearn is as hard as to learn. And therefore, in addition to the qualifications of the statesman already mentioned, he should be able to find remedies for the defects of existing constitutions, as has been said before. This he cannot do unless he knows how many forms of government there are. It is often supposed that there is only one kind of democracy and one of oligarchy. But this is a mistake; and, in order to avoid such mistakes, we must ascertain what differences there are in the constitutions of states, and in how many ways they are combined. The same political insight will enable a man to know which laws are the best, and which are suited to different constitutions; for the laws are, and ought to be, framed with a view to the constitution, and not the constitution to the laws. A constitution is the organization of offices in a state, and determines what is to be the governing body, and what is the end of each community. But laws are not to be confounded with the principles of the constitution; they are the rules according to which the magistrates should administer the state, and proceed against offenders. So that we must know the varieties, and the number of varieties, of each form of government, if only with a view to making laws. For the same laws cannot be equally suited to all oligarchies or to all democracies, since there is certainly more than one form both of democracy and of oligarchy.

2 • In our original discussion about governments we divided them into three true forms: kingly rule, aristocracy, and constitutional government, and three corresponding perversions—tyranny, oligarchy, and democracy. Of kingly rule

and of aristocracy we have already spoken, for the inquiry into the perfect state is the same thing as the discussion of the two forms thus named, since both imply a principle of excellence provided with external means. We have already determined in what aristocracy and kingly rule differ from 35 one another, and when the latter should be established. In what follows we have to describe the so-called constitutional government, which bears the common name of all constitutions, and the other forms, tyranny, oligarchy, and democracy.

It is obvious which of the three perversions is the worst, and which is the next in badness. That which is the perversion of the first and most divine is necessarily the worst. And just as a royal rule, if not a mere name, must exist by virtue 1289^{b}1 of some great personal superiority in the king, so tyranny, which is the worst of governments, is necessarily the farthest removed from a well-constituted form; oligarchy is little better, for it is a long way from aristocracy, and democracy is the most tolerable of the three.

A writer who preceded me has already made these distinc- 5 tions, but his point of view is not the same as mine. For he lays down the principle that when all the constitutions are good (the oligarchy and the rest being virtuous), democracy is the worst, but the best when all are bad. Whereas we maintain that they are in any case defective, and that one oligarchy 10 is not to be accounted better than another, but only less bad.

Not to pursue this question further at present, let us begin by determining how many varieties of constitution there are (since of democracy and oligarchy there are several); what constitution is the most generally acceptable, and what is 15 preferable in the next degree after the perfect state; and besides this what other there is which is aristocratic and well-constituted, and at the same time adapted to states in general; and of the other forms of government we must ask to what people each is suited. For democracy may meet the needs of some better than oligarchy, and conversely. In the next place we have to consider in what manner a man ought to proceed who desires to establish some one among these 20 various forms, whether of democracy or of oligarchy; and lastly, having briefly discussed these subjects to the best of our power, we will endeavour to ascertain the modes of ruin and preservation both of constitutions generally and of each separately, and to what causes they are to be attributed.

3 • The reason why there are many forms of government is that every state contains many elements. In the first place we see that all states are made up of families, and in the multitude of citizens there must be some rich and some poor, and some in a middle condition; the rich possess heavy armour, and the poor not. Of the common people, some are farmers, and some traders, and some artisans. There are also among the notables differences of wealth and property—for example, in the number of horses which they keep, for they cannot afford to keep them unless they are rich. And therefore in old times the cities whose strength lay in their cavalry were oligarchies, and they used cavalry in wars against their neighbours; as was the practice of the Eretrians and Chalcidians, and also of the Magnesians on the river Mæander, and of other peoples in Asia. Besides differences of wealth there are differences of rank and merit, and there are some other elements which were mentioned by us when in treating of aristocracy we enumerated the essentials of a state. Of these elements, sometimes all, sometimes the lesser, and sometimes the greater number, have a share in the government. It is evident then that there must be many forms of government, differing in kind, since the parts of which they are composed differ from each other in kind. For a constitution is an organization of offices, which all the citizens distribute among themselves, according to the power which different classes possess (for example the rich or the poor), or according to some principle of equality which includes both. There must therefore be as many forms of government as there are modes of arranging the offices, according to the superiorities and the differences of the parts of the state.

There are generally thought to be two principal forms: as men say of the winds that there are but two, north and south, and that the rest of them are only variations of these, so of governments there are said to be only two forms— democracy and oligarchy. For aristocracy is considered to be a kind of oligarchy, as being the rule of a few, and the so-called constitutional government to be really a democracy, just as among the winds we make the west a variation of the north, and the east of the south wind. Similarly of musical modes there are said to be two kinds, the Dorian and the Phrygian; the other arrangements of the scale are comprehended under one or other of these two. About forms of government this is a very favourite notion. But in either case the better and more exact way is to distinguish, as I have done, the one or two which are true forms, and to regard the others as perversions, whether of the most perfectly attempered or of the best form of government: the more taut and more overpowering are oligarchical, and the more relaxed and gentler are democratic.

4 • It must not be assumed, as some are fond of saying, that democracy is simply that form of government in which the greater number are sovereign, for in oligarchies, and indeed in every government, the majority rules; nor again is oligarchy that form of government in which a few are sovereign. Suppose the whole population of a city to be 1300, and that of these 1000 are rich, and do not allow the remaining 300 who are poor, but free, and in all other respects their equals, a share of the government—no one will say that this is a democracy. In like manner, if the poor were few and the masters of the rich who outnumber them, no one would ever call such a government, in which the rich majority have no share of office, an oligarchy. Therefore we should rather say that democracy is the form of government in which the free are rulers, and oligarchy in which the rich; it is only an accident that the free are the many and the rich are the few. Otherwise a government in which the offices were given according to stature, as is said to be the case in Ethiopia, or according to beauty, would be an oligarchy; for the number of tall or good-looking men is small. And yet oligarchy and

democracy are not sufficiently distinguished merely by these two characteristics of wealth and freedom. Both of them contain many other elements, and therefore we must carry our analysis further, and say that the government is not a democracy in which the freemen, being few in number, rule over the many who are not free, as at Apollonia on the Ionian Gulf, and at Thera (for in each of these states the nobles, who were also the earliest settlers, held office, although they were but a few out of many). Neither is it a democracy when the rich have the government because they exceed in number; as was the case formerly at Colophon, where the bulk of the inhabitants were possessed of large property before the Lydian War. But the form of government is a democracy when the free, who are also poor and the majority, govern, and an oligarchy when the rich and the noble govern, they being at the same time few in number.

I have said that there are many forms of government, and have explained to what causes the variety is due. Why there are more than those already mentioned, and what they are, and whence they arise, I will now proceed to consider, starting from the principle already admitted, which is that every state consists, not of one, but of many parts. If we were going to speak of the different species of animals, we should first of all determine the organs which are indispensable to every animal, as for example some organs of sense and the instruments of receiving and digesting food, such as the mouth and the stomach, besides organs of locomotion. Assuming now that there are only so many kinds of organs, but that there may be differences in them—I mean different kinds of mouths, and stomachs, and perceptive and locomotive organs—the possible combinations of these differences will necessarily furnish many varieties of animals. (For animals cannot be the same which have different kinds of mouths or of ears.) And when all the combinations are exhausted, there will be as many sorts of animals as there are combinations of the necessary organs. The same, then, is true of the forms of government which have been described; states, as I have repeatedly said, are composed, not of one, but of many elements. One element is the food-producing class, who are called farmers; a second, the class of artisans who practise the arts without which a city cannot exist—of these arts some are absolutely necessary, others contribute to luxury or to the grace of life. The third class is that of traders, and by traders I mean those who are engaged in buying and selling, whether in commerce or in retail trade. A fourth class is that of labourers. The military make up the fifth class, and they are as necessary as any of the others, if the country is not to be the slave of every invader. For how can a state which has any title to the name be of a slavish nature? The state is independent and self-sufficing, but a slave is the reverse of independent. Hence we see that this subject, though ingeniously, has not been satisfactorily treated in the *Republic*. Socrates says that a state is made up of four sorts of people who are absolutely necessary; these are a weaver, a farmer, a shoemaker, and a builder; afterwards, finding that they are not enough, he adds a smith, and again a herdsman, to look after the necessary animals; then a merchant, and then a retail trader. All these together form the complement of the first state, as if a state were established merely to supply the necessaries of life, rather than for the sake of the good, or stood equally in need of shoemakers and of farmers. But he does not admit into the state a military class until the country has increased in size, and is beginning to encroach on its neighbour's land, whereupon they go to war. Yet even amongst his four original citizens, or whatever be the number of those whom he associates in the state, there must be some one who will dispense justice and determine what is just. And as the soul may be said to be more truly part of an animal than the body, so the higher parts of states, that is to say, the warrior class, the class engaged in the administration of justice, and that engaged in deliberation, which is the special business of political understanding—these are more essential to the state than the parts which minister to the necessaries of life. Whether their several functions are the functions of different citizens, or of the same—for it may often happen that the same persons are both soldiers and farmers—is immaterial

1291ᵃ1

5

10

15

20

25

30 to the argument. The higher as well as the lower elements are to be equally considered parts of the state, and if so, the military element at any rate must be included. There are also the wealthy who minister to the state with their property; these form the seventh class. The eighth class is that of pub-

35 lic servants and of administrators; for the state cannot exist without rulers. And therefore some must be able to take office and to serve the state, either always or in turn. There only remains the class of those who deliberate and who judge be-

40 tween disputants; we were just now distinguishing them. If the presence of all these elements, and their fair and equitable organization, is necessary to states, then there must also

1291ᵇ1 be persons who have the ability of statesmen. Different functions appear to be often combined in the same individual; for example, the soldier may also be a farmer, or an artisan; or, again the counsellor a judge. And all claim to possess po-

5 litical ability, and think that they are quite competent to fill most offices. But the same persons cannot be rich and poor at the same time. For this reason the rich and the poor are

10 especially regarded as parts of a state. Again, because the rich are generally few in number, while the poor are many, they appear to be antagonistic, and as the one or the other prevails they form the government. Hence arises the common opinion that there are two kinds of government—democracy and oligarchy.

I have already explained that there are many forms of con-
15 stitution, and to what causes the variety is due. Let me now show that there are different forms both of democracy and oligarchy, as will indeed be evident from what has preceded. For both in the common people and in the notables various classes are included; of the common people, one class are farmers, another artisans; another traders, who are em-

20 ployed in buying and selling; another are the sea-faring class, whether engaged in war or in trade, as ferrymen or as fishermen. (In many places any one of these classes forms quite a large population; for example, fishermen at Tarentum and Byzantium, crews of triremes at Athens, merchant seamen

25 at Aegina and Chios, ferrymen at Tenedos.) To the classes

already mentioned may be added day-labourers, and those who, owing to their needy circumstances, have no leisure, or those who are not of free birth on both sides; and there may be other classes as well. The notables again may be divided according to their wealth, birth, excellence, education, and 30 similar differences.

Of forms of democracy first comes that which is said to be based strictly on equality. In such a democracy the law says that it is just for the poor to have no more advantage than the rich; and that neither should be masters, but both equal. For if liberty and equality, as is thought by some, are chiefly 35 to be found in democracy, they will be best attained when all persons alike share in the government to the utmost. And since the people are the majority, and the opinion of the majority is decisive, such a government must necessarily be a democracy. Here then is one sort of democracy. There is another, in which the magistrates are elected according to a 40 certain property qualification, but a low one; he who has the required amount of property has a share in the government, but he who loses his property loses his rights. Another kind 1292ᵃ1 is that in which all the citizens who are under no disqualification share in the government, but still the law is supreme. In another, everybody, if he be only a citizen, is admitted to the government, but the law is supreme as before. A fifth form of democracy, in other respects the same, is that in which not the law, but the multitude, have the supreme power, and 5 supersede the law by their decrees. This is a state of affairs brought about by the demagogues. For in democracies which are subject to the law the best citizens hold the first place, and there are no demagogues; but where the laws are not supreme, there demagogues spring up. For the people becomes 10 a monarch, and is many in one; and the many have the power in their hand, not as individuals, but collectively. Homer says that 'it is not good to have a rule of many',[1] but whether he means this corporate rule, or the rule of many individuals, is uncertain. At all events this sort of democracy, which is now 15

[1] *Iliad* II 204.

a monarchy, and no longer under the control of law, seeks to exercise monarchical sway, and grows into a despot; the flatterer is held in honour; this sort of democracy is to other democracies what tyranny is to other forms of monarchy. The spirit of both is the same, and they alike exercise a despotic rule over the better citizens. The decrees of the one correspond to the edicts of the tyrant; and the demagogue is

20 to the one what the flatterer is to the other. Both have great power—the flatterer with the tyrant, the demagogue with democracies of the kind which we are describing. The demagogues make the decrees of the people override the laws, by

25 referring all things to the popular assembly. And therefore they grow great, because the people have all things in their hands, and they hold in their hands the votes of the people, who obey them. Further, those who have any complaint to bring against the magistrates say, 'let the people be judges'; the people are happy to accept the invitation; and so the au-

30 thority of every office is undermined. Such a democracy is fairly open to the objection that it is not a constitution at all; for where the laws have no authority, there is no constitution. The law ought to be supreme over all, and the magistracies should judge of particulars, and only this[2] should be considered a constitution. So that if democracy be a real

35 form of government, the sort of system in which all things are regulated by decrees is clearly not even a democracy in the true sense of the word, for decrees relate only to particulars.

These then are the different kinds of democracy.

5 • Of oligarchies, too, there are different kinds: one where

40 the property qualification for office is such that the poor, although they form the majority, have no share in the government, yet he who acquires a qualification may obtain a share. Another sort is when there is a qualification for office, but a

1292ᵇ1 high one, and the vacancies in the governing body are filled by co-optation. If the election is made out of all the qualified persons, a constitution of this kind inclines to an aris-

---

[2] Reading ταύτην for τήν.

tocracy, if out of a privileged class, to an oligarchy. Another
sort of oligarchy is when the son succeeds the father. There is   5
a fourth form, likewise hereditary, in which the magistrates
are supreme and not the law. Among oligarchies this is what
tyranny is among monarchies, and the last-mentioned form
of democracy among democracies; and in fact this sort of oligarchy receives the name of a dynasty.   10

These are the different sorts of oligarchies and democracies. It should, however, be remembered that in many states
the constitution which is established by law, although not
democratic, owing to the education and habits of the people
may be administered democratically, and conversely in other
states the established constitution may incline to democracy,   15
but may be administered in an oligarchical spirit. This most
often happens after a revolution; for governments do not
change at once; at first the dominant party are content with
encroaching a little upon their opponents. The laws which
existed previously continue in force, but the authors of the   20
revolution have the power in their hands.

6 • From what has been already said we may safely infer
that there are these many democracies and oligarchies. For
it is necessary that either all the classes whom we mentioned
must share in the government, or some only and not others.   25
When the class of farmers and of those who possess moderate fortunes have the supreme power, the government is
administered according to law. For the citizens being compelled to live by their labour have no leisure; and so they set
up the authority of the law, and attend assemblies only when
necessary. They all obtain a share in the government when   30
they have acquired the qualification which is fixed by the law;
hence all who have acquired the property qualification are
admitted to a share in the constitution. For the absolute exclusion of any class would be oligarchical; but leisure cannot
be provided for them unless there are revenues to support
them. This is one sort of democracy, and these are the causes
which give birth to it. Another kind is based on the distinc-   35
tion which naturally comes next in order; in this, everyone

to whose birth there is no objection is eligible, but actually shares in the government only if he can find leisure. Hence in such a democracy the supreme power is vested in the laws, because the state has no means of paying the citizens. A third kind is when all freemen have a right to share in the government, but do not actually share, for the reason which has been already given; so that in this form again the law must rule. A fourth kind of democracy is that which comes latest in the history of states. For when cities have far outgrown their original size, and their revenues have increased, all the citizens have a place in the government, through the great preponderance of the multitude; and they all, including the poor who receive pay, and therefore have leisure to exercise their rights, share in the administration. Indeed, when they are paid, the common people have the most leisure, for they are not hindered by the care of their property, which often fetters the rich, who are thereby prevented from taking part in the assembly or in the courts, and so the state is governed by the poor, who are a majority, and not by the laws. Such and so many are the kinds of democracy, and they grow out of these necessary causes.

Of oligarchies, one form is that in which the majority of the citizens have some property, but not very much; and this is the first form, which allows to anyone who obtains the required amount the right of sharing in the government. The sharers in the government being a numerous body, it follows that the law must govern, and not individuals. For in proportion as they are further removed from a monarchical form of government, and in respect of property have neither so much as to be able to live without attending to business, nor so little as to need state support, they must admit the rule of law and not claim to rule themselves. But if the men of property in the state are fewer than in the former case, and own more property, there arises a second form of oligarchy. For the stronger they are, the more power they claim, and having this object in view, they themselves select those of the other classes who are to be admitted to the government; but, not being as yet strong enough to rule without the law, they make the law represent their wishes. When this power is intensified by a further diminution of their numbers and increase of their property, there arises a third and further stage of oligarchy, in which the governing class keep the offices in their own hands, and the law ordains that the son shall succeed the 30 father. When, again, the rulers have great wealth and numerous friends, this sort of family despotism approaches a monarchy; individuals rule and not the law. This is the fourth sort of oligarchy, and is analogous to the last sort of democracy.

7 • There are still two forms besides democracy and oli- 35 garchy; one of them is universally recognized and included among the four principal forms of government, which are said to be monarchy, oligarchy, democracy, and the so-called aristocracy. But there is also a fifth, which retains the generic name of constitutional government; this is not common, 40 and therefore has not been noticed by writers who attempt to enumerate the different kinds of government; like Plato, in their books about the state, they recognize four only. The 1293ᵇ1 term 'aristocracy' is rightly applied to the form of government which is described in the first part of our treatise; for that only can be rightly called aristocracy which is a government formed of the best men absolutely, and not merely of 5 men who are good relative to some hypothesis. In the perfect state the good man is absolutely the same as the good citizen; whereas in other states the good citizen is only good relatively to his own form of government. But there are some states differing from oligarchies and also differing from the so-called constitutional government; these are termed aristocracies, and in them magistrates are certainly chosen both according to their wealth and according to their merit. Such 10 a form of government differs from each of the two just now mentioned, and is termed an aristocracy. For indeed in states which do not make excellence the aim of the community, men of merit and reputation for excellence may be found. And so where a government has regard to wealth, excellence, and the populace, as at Carthage, that is aristocracy; and also where it has regard only to two out of the three, as at 15

Lacedaemon, to excellence and the populace, and the two principles of democracy and excellence temper each other. There are these two forms of aristocracy in addition to the first and perfect state, and there is a third form, viz. the constitutions which incline more than the so-called constitu-
20 tional government towards oligarchy.

8 · I have yet to speak of the so-called polity and of tyranny. I put them in this order, not because a polity or constitutional government is to be regarded as a perversion any more than
25 the above-mentioned aristocracies. The truth is, that they all fall short of the most perfect form of government, and so they are reckoned among perversions, and the really perverted forms are perversions of these, as I said in the original discussion. Last of all I will speak of tyranny, which I place last in the series because I am inquiring into the constitu-
30 tions of states, and this is the very reverse of a constitution. Having explained why I have adopted this order, I will proceed to consider constitutional government; of which the nature will be clearer now that oligarchy and democracy have been defined. For polity or constitutional government may be described generally as a fusion of oligarchy and democracy; but the term is usually applied to those forms of gov-
35 ernment which incline towards democracy, and the term aristocracy to those which incline towards oligarchy, because birth and education are commonly the accompaniments of wealth. Moreover, the rich already possess the external ad-
40 vantages the want of which is a temptation to crime, and hence they are called noblemen and gentlemen. And inasmuch as aristocracy seeks to give predominance to the best of the citizens, people say also of oligarchies that they are com-
1294ᵃ1 posed of noblemen and gentlemen. Now it appears to be an impossible thing that the state which is governed not by the best citizens but by the worst should be well-governed, and equally impossible that the state which is ill-governed should be governed by the best. But we must remember that good laws, if they are not obeyed, do not constitute good government. Hence there are two parts of good government; one

is the actual obedience of citizens to the laws, the other part   5
is the goodness of the laws which they obey; they may obey
bad laws as well as good. And there may be a further subdivi-
sion; they may obey either the best laws which are attainable
to them, or the best absolutely.

The distribution of offices according to excellence is a
special characteristic of aristocracy, for the principle of an   10
aristocracy is excellence, as wealth is of an oligarchy, and
freedom of a democracy. In all of them there of course exists the right of the majority, and whatever seems good to the
majority of those who share in the government has authority,
whether in an oligarchy, an aristocracy or a democracy. Now   15
in most states the form called polity exists, for the fusion goes
no further than the attempt to unite the freedom of the poor
and the wealth of the rich, who commonly take the place of
the noble. But as there are three grounds on which men claim   20
an equal share in the government, freedom, wealth, and excellence (for the fourth, what is called good birth, is the result
of the two last, being only ancient wealth and excellence), it
is clear that the admixture of the two elements, that is to say,
of the rich and poor, is to be called a polity or constitutional
government; and the union of the three is to be called aristocracy, and more than any other form of government, except the true and ideal, has a right to this name.   25

Thus far I have shown the existence of forms of states
other than monarchy, democracy, and oligarchy, and what
they are, and in what aristocracies differ from one another,
and polities from aristocracies—that the two latter are not
very unlike is obvious.

9 • Next we have to consider how by the side of oligarchy   30
and democracy the so-called polity or constitutional government springs up, and how it should be organized. The nature
of it will be at once understood from a comparison of oligarchy and democracy; we must ascertain their different characteristics, and taking a portion from each, fit the two together,   35
like the parts of a tally-stick. Now there are three modes in
which fusions of government may be effected. In the first

mode we must combine the laws made by both governments, say concerning the administration of justice. In oligarchies they impose a fine on the rich if they do not serve as judges, and to the poor they give no pay; but in democracies they give pay to the poor and do not fine the rich. Now the union of these two modes is a common or middle term between them, and is therefore characteristic of a constitutional government, for it is a combination of both. This is one mode of uniting the two elements. Or a mean may be taken between the enactments of the two: thus democracies require no property qualification, or only a small one, from members of the assembly, oligarchies a high one; here neither of these is the common term, but a mean between them. There is a third mode, in which something is borrowed from the oligarchical and something from the democratic principle. For example, the appointment of magistrates by lot is thought to be democratic, and the election of them oligarchical; democratic again when there is no property qualification, oligarchical when there is. In the aristocratic or constitutional state, one element will be taken from each—from oligarchy the principle of electing to offices, from democracy the disregard of qualification. Such are the various modes of combination.

There is a true union of oligarchy and democracy when the same state may be termed either a democracy or an oligarchy; those who use both names evidently feel that the fusion is complete. Such a fusion there is also in the mean; for both extremes appear in it. The Lacedaemonian constitution, for example, is often described as a democracy, because it has many democratic features. In the first place the youth receive a democratic education. For the sons of the poor are brought up with the sons of the rich, who are educated in such a manner as to make it possible for the sons of the poor to be educated like them. A similar equality prevails in the following period of life, and when the citizens are grown up to manhood the same rule is observed; there is no distinction between the rich and poor. In like manner they all have the same food at their public tables, and the rich wear only such clothing as any poor man can afford. Again, the people

elect to one of the two greatest offices of state, and in the
other they share; for they elect the Senators and share in the　30
Ephoralty. By others the Spartan constitution is said to be an
oligarchy, because it has many oligarchical elements. That all
offices are filled by election and none by lot, is one of these
oligarchical characteristics; that the power of inflicting death
or banishment rests with a few persons is another; and there
are others. In a well attempered polity there should appear
to be both elements and yet neither; also the government　35
should rely on itself, and not on foreign aid, and on itself not
through the good will of a majority[3]—they might be equally
well-disposed when there is a vicious form of government—
but through the general willingness of all classes in the state
to maintain the constitution.

Enough of the manner in which a constitutional government, and in which the so-called aristocracies, ought to be　40
framed.

10 · Of the nature of tyranny I have still to speak, in order　1295ª1
that it may have its place in our inquiry (since even tyranny is
reckoned by us to be a form of government), although there is
not much to be said about it. I have already in the former part
of this treatise discussed royalty or kingship according to the
most usual meaning of the term, and considered whether it　5
is or is not advantageous to states, and what kind of royalty
should be established, and from what source, and how.

When speaking of royalty we also spoke of two forms of
tyranny, which are both according to law, and therefore easily　10
pass into royalty. Among barbarians there are elected monarchs who exercise a despotic power; despotic rulers were also
elected in ancient Greece, called Aesymnetes. These monarchies, when compared with one another, exhibit certain
differences. And they are, as I said before, royal, in so far as　15
the monarch rules according to law over willing subjects;
but they are tyrannical in so far as he is despotic and rules according to his own fancy. There is also a third kind of tyranny,

[3] Omitting ἔξωθεν.

which is the most typical form, and is the counterpart of the
perfect monarchy. This tyranny is just that arbitrary power of
an individual which is responsible to no one, and governs all
alike, whether equals or betters, with a view to its own advantage, not to that of its subjects, and therefore against their
will. No freeman willingly endures such a government.

The kinds of tyranny are such and so many, and for the
reasons which I have given.

11 • We have now to inquire what is the best constitution
for most states, and the best life for most men, neither assuming a standard of excellence which is above ordinary
persons, nor an education which is exceptionally favoured
by nature and circumstances, nor yet an ideal state which is
an aspiration only, but having regard to the life in which the
majority are able to share, and to the form of government
which states in general can attain. As to those aristocracies,
as they are called, of which we were just now speaking, they
either lie beyond the possibilities of the greater number of
states, or they approximate to the so-called constitutional
government, and therefore need no separate discussion. And
in fact the conclusion at which we arrive respecting all these
forms rests upon the same grounds. For if what was said in
the *Ethics* is true, that the happy life is the life according to
excellence lived without impediment, and that excellence is
a mean, then the life which is in a mean, and in a mean attainable by everyone, must be the best. And the same principles
of excellence and badness are characteristic of cities and of
constitutions; for the constitution is so to speak the life of
the city.

Now in all states there are three elements: one class is very
rich, another very poor, and a third in a mean. It is admitted that moderation and the mean are best, and therefore it
will clearly be best to possess the gifts of fortune in moderation; for in that condition of life men are most ready to follow rational principle. But he who greatly excels in beauty,
strength, birth, or wealth, or on the other hand who is very
poor, or very weak, or of very low status, finds it difficult to

follow rational principle. Of these two the one sort grow
into violent and great criminals, the others into rogues and   10
petty rascals. And two sorts of offences correspond to them,
the one committed from violence, the other from roguery
[Again, the middle class is least likely to shrink from rule, or
to be over-ambitious for it],[4] both of which are injuries to the
state. Again, those who have too much of the goods of fortune, strength, wealth, friends, and the like, are neither will-   15
ing nor able to submit to authority. The evil begins at home;
for when they are boys, by reason of the luxury in which they
are brought up, they never learn, even at school, the habit
of obedience. On the other hand, the very poor, who are
in the opposite extreme, are too degraded. So that the one
class cannot obey, and can only rule despotically; the other
knows not how to command and must be ruled like slaves.   20
Thus arises a city, not of freemen, but of masters and slaves,
the one despising, the other envying; and nothing can be
more fatal to friendship and good fellowship in states than
this: for good fellowship springs from friendship; when men
are at enmity with one another, they would rather not even
share the same path. But a city ought to be composed, as far
as possible, of equals and similars; and these are generally   25
the middle classes. Wherefore the city which is composed
of middle-class citizens is necessarily best constituted in respect of the elements of which we say the fabric of the state
naturally consists. And this is the class of citizens which is
most secure in a state, for they do not, like the poor, covet
other men's goods; nor do others covet theirs, as the poor   30
covet the goods of the rich; and as they neither plot against
others, nor are themselves plotted against, they pass through
life safely. Wisely then did Phocylides pray—'Many things
are best in the mean; I desire to be of a middle condition in
my city'.

Thus it is manifest that the best political community is
formed by citizens of the middle class, and that those states   35
are likely to be well-administered in which the middle class is

[4]Excised by Dreizehnter.

large, and stronger if possible than both the other classes, or at any rate than either singly; for the addition of the middle class turns the scale, and prevents either of the extremes from being dominant. Great then is the good fortune of a state in which the citizens have a moderate and sufficient property; for where some possess much, and the others nothing, there may arise an extreme democracy, or a pure oligarchy; or a tyranny may grow out of either extreme—either out of the most rampant democracy, or out of an oligarchy; but it is not so likely to arise out of the middle constitutions and those akin to them. I will explain the reason for this hereafter, when I speak of the revolutions of states. The mean condition of states is clearly best, for no other is free from faction; and where the middle class is large, there are least likely to be factions and dissensions. For a similar reason large states are less liable to faction than small ones, because in them the middle class is large; whereas in small states it is easy to divide all the citizens into two classes who are either rich or poor, and to leave nothing in the middle. And democracies are safer and more permanent than oligarchies, because they have a middle class which is more numerous and has a greater share in the government; for when there is no middle class, and the poor are excessive in number, troubles arise, and the state soon comes to an end. A proof of the superiority of the middle class is that the best legislators have been of a middle condition; for example, Solon, as his own verses testify; and Lycurgus, for he was not a king; and Charondas, and almost all legislators.

These considerations will help us to understand why most governments are either democratic or oligarchical. The reason is that the middle class is seldom numerous in them, and whichever party, whether the rich or the common people, transgresses the mean and predominates, draws the constitution its own way, and thus arises either oligarchy or democracy. There is another reason—the poor and the rich quarrel with one another, and whichever side gets the better, instead of establishing a just or popular government, regards political supremacy as the prize of victory, and the one party sets

1296ª1

5

10

15

20

25

30

up a democracy and the other an oligarchy. Further, both the parties which had the supremacy in Greece looked only to the interest of their own form of government, and established in states, the one, democracies, and the other, oligarchies; they 35 thought of their own advantage, and of the advantage of the other states not at all. For these reasons the middle form of government has rarely, if ever, existed, and among a very few only. One man alone of all who ever ruled in Greece was induced to give this middle constitution to states.

But it has now become a habit among the citizens of states 1296ᵇ1 not even to care about equality; all men are seeking for dominion, or, if conquered, are willing to submit.

What then is the best form of government, and what makes it the best, is evident; and of other constitutions, since we say that there are many kinds of democracy and many of oligarchy, it is not difficult to see which has the first and which 5 the second or any other place in the order of excellence, now that we have determined which is the best. For that which is nearest to the best must of necessity be better, and that which is further from the mean worse, if we are judging absolutely and not relatively to given conditions: I say 'relatively to given conditions', since a particular government may be pref- 10 erable, but another form may be better for some people.

12 • We have now to consider what and what kind of government is suitable to what and what kind of men. I may begin by assuming, as a general principle common to all gov- 15 ernments, that the portion of the state which desires the permanence of the constitution ought to be stronger than that which desires the reverse. Now every city is composed of quality and quantity. By quality I mean freedom, wealth, education, good birth, and by quantity, superiority of numbers.

Quality may exist in one of the classes which make up the 20 state, and quantity in the other. For example, the meanly-born may be more in number than the well-born, or the poor than the rich, yet they may not so much exceed in quantity as they fall short in quality; and therefore there must be a comparison of quantity and quality.

25   Where the number of the poor exceeds a given proportion, there will naturally be a democracy, varying in form with the sort of people who compose it in each case. If, for example, the farmers exceed in number, the first form of de
30 mocracy will then arise; if the artisans and labouring class, the last; and so with the intermediate forms. But where the rich and the notables exceed in quality more than they fall short in quantity, there oligarchy arises, similarly assuming various forms according to the kind of superiority possessed by the oligarchs.

35   The legislator should always include the middle class in his government; if he makes his laws oligarchical, let him look to the middle class; if he makes them democratic, he should equally by his laws try to attach this class to the state. There only can the government ever be stable where the middle class exceeds one or both of the others, and in that case there
1297ᵃ1 will be no fear that the rich will unite with the poor against the rulers. For neither of them will ever be willing to serve the other, and if they look for some form of government more suitable to both, they will find none better than this, for the rich and the poor will never consent to rule in turn, because they mistrust one another. The arbiter is always the one most
5 trusted, and he who is in the middle is an arbiter. The more perfect the admixture of the political elements, the more lasting will be the constitution. Many even of those who desire to form aristocratic governments make a mistake, not only in giving too much power to the rich, but in attempting to
10 cheat the people. There comes a time when out of a false good there arises a true evil, since the encroachments of the rich are more destructive to the constitution than those of the people.

13 • The devices by which oligarchies deceive the people
15 are five in number; they relate to the assembly; the magistracies; the courts of law; the use of arms; and gymnastic exercises. The assemblies are thrown open to all, but either the rich only are fined for non-attendance, or a much larger fine is inflicted upon them. As to the magistracies, those who are

qualified by property cannot decline office upon oath, but the 20
poor may. In the law-courts the rich, and the rich only, are
fined if they do not serve, the poor are let off with impunity,
or, as in the laws of Charondas, a larger fine is inflicted on the
rich, and a smaller one on the poor. In some states all citizens
who have registered themselves are allowed to attend the assembly and to try causes; but if after registration they do not 25
attend either in the assembly or at the courts, heavy fines
are imposed upon them. The intention is that through fear
of the fines they may avoid registering themselves, and then
they cannot sit in the law-courts or in the assembly. Concerning the possession of arms, and gymnastic exercises,
they legislate in a similar spirit. For the poor are not obliged
to have arms, but the rich are fined for not having them; 30
and in like manner no penalty is inflicted on the poor for
non-attendance at the gymnasium, and consequently, having nothing to fear, they do not attend, whereas the rich are
liable to a fine, and therefore they take care to attend.

These are the devices of oligarchical legislators, and in democracies they have counter-devices. They pay the poor for 35
attending the assemblies and the law-courts, and they inflict
no penalty on the rich for non-attendance. It is obvious that
he who would duly mix the two principles should combine
the practice of both, and provide that the poor should be paid
to attend, and the rich fined if they do not attend, for then 40
all will take part; if there is no such combination, power will
be in the hands of one party only. The government should be
confined to those who carry arms. As to the property quali- 1297^{b}1
fication, no absolute rule can be laid down, but we must see
what is the highest qualification sufficiently comprehensive
to secure that the number of those who have the rights of citizens exceeds the number of those excluded. Even if they have 5
no share in office, the poor, provided only that they are not
outraged or deprived of their property, will be quiet enough.

But to secure gentle treatment for the poor is not an easy
thing, since a ruling class is not always humane. And in
time of war the poor are apt to hesitate unless they are fed; 10
when fed, they are willing enough to fight. In some states the

government is vested, not only in those who are actually serving, but also in those who have served; among the Malians,
15 for example, the governing body consisted of the latter, while
the magistrates were chosen from those actually on service. And the earliest government which existed among the
Greeks, after the overthrow of the kingly power, grew up out
of the warrior class, and was originally taken from the knights
(for strength and superiority in war at that time depended on
20 cavalry; indeed, without discipline, infantry are useless, and
in ancient times there was no military knowledge or tactics,
and therefore the strength of armies lay in their cavalry). But
when cities increased and the heavy-armed grew in strength,
more had a share in the government; and this is the reason
25 why the states which we call constitutional governments have
been hitherto called democracies. Ancient constitutions, as
might be expected, were oligarchical and royal; their population being small they had no considerable middle class; the
people were weak in numbers and organization, and were
therefore more content to be governed.

I have explained why there are various forms of govern-
30 ment, and why there are more than is generally supposed; for
democracy, as well as other constitutions, has more than one
form: also what their differences are, and whence they arise,
and what is the best form of government, speaking generally, and to whom the various forms of government are best
suited; all this has now been explained.

35 14 • Having thus gained an appropriate basis of discussion
we will proceed to speak of the points which follow next in
order. We will consider the subject not only in general but
with reference to particular constitutions. All constitutions
have three elements, concerning which the good lawgiver
has to regard what is expedient for each constitution. When
40 they are well-ordered, the constitution is well-ordered, and
as they differ from one another, constitutions differ. There is
one element which deliberates about public affairs; secondly
1298ᵃ1 that concerned with the magistracies—the questions being,
what they should be, over what they should exercise author-

ity, and what should be the mode of electing to them; and thirdly that which has judicial power.

The deliberative element has authority in matters of war and peace, in making and unmaking alliances; it passes laws, inflicts death, exile, confiscation, elects magistrates and audits their accounts. These powers must be assigned either all to all the citizens or all to some of them (for example, to one or more magistracies, or different causes to different magistracies), or some of them to all, and others of them only to some. That all things should be decided by all is characteristic of democracy; this is the sort of equality which the people desire. But there are various ways in which all may share in the government; they may deliberate, not all in one body, but by turns, as in the constitution of Telecles the Milesian. There are other constitutions in which the boards of magistrates meet and deliberate, but come into office by turns, and are elected out of the tribes and the very smallest divisions of the state, until every one has obtained office in his turn. The citizens, on the other hand, are assembled only for the purposes of legislation, and to consult about the constitution, and to hear the edicts of the magistrates. In another variety of democracy the citizens form one assembly, but meet only to elect magistrates, to pass laws, to advise about war and peace, and to make scrutinies. Other matters are referred severally to special magistrates, who are elected by vote or by lot out of all the citizens. Or again, the citizens meet about election to offices and about scrutinies, and deliberate concerning war or alliances while other matters are administered by the magistrates, who, as far as is possible, are elected by vote. I am speaking of those magistracies in which special knowledge is required. A fourth form of democracy is when all the citizens meet to deliberate about everything, and the magistrates decide nothing, but only make the preliminary inquiries; and that is the way in which the last form of democracy, corresponding, as we maintain, to the close family oligarchy and to tyranny, is at present administered. All these modes are democratic.

On the other hand, that some should deliberate about all is oligarchical. This again is a mode which, like the democratic,

35   has many forms. When the deliberative class being elected out of those who have a moderate qualification are numerous and they respect and obey the prohibitions of the law without altering it, and anyone who has the required qualification shares in the government, then, just because of this moderation, the oligarchy inclines towards polity. But when only selected individuals and not the whole people share in the deliberations of

1298ᵇ1   the state, then, although, as in the former case, they observe the law, the government is a pure oligarchy. Or, again, when those who have the power of deliberation are self-elected, and son succeeds father, and they and not the laws are supreme— the government is of necessity oligarchical. Where, again,

5   particular persons have authority in particular matters—for example, when the whole people decide about peace and war and hold scrutinies, but the magistrates regulate everything else, and they are elected by vote or by lot—there the government is an aristocracy or a constitutional government. And if some questions are decided by magistrates elected by vote, and others by magistrates elected by lot, either absolutely or out of select candidates, or elected partly by vote, partly by

10   lot—these practices are partly characteristic of an aristocratic government, and partly of a pure constitutional government.

    These are the various forms of the deliberative body; they correspond to the various forms of government. And the government of each state is administered according to one or other of the principles which have been laid down. Now it is for the interest of democracy, according to the most prevalent notion of it (I am speaking of that extreme form of democracy

15   in which the people are supreme even over the laws), with a view to better deliberation to adopt the custom of oligarchies respecting courts of law. For in oligarchies the rich who are wanted to be judges are compelled to attend under pain of a fine, whereas in democracies the poor are paid to attend. And this practice of oligarchies should be adopted by democracies in their public assemblies, for they will advise better if they all

20   deliberate together, the people with the notables and the notables with the people. It is also a good plan that those who deliberate should be elected by vote or by lot in equal numbers

out of the different classes; and that if the people greatly exceed in number those who have political training, pay should not be given to all, but only to as many as would balance the number of the notables, or that the number in excess should be eliminated by lot. But in oligarchies either certain persons should be co-opted from the mass, or a class of officers should be appointed such as exist in some states, who are termed Probuli and guardians of the law; and the citizens should occupy themselves exclusively with matters on which they have previously deliberated; for in that way the people will have a share in the deliberations of the state, but will not be able to disturb the principles of the constitution. Again, in oligarchies either the people ought to accept the measures of the government, or not to pass anything contrary to them; or, if all are allowed to share in counsel, the decision should rest with the magistrates. The opposite of what is done in constitutional governments should be the rule in oligarchies; the veto of the majority should be final, their assent not final, but the proposal should be referred back to the magistrates. Whereas in constitutional governments they take the contrary course; the few have the negative, not the affirmative power; the affirmation of everything rests with the multitude.

These, then, are our conclusions respecting the deliberative, that is, the supreme element in states.

15 • Next we will proceed to consider the distribution of offices; this, too, being a part of politics concerning which many questions arise:—What shall their number be? Over what shall they preside, and what shall be their duration? Sometimes they last for six months, sometimes for less; sometimes they are annual, whilst in other cases offices are held for still longer periods. Shall they be for life or for a long term of years; or, if for a short term only, shall the same persons hold them over and over again, or once only? Also about the appointment to them—from whom are they to be chosen, by whom, and how? We should first be in a position to say what are the possible varieties of them, and then we may proceed to determine which are suited to different

forms of government. But what are to be included under the
term 'offices'? That is a question not quite so easily answered.
For a political community requires many officers; and not
every one who is chosen by vote or by lot is to be regarded
as a ruler. In the first place there are the priests, who must
be distinguished from political officers; masters of choruses
and heralds, even ambassadors, are elected by vote. Some duties of superintendence again are political, extending either
to all the citizens in a single sphere of action, like the office
of the general who superintends them when they are in the
field, or to a section of them only, like the inspectorships of
women or of youth. Other offices are concerned with household management, like that of the corn measurers who exist
in many states and are elected officers. There are also menial
offices which the rich have executed by their slaves. Speaking
generally, those are to be called offices to which the duties are
assigned of deliberating about certain measures and of judging and commanding, especially the last; for to command
is the especial duty of a magistrate. But the question is not
of any importance in practice; no one has ever brought into
court the meaning of the word, although such problems have
a speculative interest.

What kinds of offices, and how many, are necessary to the
existence of a state, and which, if not necessary, yet conduce
to its well-being, are much more important considerations,
affecting all constitutions, but more especially small states.
For in great states it is possible, and indeed necessary, that
every office should have a special function; where the citizens
are numerous, many may hold office. And so it happens that
some offices a man holds a second time only after a long interval, and others he holds once only; and certainly every work
is better done which receives the sole and not the divided attention of the worker. But in small states it is necessary to
combine many offices in a few hands, since the small number
of citizens does not admit of many holding office—for who
will there be to succeed them? And yet small states at times
require the same offices and laws as large ones; the difference
is that the one want them often, the others only after long in-

tervals. Hence there is no reason why the care of many offices
should not be imposed on the same person, for they will not
interfere with each other. When the population is small, offices should be like the spits which also serve to hold a lamp.
We must first ascertain how many magistrates are necessary   10
in every state, and also how many are not exactly necessary,
but are nevertheless useful, and then there will be no difficulty
in seeing what offices can be combined in one. We should also
know over which matters several local tribunals are to have
jurisdiction, and in which cases authority should be central-   15
ized: for example, should one person keep order in the
market and another in some other place, or should the same
person be responsible everywhere? Again, should offices be
divided according to the subjects with which they deal, or according to the persons with whom they deal: I mean to say,
should one person see to good order in general, or one look
after the boys, another after the women, and so on? Further,   20
under different constitutions, should the magistrates be the
same or different? For example, in democracy, oligarchy, aristocracy, monarchy, should there be the same magistrates,
although they are elected not out of equal or similar classes of
citizens, but differently under different constitutions—in aristocracies, for example, they are chosen from the educated,
in oligarchies from the wealthy, and in democracies from the   25
free—or are there certain differences in the offices answering
to them as well, and may the same be suitable to some, but
different offices to others? For in some states it may be convenient that the same office should have a more extensive, in
other states a narrower sphere. Special offices are peculiar to   30
certain forms of government—for example that of Probuli,
which is not a democratic office, although a council is democratic. There must be some body of men whose duty is to prepare measures for the people in order that they may not be
diverted from their business; when these are few in number,
the state inclines to an oligarchy: or rather the Probuli must
always be few, and are therefore an oligarchical element. But   35
when both institutions exist in a state, the Probuli are a check
on the council; for the counsellor is a democratic element,

but the Probuli are oligarchical. Even the power of the council disappears when democracy has taken that extreme form in which the people themselves are always meeting and deliberating about everything. This is the case when the members of the assembly receive abundant pay; for they have nothing to do and are always holding assemblies and deciding everything for themselves. A magistracy which controls the boys or the women, or any similar office, is suited to an aristocracy rather than to a democracy; for how can the magistrates prevent the wives of the poor from going out of doors? Neither is it an oligarchical office; for the wives of the oligarchs are too grand.

Enough of these matters. I will now inquire into appointments to offices. The varieties depend on three terms, and the combinations of these give all possible modes: first, who appoints? secondly, from whom? and thirdly, how? Each of these three admits of two varieties. For either all the citizens, or only some, appoint. Either the magistrates are chosen out of all or out of some who are distinguished either by a property qualification, or by birth, or excellence, or for some special reason, as at Megara only those were eligible who had returned from exile and fought together against the democracy. They may be appointed either by vote or by lot. Again, these several varieties may be coupled, I mean that some officers may be elected by some, others by all, and some again out of some, and others out of all, and some by vote and others by lot. Each variety of these terms admits of four modes.

For either all may appoint from all by vote, or all from all by lot, or all from some by vote, or all from some by lot. Again, if it is only some who appoint, they may do so from all by vote or from all by lot or from some by vote or from some by lot. And if from all, either by sections, as, for example, by tribes, and wards, and phratries, until all the citizens have been gone through; or the citizens may be in all cases eligible indiscriminately; or sometimes in one way, sometimes in the other—I mean, from all by vote in some cases, by lot in others. Thus the modes that arise, apart from the two couplings, number twelve. Of these systems two are popular, that all should appoint from all by vote or by lot—or by both, some of the offices by lot, others by vote. That all should not appoint at once, but should appoint from all or from some either by lot or by vote or by both, or appoint to some offices from all and to others from some ('by both' meaning to some offices by lot, to others by vote), is characteristic of a polity. [And that some should appoint from all, to some offices by vote, to others by lot or by both—some by lot, others by vote—is oligarchical; and it is more oligarchical to appoint by both. And to appoint to some offices from all, to others from some, is characteristic of a polity with a leaning towards aristocracy—or to appoint some by vote, others by lot.]⁵ That some should appoint from some is oligarchical— even that some should appoint from some by lot (and if this does not actually occur, it is none the less oligarchical in character), or that some should appoint from some by both. That some should appoint from all, and that sometimes all should appoint from some, by vote, is aristocratic.

These are the different modes of constituting magistrates, and these correspond to different forms of government:— which are proper to which, or how they ought to be established, will be evident when we determine the nature of their powers. By powers I mean such powers as a magistrate exercises over the revenue or in defence of the country; for there are various kinds of power: the power of the general, for example, is not the same as that which regulates contracts in the market.

Of the three parts of government the judicial remains to be considered, and this we shall divide on the same principle. There are three points on which the varieties of law-courts depend: the persons from whom they are appointed, the matters with which they are concerned, and the manner of their appointment. I mean, are the judges taken from all, or from some only? how many kinds of law-courts are there? are the judges chosen by vote or by lot?

⁵ Excised by Dreizehnter. The text is uncertain throughout this paragraph.

First, let me determine how many kinds of law-courts there are. They are eight in number: one is the court of audits or
20 scrutinies; a second takes cognizance of ordinary offences against the state; a third is concerned with treason against the constitution; the fourth determines disputes respecting penalties, whether raised by magistrates or by private persons; the fifth decides the more important civil cases; the sixth tries
25 cases of homicide, which are of various kinds, premeditated, involuntary, and cases in which the guilt is confessed but the justice is disputed; and there may be a fourth court in which murderers who have fled from justice are tried after their return, such as the Court of Phreatto is said to be at Athens. But cases of this sort rarely happen at all even in large cities. The
30 different kinds of homicide may be tried either by the same or by different courts. There are courts for strangers:—of these there are two subdivisions, one for the settlement of their disputes with one another, the other for the settlement of disputes between them and the citizens. And besides all these there must be courts for small suits about sums of a drachma up to five drachmas, or a little more, which have to be deter-
35 mined, but do not require many judges.

Nothing more need be said of these small suits, nor of the courts for homicide and for strangers:—I would rather speak of political cases, which, when mismanaged, create division and disturbances in constitutions.

Now if all the citizens judge, in all the different cases which I have distinguished, they may be appointed by vote or
40 by lot, or sometimes by lot and sometimes by vote. Or when a single class of causes are tried, the judges who decide them may be appointed, some by vote, and some by lot. These then are the four modes of appointing judges from the whole peo-
1301ᵃ1 ple, and there will be likewise four modes, if they are elected from a part only; for they may be appointed from some by vote and judge in all causes; or they may be appointed from some by lot and judge in all causes; or they may be elected in some cases by vote, and in some cases taken by lot, or some courts, even when judging the same causes, may be com-
5 posed of members some appointed by vote and some by lot.

These modes, then, as was said, answer to those previously mentioned.

Once more, the modes of appointment may be combined; I mean, that some may be chosen out of the whole people, others out of some, some out of both; for example, the same tribunal may be composed of some who were elected out of all, and of others who were elected out of some, either by vote or by lot or by both.

In how many forms law-courts can be established has now been considered. The first form, viz. that in which the judges are taken from all the citizens, and in which all causes are tried, is democratic; the second, which is composed of a few only who try all causes, oligarchical; the third, in which some courts are taken from all classes, and some from certain classes only, aristocratic and constitutional.

BOOK V

1 • The design which we proposed to ourselves is now nearly completed. Next in order follow the causes of revolution in states, how many, and of what nature they are; what modes of destruction apply to particular states, and out of what, and into what they mostly change; also what are the modes of preservation in states generally, or in a particular state, and by what means each state may be best preserved: these questions remain to be considered.

In the first place we must assume as our starting-point that in the many forms of government which have sprung up there has always been an acknowledgement of justice and proportionate equality, although mankind fail in attaining them, as indeed I have already explained. Democracy, for example, arises out of the notion that those who are equal in any respect are equal in all respects; because men are equally free, they claim to be absolutely equal. Oligarchy is based on the notion that those who are unequal in one respect are in all respects unequal; being unequal, that is, in property, they suppose themselves to be unequal absolutely. The democrats think that as they are equal they ought to be equal in all things; while the oligarchs, under the idea that they are unequal, claim too much, which is one form of inequality. All these forms of government have a kind of justice, but, tried by an absolute standard, they are faulty; and, therefore, both parties, whenever their share in the government does not accord with their preconceived ideas, stir up revolution. Those who excel in excellence have the best right of all to rebel (for they alone can with reason be deemed absolutely unequal), but then they are of all men the least inclined to do so. There is also a superiority which is claimed by men of rank; for they are thought noble because they spring from wealthy and excellent ancestors. Here then, so to speak, are opened the very springs and fountains of revolution; and hence arise two sorts of changes in governments; the one affecting the constitution, when men seek to change from an existing form into some other, for example, from democracy into oligarchy, and from oligarchy into democracy, or from either of them into constitutional government or aristocracy, and conversely; the other not affecting the constitution, when, without disturbing the form of government, whether oligarchy, or monarchy, or any other, they try to get the administration into their own hands. Further, there is a question of degree; an oligarchy, for example, may become more or less oligarchical, and a democracy more or less democratic; and in like manner the characteristics of the other forms of government may be more or less strictly maintained. Or the revolution may be directed against a portion of the constitution only, e.g., the establishment or overthrow of a particular office: as at Sparta it is said that Lysander attempted to overthrow the monarchy, and king Pausanias, the ephoralty. At Epidamnus, too, the change was partial. For instead of phylarchs or heads of tribes, a council was appointed; but to this day the magistrates are the only members of the ruling class who are compelled to go to the Heliaea when an election takes place, and the office of the single archon was another oligarchical feature. Everywhere inequality is a cause of revolution, but an inequality in which there is no proportion—for instance, a perpetual monarchy among equals; and always it is the desire for equality which rises in rebellion.

Now equality is of two kinds, numerical and proportional; by the first I mean sameness or equality in number or size; by the second, equality of ratios. For example, the excess of three over two is numerically equal to the excess of two over one; whereas four exceeds two in the same ratio in which two exceeds one, for two is the same part of four that one is of two, namely, the half. As I was saying before, men agree that justice in the abstract is proportion, but they differ in that some think that if they are equal in any respect they are equal absolutely, others that if they are unequal in any respect they should be unequal in all. Hence there are two principal forms of government, democracy and oligarchy; for good birth and excellence are rare, but wealth and numbers are more common. In what city shall we find a hundred persons of good birth and of excellence? whereas the rich everywhere abound. That a state should be ordered, simply and wholly, according to either kind of equality, is not a good thing; the proof is the fact that such forms of government never last. They are originally based on a mistake, and, as they begin badly, cannot fail to end badly. The inference is that both kinds of equality should be employed; numerical in some cases, and proportionate in others.

Still democracy appears to be safer and less liable to revolution than oligarchy. For in oligarchies there is the double danger of the oligarchs falling out among themselves and also with the people; but in democracies there is only the danger of a quarrel with the oligarchs. No dissension worth mentioning arises among the people themselves. And we may further remark that a government which is composed of the middle class more nearly approximates to democracy than to oligarchy, and is the safest of the imperfect forms of government.

2 • In considering how dissensions and political revolutions arise, we must first of all ascertain the beginnings and causes of them which affect constitutions generally. They

may be said to be three in number; and we have now to give an outline of each. We want to know what is the state of mind and what are the motives of those who make them and whence arise political disturbances and quarrels. The universal and chief cause of this revolutionary feeling has been already mentioned; viz. the desire for equality, when men think that they are equal to others who have more than themselves; or, again, the desire for inequality and superiority, when conceiving themselves to be superior they think that they have not more but the same or less than their inferiors; pretensions which may or may not be just. Inferiors revolt in order that they may be equal, and equals that they may be superior. Such is the state of mind which creates revolutions. The motives for making them are the desire for gain and honour, or the fear of dishonour and loss; the authors of them want to divert punishment or dishonour from themselves or their friends. The causes and reasons of revolutions, whereby men are themselves affected in the way described, and about the things which I have mentioned, viewed in one way may be regarded as seven, and in another as more than seven. Two of them have been already noticed; but they act in a different manner, for men are excited against one another by the love of gain and honour—not, as in the case which I have just supposed, in order to obtain them for themselves, but at seeing others, justly or unjustly, monopolising them. Other causes are insolence, fear, excessive predominance, contempt, disproportionate increase in some part of the state; causes of another sort are election intrigues, carelessness, neglect about trifles, dissimilarity of elements.

3 • What share insolence and avarice have in creating revolutions, and how they work, is plain enough. When the magistrates are insolent and grasping they conspire against one another and also against the constitution from which they derive their power, making their gains either at the expense of individuals or of the public. It is evident, again, what an influence honour exerts and how it is a cause of revolution. Men who are themselves dishonoured and who see others

obtaining honours rise in rebellion; the honour or dishonour when undeserved is unjust; and just when awarded according to merit. Again, superiority is a cause of revolution when one or more persons have a power which is too much for the state and the power of the government; this is a condition of affairs out of which there tends to arise a monarchy, or a family oligarchy. And therefore, in some places, as at Athens and Argos, they have recourse to ostracism. But how much better to provide from the first that there should be no such pre-eminent individuals instead of letting them come into existence and then finding a remedy.

Another cause of revolution is fear. Either men have committed wrong, and are afraid of punishment, or they are expecting to suffer wrong and are desirous of anticipating their enemy. Thus at Rhodes the notables conspired against the people through fear of the suits that were brought against them. Contempt is also a cause of insurrection and revolution; for example, in oligarchies—when those who have no share in the state are the majority, they revolt, because they think that they are the stronger. Or, again, in democracies, the rich despise the disorder and anarchy of the state; at Thebes, for example, where, after the battle of Oenophyta, the bad administration of the democracy led to its ruin. At Megara the fall of the democracy was due to a defeat occasioned by disorder and anarchy. And at Syracuse the democracy aroused contempt before the tyranny of Gelo arose; at Rhodes, before the insurrection.

Political revolutions also spring from a disproportionate increase in any part of the state. For as a body is made up of many members, and every member ought to grow in proportion so that symmetry may be preserved, but it loses its nature if the foot is four cubits long and the rest of the body two spans; and, should the abnormal increase be one of quality as well as of quantity, it may even take the form of another animal: even so a state has many parts, of which some one may often grow imperceptibly; for example, the number of poor in democracies and in constitutional states. And this disproportion may sometimes happen by an accident, as at

15

20

25

30

35

1303ᵃ1

Tarentum, from a defeat in which many of the notables were
slain in a battle with the Iapygians just after the Persian War,
5 the constitutional government in consequence becoming a
democracy; or as was the case at Argos, where the Argives,
after their army had been cut to pieces on the seventh day of
the month by Cleomenes the Lacedaemonian, were compelled to admit to citizenship some of their serfs; and at Athens, when, after frequent defeats of their infantry at the time
of the Peloponnesian War, the notables were reduced in
10 number, because the soldiers had to be taken from the roll
of citizens. Revolutions arise from this cause as well, in democracies as in other forms of government, but not to so
great an extent. When the rich grow numerous or properties increase, the form of government changes into an oligarchy or a government of families. Forms of government
also change—sometimes even without revolution, owing
to election contests, as at Heraea (where, instead of electing
15 their magistrates, they took them by lot, because the electors
were in the habit of choosing their own partisans); or owing
to carelessness, when disloyal persons are allowed to find
their way into the highest offices, as at Oreum, where, upon
the accession of Heracleodorus to office, the oligarchy was
overthrown, and changed by him into a constitutional and
20 democratic government.

Again, the revolution may be facilitated by the slightness
of the change; I mean that a great change may sometimes
slip into the constitution through neglect of a small matter;
at Ambracia, for instance, the qualification for office, small
at first, was eventually reduced to nothing. For the Ambraci-
ots thought that a small qualification was much the same as
none at all.

25 Another cause of revolution is difference of races which
do not at once acquire a common spirit; for a state is not the
growth of a day, any more than it grows out of a multitude
brought together by accident. Hence the reception of strangers in colonies, either at the time of their foundation or afterwards, has generally produced revolution; for example, the
Achaeans who joined the Troezenians in the foundation of

Sybaris, becoming later the more numerous, expelled them; hence the curse fell upon Sybaris. At Thurii the Sybarites quarrelled with their fellow-colonists; thinking that the land belonged to them, they wanted too much of it and were driven out. At Byzantium the new colonists were detected in a conspiracy, and were expelled by force of arms; the people of Antissa, who had received the Chian exiles, fought with them, and drove them out; and the Zancleans, after having received the Samians, were driven by them out of their own city. The citizens of Apollonia on the Euxine, after the introduction of a fresh body of colonists, had a revolution; the Syracusans, after the expulsion of their tyrants, having admitted strangers and mercenaries to the rights of citizenship, quarrelled and came to blows; the people of Amphipolis, having received Chalcidian colonists, were nearly all expelled by them.

Now, in oligarchies the masses make revolution under the idea that they are unjustly treated, because, as I said before, they are equals, and have not an equal share, and in democracies the notables revolt, because they are not equals, and yet have only an equal share.

Again, the situation of cities is a cause of revolution when the country is not naturally adapted to preserve the unity of the state. For example, the Chytians at Clazomenae did not agree with the people of the island; and the people of Colophon quarrelled with the Notians; at Athens, too, the inhabitants of the Piraeus are more democratic than those who live in the city. For just as in war the impediment of a ditch, however small, may break a regiment, so every cause of difference makes a breach in a city. The greatest opposition is confessedly that of excellence and badness; next comes that of wealth and poverty; and there are other antagonistic elements, greater or less, of which one is this difference of place.

4 • In revolutions the occasions may be trifling, but great interests are at stake. Even trifles are most important when they concern the rulers, as was the case of old at Syracuse; for the Syracusan constitution was once changed by a love-quarrel of two young men, who were in the government. The

story is that while one of them was away from home his beloved was gained over by his companion, and he to revenge
25 himself seduced the other's wife. They then drew the members of the ruling class into their quarrel and so split all the
people into portions. We learn from this story that we should
be on our guard against the beginnings of such evils, and
should put an end to the quarrels of chiefs and mighty men.
The mistake lies in the beginning—as the proverb says—
30 'Well begun is half done'; so an error at the beginning, though
quite small, bears the same ratio to the errors in the other
parts. In general, when the notables quarrel, the whole city
is involved, as happened in Hestiaea after the Persian War.
The occasion was the division of an inheritance; one of two
brothers refused to give an account of their father's property
35 and the treasure which he had found: so the poorer of the
two quarrelled with him and enlisted in his cause the popular
party, the other, who was very rich, the wealthy classes.

At Delphi, again, a quarrel about a marriage was the be-
1304ª1 ginning of all the troubles which followed. In this case the
bridegroom, fancying some occurrence to be of evil omen,
came to the bride, and went away without taking her. Whereupon her relations, thinking that they were insulted by him,
put some of the sacred treasure among his offerings while he
was sacrificing, and then slew him, pretending that he had
5 been robbing the temple. At Mytilene, too, a dispute about
heiresses was the beginning of many misfortunes, and led to
the war with the Athenians in which Paches took their city.
A wealthy citizen, named Timophanes, left two daughters;
Dexander, another citizen, wanted to obtain them for his
sons; but he was rejected in his suit, whereupon he stirred up
a revolution, and instigated the Athenians (of whom he was
10 representative) to interfere. A similar quarrel about an heiress arose at Phocis between Mnaseas the father of Mnason,
and Euthycrates the father of Onomarchus; this was the beginning of the Sacred War. A marriage-quarrel was also the
cause of a change in the government of Epidamnus. A certain
man betrothed his daughter to a person whose father, having
15 been made a magistrate, fined the father of the girl, and the

latter, stung by the insult, conspired with the unenfranchised classes to overthrow the state.

Governments also change into oligarchy or into democracy or into a constitutional government because the magistrates, or some other section of the state, increase in power or renown. Thus at Athens the reputation gained by the court of the Areopagus, in the Persian War, seemed to tighten the reins of government. On the other hand, the victory of Salamis, which was gained by the common people who served in the fleet, and won for the Athenians the empire due to command of the sea, strengthened the democracy. At Argos, the notables, having distinguished themselves against the Lacedaemonians in the battle of Mantinea, attempted to put down the democracy. At Syracuse, the people, having been the chief authors of the victory in the war with the Athenians, changed the constitutional government into democracy. At Chalcis, the people, uniting with the notables, killed Phoxus the tyrant, and then seized the government. At Ambracia, the people, in like manner, having joined with the conspirators in expelling the tyrant Periander, transferred the government to themselves. And generally, it should be remembered that those who have secured power to the state, whether private citizens, or magistrates, or tribes, or any other part or section of the state, are apt to cause revolutions. For either envy of their greatness draws others into rebellion, or they themselves, in their pride of superiority, are unwilling to remain on a level with others.

Revolutions also break out when opposite parties, e.g. the rich and the people, are equally balanced, and there is little or no middle class; for, if either party were manifestly superior, the other would not risk an attack upon them. And for this reason, those who are eminent in excellence usually do not stir up insurrections, being always a minority. Such in general are the beginnings and causes of the disturbances and revolutions to which every form of government is liable.

Revolutions are effected in two ways, by force and by fraud. Force may be applied either at the time of making the revolution or afterwards. Fraud, again, is of two kinds; for sometimes the citizens are deceived into acquiescing in a change of government, and afterwards they are held in subjection against their will. This was what happened in the case of the Four Hundred, who deceived the people by telling them that the king would provide money for the war against the Lacedaemonians, and, having cheated the people, still endeavoured to retain the government. In other cases the people are persuaded at first, and afterwards, by a repetition of the persuasion, their goodwill and allegiance are retained. The revolutions which affect constitutions generally spring from the above-mentioned causes.

5 • And now, taking each constitution separately, we must see what follows from the principles already laid down.

Revolutions in democracies are generally caused by the intemperance of demagogues, who either in their private capacity lay information against rich men until they compel them to combine (for a common danger unites even the bitterest enemies), or coming forward in public stir up the people against them. The truth of this remark is proved by a variety of examples. At Cos the democracy was overthrown because wicked demagogues arose, and the notables combined. At Rhodes the demagogues not only provided pay for the multitude, but prevented them from making good to the trierarchs the sums which had been expended by them; and they, in consequence of the suits which were brought against them, were compelled to combine and put down the democracy. The democracy at Heraclea was overthrown shortly after the foundation of the colony by the injustice of the demagogues, which drove out the notables, who came back in a body and put an end to the democracy. Much in the same manner the democracy at Megara was overturned; there the demagogues drove out many of the notables in order that they might be able to confiscate their property. At length the exiles, becoming numerous, returned, and, engaging and defeating the people, established the oligarchy. The same thing happened with the democracy of Cyme, which was over-

thrown by Thrasymachus. And we may observe that in most   1305ª1
states the changes have been of this character. For sometimes
the demagogues, in order to curry favour with the people,
wrong the notables and so force them to combine—either
they make a division of their property, or diminish their in-   5
comes by the imposition of public services, and sometimes
they bring accusations against the rich so that they may have
their wealth to confiscate.

Of old, the demagogue was also a general, and then democracies changed into tyrannies. Most of the ancient tyrants were originally demagogues. They are not so now, but   10
they were then; and the reason is that they were generals
and not orators, for oratory had not yet come into fashion.
Whereas in our day, when the art of rhetoric has made such
progress, the orators lead the people, but their ignorance of
military matters prevents them from usurping power; at any
rate instances to the contrary are few and slight. Tyrannies   15
were more common formerly than now, for this reason also,
that great power was placed in the hands of individuals; thus a
tyranny arose at Miletus out of the office of the Prytanis, who
had supreme authority in many important matters. Moreover, in those days, when cities were not large, the people
dwelt in the fields, busy at their work; and their chiefs, if they   20
possessed any military talent, seized the opportunity, and
winning the confidence of the masses by professing their hatred of the wealthy, they succeeded in obtaining the tyranny.
Thus at Athens Peisistratus led a faction against the men of
the plain, and Theagenes at Megara slaughtered the cattle of
the wealthy, which he found by the river side, where they had   25
put them to graze. Dionysius, again, was thought worthy of
the tyranny because he denounced Daphnaeus and the rich;
his enmity to the notables won for him the confidence of the
people. Changes also take place from the ancient to the latest
form of democracy; for where there is a popular election of
the magistrates and no property qualification, the aspirants   30
for office get hold of the people, and contrive at last even to
set them above the laws. A more or less complete cure for this

state of things is for the separate tribes, and not the whole people, to elect the magistrates.

35   These are the principal causes of revolutions in democracies.

6 • There are two patent causes of revolutions in oligarchies: first, when the oligarchs oppress the people, for then anybody is good enough to be their champion, especially if he be himself a member of the oligarchy, as Lygdamis at Naxos, who afterwards came to be tyrant. But revolutions 1305ᵇ1 which commence outside the governing class may be further subdivided. Sometimes, when the government is very exclusive, the revolution is brought about by persons of the wealthy class who are excluded, as happened at Massalia and 5 Istros and Heraclea, and other cities.

Those who had no share in the government created a disturbance, until first the elder brothers, and then the younger, were admitted; for in some places father and son, in others, elder and younger brothers, do not hold office together. At 10 Massalia the oligarchy became more like a constitutional government, but at Istros ended in a democracy, and at Heraclea was enlarged to 600. At Cnidos, again, the oligarchy underwent a considerable change. For the notables fell out among themselves, because only a few shared in the government; there existed among them the rule already mentioned, that father and son could not hold office together, and, if 15 there were several brothers, only the eldest was admitted. The people took advantage of the quarrel, and choosing one of the notables to be their leader, attacked and conquered the oligarchs, who were divided, and division is always a source of weakness. The city of Erythrae, too, in old times was 20 ruled, and ruled well, by the Basilidae, but the people took offence at the narrowness of the oligarchy and changed the constitution.

Of internal causes of revolutions in oligarchies one is the personal rivalry of the oligarchs, which leads them to play the demagogue. Now, the oligarchical demagogue is of two sorts: either he practises upon the oligarchs themselves (for, although the oligarchy are quite a small number, there may

be a demagogue among them, as at Athens Charicles' party   25
won power by courting the Thirty, that of Phrynichus by
courting the Four Hundred); or the oligarchs may play the
demagogue with the people. This was the case at Larissa,
where the guardians of the citizens endeavoured to gain over
the people because they were elected by them; and such is the   30
fate of all oligarchies in which the magistrates are elected, as
at Abydos, not by the class in which they belong, but by the
heavy-armed or by the people, although they may be required
to have a high qualification, or to be members of a political
club; or, again, where the law-courts are composed of persons outside the government, the oligarchs flatter the people
in order to obtain a decision in their own favour, and so they
change the constitution; this happened at Heraclea in Pon-   35
tus. Again, oligarchies change whenever any attempt is made
to narrow them; for then those who desire equal rights are
compelled to call in the people. Changes in the oligarchy also
occur when the oligarchs waste their private property by extravagant living; for then they want to innovate, and either
try to make themselves tyrants, or install some one else in the
tyranny, as Hipparinus did Dionysius at Syracuse, and as at   1306ª1
Amphipolis a man named Cleotimus introduced Chalcidian
colonists, and when they arrived, stirred them up against the
rich. For a like reason in Aegina the person who carried on
the negotiation with Chares endeavoured to revolutionize
the state. Sometimes a party among the oligarchs try directly   5
to create a political change; sometimes they rob the treasury,
and then either the thieves or, as happened at Apollonia in
Pontus, those who resist them in their thieving quarrel with
the rulers. But an oligarchy which is at unity with itself is not   10
easily destroyed from within; of this we may see an example
at Pharsalus, for there, although the rulers are few in number, they govern a large city, because they have a good understanding among themselves.

Oligarchies, again, are overthrown when another oligarchy is created within the original one, that is to say, when the
whole governing body is small and yet they do not all share   15
in the highest offices. Thus at Elis the governing body was a

small senate; and very few ever found their way into it, because the senators were only ninety in number, and were elected for life and out of certain families in a manner similar
20 to the Lacedaemonian elders. Oligarchy is liable to revolutions alike in war and in peace; in war because, not being able to trust the people, the oligarchs are compelled to hire mercenaries, and the general who is in command of them often ends in becoming a tyrant, as Timophanes did at Corinth; or if there are more generals than one they make themselves
25 into a junta. Sometimes the oligarchs, fearing this danger, give the people a share in the government because their services are necessary to them. And in time of peace, from mutual distrust, the two parties hand over the defence of the state to the army and to an arbiter between the two factions, who often ends the master of both. This happened at Larissa when
30 Simos the Aleuad had the government, and at Abydos in the days of Iphiades and the political clubs. Revolutions also arise out of marriages or lawsuits which lead to the overthrow of one party among the oligarchs by another. Of quarrels about
35 marriages I have already mentioned some instances; another occurred at Eretria, where Diagoras overturned the oligarchy of the knights because he had been wronged about a marriage. A revolution at Heraclea, and another at Thebes, both arose out of decisions of law-courts upon a charge of adultery; in both cases the punishment was just, but executed in
1306ᵇ1 the spirit of party, at Heraclea upon Eurytion, and at Thebes upon Archias; for their enemies were jealous of them and so had them pilloried in the agora. Many oligarchies have been destroyed by some members of the ruling class taking offence
5 at their excessive despotism; for example, the oligarchy at Cnidus and at Chios.

Changes of constitutional governments, and also of oligarchies which limit the office of counsellor, judge, or other magistrate to persons having a certain money qualification, often occur by accident. The qualification may have been
10 originally fixed according to the circumstances of the time, in such a manner as to include in an oligarchy a few only, or

in a constitutional government the middle class. But after a time of prosperity, whether arising from peace or some other good fortune, the same property becomes many times as valuable, and then everybody participates in every office; this happens sometimes gradually and insensibly, and some- 15 times quickly. These are the causes of changes and revolutions in oligarchies.

We must remark generally, both of democracies and oligarchies, that they sometimes change, not into the opposite forms of government, but only into another variety of the same class; I mean to say, from those forms of democracy 20 and oligarchy which are regulated by law into those which are arbitrary, and conversely.

7 • In aristocracies revolutions are stirred up when a few only share in the honours of the state; a cause which has been already shown to affect oligarchies; for an aristocracy is a sort of oligarchy, and, like an oligarchy, is the government of a few, although few not for the same reason; hence 25 the two are often confused. And revolutions will be most likely to happen, and must happen, when the mass of the people are of the high-spirited kind, and have a notion that they are as good as their rulers. Thus at Lacedaemon the so-called Partheniae, who were the sons of the Spartan peers, 30 attempted a revolution, and, being detected, were sent away to colonize Tarentum. Again, revolutions occur when great men who are at least of equal excellence are denied honours by those higher in office, as Lysander was by the kings of Sparta; or, when a brave man is excluded from the honours of the state, like Cinadon, who conspired against the Spartans in the reign of Agesilaus; or, again, when some are very 35 poor and others very rich, a state of society which is most often the result of war, as at Lacedaemon in the days of the Messenian War; this is proved from the poem of Tyrtaeus, entitled 'Good Order'; for he speaks of certain citizens who 1307ᵃ1 were ruined by the war and wanted to have a redistribution of the land. Again, revolutions arise when an individual who is

great, and might be greater, wants to rule alone, as, at Lacedaemon, Pausanias, who was general in the Persian War, or
like Hanno at Carthage.

Constitutional governments and aristocracies are commonly overthrown owing to some deviation from justice in
the constitution itself; the cause of the downfall is, in the
former, the ill-mingling of the two elements democracy and
oligarchy; in the latter, of the three elements, democracy, oligarchy, and excellence, but especially democracy and oligarchy. For to combine these is the endeavour of constitutional
governments; and most of the so-called aristocracies have a
like aim, but differ from polities in the mode of combination;
hence some of them are more and some less permanent.
Those which incline more to oligarchy are called aristocracies, and those which incline to democracy constitutional
governments. And therefore the latter are the safer of the
two; for the greater the number, the greater the strength,
and when men are equal they are contented. But the rich,
if the constitution gives them power, are apt to be insolent
and avaricious; and, in general, whichever way the constitution inclines, in that direction it changes as either party gains
strength, a constitutional government becoming a democracy, an aristocracy an oligarchy. But the process may be re-
versed, and aristocracy may change into democracy. This
happens when the poor, under the idea that they are being
wronged, force the constitution to take an opposite form. In
like manner constitutional governments change into oligarchies. The only stable principle of government is equality according to merit, and for every man to enjoy his own.

What I have just mentioned actually happened at Thurii,
where the qualification for office, at first high, was therefore
reduced, and the magistrates increased in number. The notables had previously acquired the whole of the land contrary
to law; for the government tended to oligarchy, and they
were able to encroach. . . .[1] But the people, who had been

---

[1] Dreizehnter marks a lacuna.

trained by war, soon got the better of the guards kept by the oligarchs, until those who had too much gave up their land.

Again, since all aristocratic governments incline to oligarchy, the notables are apt to be grasping; thus at Lacedaemon, where property tends to pass into few hands, the notables can do too much as they like, and are allowed to marry whom they please. The city of Locri was ruined by a marriage connexion with Dionysius, but such a thing could never have happened in a democracy, or in a well-balanced aristocracy.

I have already remarked that in all states revolutions are occasioned by trifles.

In aristocracies, above all, they are of a gradual and imperceptible nature. The citizens begin by giving up some part of the constitution, and so with greater ease the government change something else which is a little more important, until they have undermined the whole fabric of the state. At Thurii there was a law that generals should only be re-elected after an interval of five years, and some young men who were popular with the soldiers of the guard for their military prowess, despising the magistrates and thinking that they would easily gain their purpose, wanted to abolish this law and allow their generals to hold perpetual commands; for they well knew that the people would be glad enough to elect them. Whereupon the magistrates who had charge of these matters, and who are called councillors, at first determined to resist, but they afterwards consented, thinking that, if only this one law was changed, no further inroad would be made on the constitution. But other changes soon followed which they in vain attempted to oppose; and the state passed into the hands of the revolutionists, who established a dynastic oligarchy.

All constitutions are overthrown either from within or from without; the latter, when there is some government close at hand having an opposite interest, or at a distance, but powerful. This was exemplified by the Athenians and the Lacedaemonians; the Athenians everywhere put down the oligarchies, and the Lacedaemonians the democracies.

I have now explained what are the chief causes of revolutions and dissensions in states.

8 • We have next to consider what means there are of preserving constitutions in general, and in particular cases. In the first place it is evident that if we know the causes which destroy constitutions, we also know the causes which preserve them; for opposites produce opposites, and destruction is the opposite of preservation.

In all well-balanced governments there is nothing which should be more jealously maintained than the spirit of obedience to law, more especially in small matters; for transgression creeps in unperceived and at last ruins the state, just as the constant recurrence of small expenses in time eats up a fortune. The expense does not take place all at once, and therefore is not observed; the mind is deceived, as in the fallacy which says that 'if each part is little, then the whole is little'. And this is true in one way, but not in another, for the whole and the all are not little, although they are made up of littles.

In the first place, then, men should guard against the beginning of change, and in the second place they should not rely upon the political devices of which I have already spoken, invented only to deceive the people, for they are proved by experience to be useless. Further, we note that oligarchies as well as aristocracies may last, not from any inherent stability in such forms of government, but because the rulers are on good terms both with the unenfranchised and with the governing classes, not maltreating any who are excluded from the government, but introducing into it the leading spirits among them. They should never wrong the ambitious in a matter of honour, or the common people in a matter of money; and they should treat one another and their fellow-citizens in a spirit of equality. The equality which the friends of democracy seek to establish for the multitude is not only just but likewise expedient among equals. Hence, if the governing class are numerous, many democratic institutions are useful; for example, the restriction of the tenure of offices to six months, so that all those who are of equal rank may share in them.

Indeed, a group of equals is a kind of democracy, and therefore demagogues are very likely to arise among them, as I have already remarked. The short tenure of office prevents oligarchies and aristocracies from falling into the hands of families; it is not easy for a person to do any great harm when his tenure of office is short, whereas long possession begets 20 tyranny in oligarchies and democracies. For the aspirants to tyranny are either the principal men of the state, who in democracies are demagogues and in oligarchies members of ruling houses, or those who hold great offices, and have a long tenure of them.

Constitutions are preserved when their destroyers are at a distance, and sometimes also because they are near, for the 25 fear of them makes the government keep in hand the constitution. Wherefore the ruler who has a care of the constitution should invent terrors, and bring distant dangers near, in order that the citizens may be on their guard, and, like sentinels in a night-watch, never relax their attention. He should 30 endeavour too by help of the laws to control the contentions and quarrels of the notables, and to prevent those who have not hitherto taken part in them from catching the spirit of contention. No ordinary man can discern the beginning of evil, but only the true statesman.

As to the change produced in oligarchies and constitutional governments by the alternation of the qualification, 35 when this arises, not out of any variation in the qualification but only out of the increase of money, it is well to compare the new valuation of property with that of past years, annually in those cities in which the census is taken annually, and in larger cities every third or fifth year. If the whole is 1308ᵇ1 many times greater or many times less than when the ratings recognized by the constitution were fixed, there should be power given by law to raise or lower the qualification as the amount is greater or less. Where this is not done a constitu- 5 tional government passes into an oligarchy, and an oligarchy is narrowed to a rule of families; or in the opposite case constitutional government becomes democracy, and oligarchy either constitutional government or democracy. 10

It is a principle common to democracy, oligarchy, and every other form of government not to allow the disproportionate increase of any citizen, but to give moderate honour

for a long time rather than great honour for a short time. For
15 men are easily spoilt; not every one can bear prosperity. But
if this rule is not observed, at any rate the honours which are
given all at once should be taken away by degrees and not all
at once. Especially should the laws provide against any one
having too much power, whether derived from friends or
money; if he has, he should be sent clean out of the coun-
20 try. And since innovations creep in through the private life
of individuals also, there ought to be a magistracy which will
have an eye to those whose life is not in harmony with the
government, whether oligarchy or democracy or any other.
25 And for a like reason an increase of prosperity in any part
of the state should be carefully watched. The proper remedy
for this evil is always to give the management of affairs and
offices of state to opposite elements; such opposites are the
good and the many, or the rich and the poor. Another way is
30 to combine the poor and the rich in one body, or to increase
the middle class: thus an end will be put to the revolutions
which arise from inequality.

But above all every state should be so administered and so
regulated by law that its magistrates cannot possibly make
money. In oligarchies special precautions should be used
against this evil. For the people do not take any great offence
35 at being kept out of the government—indeed they are rather
pleased than otherwise at having leisure for their private
business—but what irritates them is to think that their rulers are stealing the public money; then they are doubly annoyed; for they lose both honour and profit. If office brought
no profit, then and then only could democracy and aristoc-
1309ᵃ1 racy be combined; for both notables and people might have
their wishes gratified. All would be able to hold office, which
is the aim of democracy, and the notables would be magistrates, which is the aim of aristocracy. And this result may be
accomplished when there is no possibility of making money
5 out of the offices; for the poor will not want to have them
when there is nothing to be gained from them—they would
rather be attending to their own concerns; and the rich, who
do not want money from the public treasury, will be able to

take them; and so the poor will keep to their work and grow rich, and the notables will not be governed by the lower class. In order to avoid peculation of the public money, the transfer of the revenue should be made at a general assembly of the citizens, and duplicates of the accounts deposited with the different brotherhoods, companies, and tribes. And honours should be given by law to magistrates who have the reputation of ruling without gain. In democracies the rich should be spared; not only should their property not be divided, but their incomes also, which in some states are taken from them imperceptibly, should be protected. It is a good thing to prevent the wealthy citizens, even if they are willing, from undertaking expensive and useless public services, such as the giving of choruses, torch-races, and the like.

In an oligarchy, on the other hand, great care should be taken of the poor, and lucrative offices should go to them; if any of the wealthy classes insult them, the offender should be punished more severely than if he had wronged one of his own class. Provision should be made that estates pass by inheritance and not by gift, and no person should have more than one inheritance; for in this way properties will be equalized, and more of the poor rise to wealth. It is also expedient both in a democracy and in an oligarchy to assign to those who have less share in the government (i.e. to the rich in a democracy and to the poor in an oligarchy) an equality or preference in all but the principal offices of state. The latter should be entrusted chiefly or only to members of the governing class.

9 · There are three qualifications required in those who have to fill the highest offices—first of all, loyalty to the established constitution; then the greatest administrative capacity; and excellence and justice of the kind proper to each form of government; for, if what is just is not the same in all governments, the quality of justice must also differ. There may be a doubt, however, when all these qualities do not meet in the same person; suppose, for example, a good general is a bad man and not a friend to the constitution, and another man is

1309^b1

loyal and just, which should we choose? In making the election ought we not to consider two points? what qualities are common, and what are rare. Thus in the choice of a general, we should regard his experience rather than his excellence; for few have military experience, but many have excellence. In any office of trust or stewardship, on the other hand, the opposite rule should be observed; for more excellence than ordinary is required in the holder of such an office, but the necessary knowledge is of a sort which all men possess.

It may, however, be asked what a man wants with excellence if he has political ability and is loyal, since these two qualities alone will make him do what is for the public interest. But may not men have both of them and yet be deficient in self-control?—If, knowing and loving their own interests, they do not always attend to them, may they not be equally negligent of the interests of the public?

Speaking generally, we may say that whatever legal enactments are held to be for the interest of various constitutions, all these preserve them. And the great preserving principle is the one which has been repeatedly mentioned—to have a care that the loyal citizens should be stronger than the disloyal. Neither should we forget the mean, which at the present day is lost sight of in perverted forms of government; for many practices which appear to be democratic are the ruin of democracies, and many which appear to be oligarchical are the ruin of oligarchies. Those who think that all excellence is to be found in their own party principles push matters to extremes; they do not consider that disproportion destroys a state. A nose which varies from the ideal of straightness to a hook or snub may still be of good shape and agreeable to the eye; but if the excess is very great, all symmetry is lost, and the nose at last ceases to be a nose at all on account of some excess in one direction or defect in the other; and this is true of every other part of the human body. The same law of proportion equally holds in states. Oligarchy or democracy, although a departure from the most perfect form, may yet be a good enough government, but if any one attempts to push the principles of either to an extreme, he will begin by spoil-

ing the government and end by having none at all. Therefore
the legislator and the statesman ought to know what dem-   35
ocratic measures save and what destroy a democracy, and
what oligarchical measures save or destroy an oligarchy. For
neither the one nor the other can exist or continue to exist
unless both rich and poor are included in it. If equality of
property is introduced, the state must of necessity take another form; for when by laws carried to excess one or other
element in the state is ruined, the constitution is ruined.   1310ᵃ1

There is an error common both to oligarchies and to democracies:—in the latter the demagogues, when the multitude are above the law, are always cutting the city in two by
quarrels with the rich, whereas they should always profess   5
to be maintaining their cause; just as in oligarchies the oligarchs should profess to maintain the cause of the people,
and should take oaths the opposite of those which they now
take. For there are cities in which they swear—'I will be an
enemy to the people, and will devise all the harm against
them which I can'; but they ought to exhibit and to enter-
tain the very opposite feeling; in the form of their oath there   10
should be an express declaration—'I will do no wrong to the
people'.

But of all the things which I have mentioned that which
most contributes to the permanence of constitutions is the
adaptation of education to the form of government, and yet
in our own day this principle is universally neglected. The
best laws, though sanctioned by every citizen of the state,   15
will be of no avail unless the young are trained by habit and
education in the spirit of the constitution, if the laws are
democratic, democratically, or oligarchically, if the laws are
oligarchical. For there may be a want of self-discipline in
states as well as in individuals. Now, to have been educated   20
in the spirit of the constitution is not to perform the actions
in which oligarchs or democrats delight, but those by which
the existence of an oligarchy or of a democracy is made possible. Whereas among ourselves the sons of the ruling class
in an oligarchy live in luxury, but the sons of the poor are
hardened by exercise and toil, and hence they are both more   25

inclined and better able to make a revolution. And in democracies of the more extreme type there has arisen a false idea
of freedom which is contradictory to the true interests of the
state. For two principles are characteristic of democracy, the
30 government of the majority and freedom. Men think that
what is just is equal; and that equality is the supremacy of the
popular will; and that freedom means doing what one likes.
In such democracies every one lives as he pleases, or in the
words of Euripides, 'according to his fancy'. But this is all
wrong; men should not think it slavery to live according to
35 the rule of the constitution; for it is their salvation.

I have now discussed generally the cause of the revolution
and destruction of states, and the means of their preservation and continuance.

10 • I have still to speak of monarchy, and the causes of
its destruction and reservation. What I have said already re-
1310ᵇ1 specting forms of constitutional government applies almost
equally to royal and to tyrannical rule. For royal rule is of
the nature of an aristocracy, and a tyranny is a compound
5 of oligarchy and democracy in their most extreme forms;
it is therefore most injurious to its subjects, being made up
of two evil forms of government, and having the perversions and errors of both. These two forms of monarchy are
contrary in their very origin. The appointment of a king is
the resource of the better classes against the people, and he
10 is elected by them out of their own number, because either
he himself or his family excel in excellence and excellent actions; whereas a tyrant is chosen from the people to be their
protector against the notables, and in order to prevent them
from being injured. History shows that almost all tyrants
15 have been demagogues who gained the favour of the people
by their accusation of the notables. At any rate this was the
manner in which the tyrannies arose in the days when cities
had increased in power. Others which were older originated
in the ambition of kings wanting to overstep the limits of
their hereditary power and become despots. Others again
grew out of the class which were chosen to be chief magis-

trates; for in ancient times the people who elected them 20
gave the magistrates, whether civil or religious, a long tenure. Others arose out of the custom which oligarchies had of
making some individual supreme over the highest offices. In
any of these ways an ambitious man had no difficulty, if he
desired, in creating a tyranny, since he had the power in his
hands already, either as king or as one of the officers of state. 25
Thus Pheidon at Argos and several others were originally
kings, and ended by becoming tyrants; Phalaris, on the other
hand, and the Ionian tyrants, acquired the tyranny by holding great offices. Whereas Panaetius at Leontini, Cypselus at
Corinth, Peisistratus at Athens, Dionysius at Syracuse, and 30
several others who afterwards became tyrants, were at first
demagogues.

And so, as I was saying, royalty ranks with aristocracy,
for it is based upon merit, whether of the individual or of
his family, or on benefits conferred, or on these claims with
power added to them. For all who have obtained this honour
have benefited, or had in their power to benefit, states and 35
nations; some, like Codrus, have prevented the state from
being enslaved in war; others, like Cyrus, have given their
country freedom, or have settled or gained a territory, like
the Lacedaemonian, Macedonian, and Molossian kings. The
idea of a king is to be a protector of the rich against unjust
treatment, of the people against insult and oppression. 1311ᵃ1

Whereas a tyrant, as has often been repeated, has no regard to any public interest, except as conducive to his private
ends; his aim is pleasure, the aim of a king, honour. Therefore they differ also in their excesses; the tyrant accumulates
riches, the king seeks what brings honour. And the guards of 5
a king are citizens, but of a tyrant mercenaries.

That tyranny has all the vices both of democracy and oligarchy is evident. As of oligarchy so of tyranny, the end is wealth
(for by wealth only can the tyrant maintain his guard and 10
his luxury). Both mistrust the people, and therefore deprive
them of their arms. Both agree too in injuring the people and
driving them out of the city and dispersing them. From democracy tyrants have borrowed the art of making war upon

the notables and destroying them secretly or openly, or of ex-
iling them because they are rivals and stand in the way of their
power; and also because plots against them are contrived by
men of this class, who either want to rule or to escape subjection. Hence Periander advised Thrasybulus by cutting off the
tops of the tallest ears of corn, meaning that he must always
put out of the way the citizens who overtop the rest. And so,
as I have already intimated, the beginnings of change are
the same in monarchies as in forms of constitutional government; subjects attack their sovereigns out of fear or contempt, or because they have been unjustly treated by them.
And of injustice the most common form is insult, another is
confiscation of property.

The ends sought by conspiracies against monarchies,
whether tyrannies or royalties, are the same as the ends
sought by conspiracies against other forms of government.
Monarchs have great wealth and honour, which are objects
of desire to all mankind. The attacks are made sometimes
against their lives, sometimes against the office; where the
sense of insult is the motive, against their lives. Any sort of
insult (and there are many) may stir up anger, and when men
are angry, they commonly act out of revenge, and not from
ambition. For example, the attempt made upon the Peisistratidae arose out of the public dishonour offered to the
sister of Harmodius and the insult to himself. He attacked
the tyrant for his sister's sake, and Aristogeiton joined in
the attack for the sake of Harmodius. A conspiracy was also
formed against Periander, the tyrant of Ambracia, because,
when drinking with a favourite youth, he asked him whether
by this time he was not with child by him. Philip, too, was attacked by Pausanias because he permitted him to be insulted
by Attalus and his friends, and Amyntas the Little, by Derdas,
because he boasted of having enjoyed his youth. Evagoras of
Cyprus, again, was slain by the eunuch to revenge an insult;
for his wife had been carried off by Evagoras's son. Many
conspiracies have originated in shameful attempts made by
sovereigns on the persons of their subjects. Such was the
attack of Crataeas upon Archelaus; he had always hated his

intercourse with the king, and so, when Archelaus, having   10
promised him one of his two daughters in marriage, did not
give him either of them, but broke his word and married the
elder to the king of Elymeia, when he was hard pressed in a
war against Sirrhas and Arrhabaeus, and the younger to his
own son Amyntas, under the idea that Amyntas would then
be less likely to quarrel with his son by Cleopatra—Crataeas   15
made this slight a pretext for attacking Archelaus, though
even a less reason would have sufficed, for the real cause of
the estrangement was the disgust which he felt at his sexual
subjection. And from a like motive Hellanocrates of Larissa
conspired with him; for when Archelaus, who was his lover,
did not fulfil his promise of restoring him to his country, he
thought that the intercourse between them had originated,   20
not in sexual desire, but in the wish to insult him. Pytho, too,
and Heracleides of Aenos, slew Cotys in order to avenge their
father, and Adamas revolted from Cotys in revenge for the
wanton outrage which he had committed in castrating him
when a child.

Many, too, enraged by blows inflicted on the person
which they deemed an insult, have either killed or attempted   25
to kill officers of state and royal princes by whom they have
been injured. Thus, at Mytilene, Megacles and his friends
attacked and slew the Penthilidae, as they were going about
and striking people with clubs. At a later date Smerdis, who
had been beaten and torn away from his wife by Penthilus,   30
slew him. In the conspiracy against Archelaus, Decamnichus
stimulated the fury of the assassins and led the attack; he was
enraged because Archelaus had delivered him to Euripides to
be scourged; for the poet had been irritated at some remark
made by Decamnichus on the foulness of his breath. Many
other examples might be cited of murders and conspiracies   35
which have arisen from similar causes.

Fear is another motive which, as we have said, has caused
conspiracies as well in monarchies as in more popular forms
of government. Thus Artapanes conspired against Xerxes and
slew him, fearing that he would be accused of hanging Darius
against his orders—he having been under the impression that

Xerxes would forget what he had said in the middle of a meal, and that the offence would be forgiven.

Another motive is contempt, as in the case of Sardanapalus, whom someone saw carding wool with his women, if the story-tellers say truly; and the tale may be true, if not of him, of someone else. Dion attacked the younger Dionysius because he despised him, and saw that he was equally despised by his own subjects, and that he was always drunk. Even the friends of a tyrant will sometimes attack him out of contempt; for the confidence which he reposes in them breeds contempt, and they think that they will not be found out. The expectation of success is likewise a sort of contempt; the assailants are ready to strike, and think nothing of the danger, because they seem to have the power in their hands. Thus generals of armies attack monarchs; as, for example, Cyrus attacked Astyages, despising the effeminacy of his life, and believing that his power was worn out. Thus again, Seuthes the Thracian conspired against Amadocus, whose general he was.

And sometimes men are actuated by more than one motive, like Mithridates, who conspired against Ariobarzanes, partly out of contempt and partly from the love of gain.

Bold natures, placed by their sovereigns in a high military position, are most likely to make the attempt in the expectation of success; for courage is emboldened by power, and the union of the two inspires them with the hope of an easy victory.

Attempts of which the motive is ambition arise in a different way as well as in those already mentioned. There are men who will not risk their lives in the hope of gains and honours however great, but who nevertheless regard the killing of a tyrant simply as an extraordinary action which will make them famous and notable in the world; they wish to acquire, not a kingdom, but a name. It is rare, however, to find such men; he who would kill a tyrant must be prepared to lose his life if he fails. He must have the resolution of Dion, who, when he made war upon Dionysius, took with him very few troops, saying 'that whatever measure of success he might attain would be enough for him, even if he were to die the moment he landed; such a death would be welcome to him'. But this is a temper to which few can attain.

Once more, tyrannies, like all other governments, are destroyed from without by some opposite and more powerful form of government. That such a government will have the will to attack them is clear; for the two are opposed in principle; and all men, if they can, do what they want to. Democracy is antagonistic to tyranny, on the principle of Hesiod, 'Potter hates Potter', because they are nearly akin, for the extreme form of democracy is tyranny; and royalty and aristocracy are both alike opposed to tyranny, because they are constitutions of a different type. And therefore the Lacedaemonians put down most of the tyrannies, and so did the Syracusans during the time when they were well governed.

Again, tyrannies are destroyed from within, when the reigning family are divided among themselves, as that of Gelo was, and more recently that of Dionysius; in the case of Gelo because Thrasybulus, the brother of Hiero, flattered the son of Gelo and led him into excesses in order that he might rule in his name. Whereupon the family got together a party to get rid of Thrasybulus and save the tyranny; but those of the people who conspired with them seized the opportunity and drove them all out. In the case of Dionysius, Dion, his own relative, attacked and expelled him with the assistance of the people; he afterwards perished himself.

There are two chief motives which induce men to attack tyrannies—hatred and contempt. Hatred of tyrants is inevitable, and contempt is also a frequent cause of their destruction. Thus we see that most of those who have acquired, have retained their power, but those who have inherited, have lost it, almost at once; for, living in luxurious ease, they have become contemptible, and offer many opportunities to their assailants. Anger, too, must be included under hatred, and produces the same effects. It is often even more ready to strike—the angry are more impetuous in making an attack, for they do not follow rational principle. And men are very apt to give way to their passions when they are insulted. To this cause is to be attributed the fall of the Peisistratidae and of many others.

1312ᵇ1

5

10

15

20

25

30

Hatred is more reasonable, for anger is accompanied by pain, which is an impediment to reason, whereas hatred is painless.

35   In a word, all the causes which I have mentioned as destroying the last and most unmixed form of oligarchy, and the extreme form of democracy, may be assumed to affect tyranny; indeed the extreme forms of both are only tyrannies distributed among several persons. Kingly rule is little affected by external causes, and is therefore lasting; it is generally destroyed from within. And there are two ways in which

1313ᵃ1   the destruction may come about; when the members of the royal family quarrel among themselves, and when the kings attempt to administer the state too much after the fashion of a tyranny, and to extend their authority contrary to the law. Royalties do not now come into existence; where such forms

5   of government arise, they are rather monarchies or tyrannies. For the rule of a king is over voluntary subjects, and he is supreme in all important matters; but in our own day men are more upon an equality, and no one is so immeasurably superior to others as to represent adequately the greatness and dignity of the office. Hence mankind will not, willingly,

10   endure it, and any one who obtains power by force or fraud is at once thought to be a tyrant. In hereditary monarchies a further cause of destruction is the fact that kings often fall into contempt, and, although possessing not tyrannical power, but only royal dignity, are apt to outrage others. Their overthrow is then readily effected; for there is an end to the

15   king when his subjects do not want to have him, but the tyrant lasts, whether they like him or not.

    The destruction of monarchies is to be attributed to these and the like causes.

11 • And they are preserved, to speak generally, by the opposite causes; or, if we consider them separately, royalty is

20   preserved by the limitation of its powers. The more restricted the functions of kings, the longer their power will last unimpaired; for then they are more moderate and not so despotic in their ways; and they are less envied by their subjects. This is the reason why the kingly office has lasted so long among the

Molossians. And for a similar reason it has continued among the Lacedaemonians, because there it was always divided between two, and afterwards further limited by Theopompus in various respects, more particularly by the establishment of the Ephoralty. He diminished the power of the kings, but established on a more lasting basis the kingly office, which was thus made in a certain sense not less, but greater. There is a story that when his wife once asked him whether he was not ashamed to leave to his sons a royal power which was less than he had inherited from his father, 'No indeed', he replied, 'for the power which I leave to them will be more lasting'.

As to tyrannies, they are preserved in two quite opposite ways. One of them is the old traditional method in which most tyrants administer their government. Of such arts Periander of Corinth is said to have been the great master, and many similar devices may be gathered from the Persians in the administration of their government. There are firstly the prescriptions mentioned some distance back, for the preservation of a tyranny, in so far as this is possible; viz. that the tyrant should lop off those who are too high; he must put to death men of spirit; he must not allow common meals, clubs, education, and the like; he must be upon his guard against anything which is likely to inspire either courage or confidence among his subjects; he must prohibit schools or other meetings for discussion, and he must take every means to prevent people from knowing one another (for acquaintance begets mutual confidence). Further, he must compel all persons staying in the city to appear in public and live at his gates; then he will know what they are doing: if they are always kept under, they will learn to be humble. In short, he should practise these and the like Persian and barbaric arts, which all have the same object. A tyrant should also endeavour to know what each of his subjects says or does, and should employ spies, like the 'female detectives' at Syracuse, and the eavesdroppers whom Hiero was in the habit of sending to any place of resort or meeting; for the fear of informers prevents people from speaking their minds, and if they do, they are more easily found out. Another art of the tyrant is to sow

quarrels among the citizens; friends should be embroiled with friends, the people with the notables, and the rich with one another. Also he should impoverish his subjects; he thus provides against the maintenance of a guard by the citizens,
20 and the people, having to keep hard at work, are prevented from conspiring. The Pyramids of Egypt afford an example of this policy; also the offerings of the family of Cypselus, and the building of the temple of Olympian Zeus by the Peisistratidae, and the great Polycratean monuments at Samos; all these works were alike intended to occupy the people and
25 keep them poor. Another practice of tyrants is to multiply taxes, after the manner of Dionysius at Syracuse, who contrived that within five years his subjects should bring into the treasury their whole property. The tyrant is also fond of making war in order that his subjects may have something to do and be always in want of a leader. And whereas the power of a
30 king is preserved by his friends, the characteristic of a tyrant is to distrust his friends, because he knows that all men want to overthrow him, and they above all have the power to do so.

Again, the practices of the last and worst form of democracy are all found in tyrannies. Such are the power given to
35 women in their families in the hope that they will inform against their husbands, and the licence which is allowed to slaves in order that they may betray their masters; for slaves and women do not conspire against tyrants; and they are of course friendly to tyrannies and also to democracies, since under them they have a good time. For the people too would fain be a monarch, and therefore by them, as well as by the ty-
40 rant, the flatterer is held in honour; in democracies he is the demagogue; and the tyrant also has those who associate with him in a humble spirit, which is a work of flattery.

1314ª1 Hence tyrants are always fond of bad men, because they love to be flattered, but no man who has the spirit of a freeman in him will lower himself by flattery; good men love others, or at any rate do not flatter them. Moreover, the bad are
5 useful for bad purposes; 'nail knocks out nail', as the proverb says. It is characteristic of a tyrant to dislike every one who has dignity or independence; he wants to be alone in

his glory, but anyone who claims a like dignity or asserts his independence encroaches upon his prerogative, and is hated by him as an enemy to his power. Another mark of a tyrant is that he likes foreigners better than citizens, and lives with them and invites to his table; for the one are enemies, but the others enter into no rivalry with him.

Such are the marks of the tyrant and the arts by which he preserves his power; there is no wickedness too great for him. All that we have said may be summed up under three heads, which answer to the three aims of the tyrant. These are, the humiliation of his subjects, for he knows that a mean-spirited man will not conspire against anybody: the creation of mistrust among them; for a tyrant is not overthrown until men begin to have confidence in one another; and this is the reason why tyrants are at war with the good; they are under the idea that their power is endangered by them, not only because they will not be ruled despotically, but also because they are loyal to one another, and to other men, and do not inform against one another or against other men: the tyrant desires that his subjects shall be incapable of action, for no one attempts what is impossible, and they will not attempt to overthrow a tyranny if they are powerless. Under these three heads the whole policy of a tyrant may be summed up, and to one or other of them all his ideas may be referred: he sows distrust among his subjects; he takes away their power; and he humbles them.

This then is one of the two methods by which tyrannies are preserved; and there is another which proceeds upon an almost opposite principle of action. The nature of this latter method may be gathered from a comparison of the causes which destroy kingdoms, for as one mode of destroying kingly power is to make the office of king more tyrannical, so the salvation of a tyranny is to make it more like the rule of a king. But of one thing the tyrant must be careful; he must keep power enough to rule over his subjects, whether they like him or not, for if he once gives this up he gives up his tyranny. But though power must be retained as the foundation, in all else the tyrant should act or appear to act in the character of a king.

1314ᵇ1 In the first place he should pretend concern for the public revenues, and not waste money in making presents of a sort at which the common people get excited when they see their hard-won earnings snatched from them and lavished on courtesans and foreigners and artists. He should give an account

5 of what he receives and of what he spends (a practice which has been adopted by some tyrants); for then he will seem to be a steward of the public rather than a tyrant; nor need he fear that, while he is the lord of the city, he will ever be in want of money. Such a policy is at all events much more advantageous

10 for the tyrant when he goes from home, than to leave behind him a hoard, for then the garrison who remain in the city will be less likely to attack his power; and a tyrant, when he is absent from home, has more reason to fear the guardians of his treasure than the citizens, for the one accompany him, but the others remain behind. In the second place, he should be seen to collect taxes and to require public services only for state

15 purposes, and so as to form a fund in case of war, and generally he ought to make himself the guardian and treasurer of them, as if they belonged, not to him, but to the public. He should appear, not harsh, but dignified, and when men meet him they

20 should look upon him with reverence, and not with fear. Yet it is hard for him to be respected if he inspires no respect, and therefore whatever virtues he may neglect, at least he should maintain the character of a great soldier, and produce the impression that he is one. Neither he nor any of his associates should ever assault the young of either sex who are his sub-

25 jects, and the women of his family should observe a like self-control towards other women; the insolence of women has ruined many tyrannies. In the indulgence of pleasures he should be the opposite of our modern tyrants, who not only begin at

30 dawn and pass whole days in sensuality, but want other men to see them, so that they may admire their happy and blessed lot. In these things a tyrant should if possible be moderate, or at any rate should not parade his vices to the world; for a drunken and drowsy tyrant is soon despised and attacked; not

35 so he who is temperate and wide awake.

His conduct should be the very reverse of nearly everything which has been said before about tyrants. He ought to
adorn and improve his city, as though he were not a tyrant,
but the guardian of the state. Also he should appear to be particularly earnest in the service of the gods; for if men think
that a ruler is religious and has a reverence for the gods, they   1315ᵃ1
are less afraid of suffering injustice at his hands, and they are
less disposed to conspire against him, because they believe
him to have the very gods fighting on his side. At the same
time his religion must not be thought foolish. And he should
honour men of merit, and make them think that they would
not be held in more honour by the citizens if they had a free   5
government. The honour he should distribute himself, but
the punishment should be inflicted by officers and courts of
law. It is a precaution which is taken by all monarchs not to
make one person great; but if one, then two or more should
be raised, that they may keep an eye on one another. If after
all some one has to be made great, he should not be a man   10
of bold spirit; for such dispositions are ever most inclined to
strike. And if any one is to be deprived of his power, let it be
diminished gradually, not taken from him all at once. The tyrant should abstain from all outrage; in particular from personal violence and from wanton conduct towards the young.   15
He should be especially careful of his behaviour to men who
are lovers of honour; for as the lovers of money are offended
when their property is touched, so are the lovers of honour
and the good when their honour is affected. Therefore a tyrant
ought either not to commit such acts at all; or he should be   20
thought only to employ fatherly correction, and not to tram-
ple upon others—and his acquaintance with youth should
be supposed to arise from desire, and not from the insolence
of power, and in general he should compensate the appearance of dishonour by the increase of honour.

Of those who attempt assassination they are the most   25
dangerous, and require to be most carefully watched, who
do not care to survive, if they effect their purpose. Therefore
special precaution should be taken about any who think that

either they or those for whom they care have been insulted;
for when men are led away by passion to assault others they
are regardless of themselves. As Heracleitus says, 'It is difficult to fight against anger; for a man will buy revenge with
his soul'.

And whereas states consist of two classes, of poor men
and of rich, the tyrant should lead both to imagine that they
are preserved and prevented from harming one another by
his rule, and whichever of the two is stronger he should attach to his government; for, having this advantage, he has no
need either to emancipate slaves or to disarm the citizens;
either party added to the force which he already has, will
make him stronger than his assailants.

But enough of these details—what should be the general
policy of the tyrant is obvious. He ought to show himself to
his subjects in the light, not of a tyrant, but of a steward and
a king. He should not appropriate what is theirs, but should
be their guardian; he should be moderate, not extravagant
in his way of life; he should win the notables by companionship, and the multitude by flattery. For then his rule will of
necessity be nobler and happier, because he will rule over better men whose spirits are not crushed, and who do not hate
and fear him. His power too will be more lasting. His disposition will be virtuous, or at least half virtuous; and he will
not be wicked, but half wicked only.

12 • Yet no forms of government are so short-lived as oligarchy and tyranny. The tyranny which lasted longest was
that of Orthagoras and his sons at Sicyon; this continued for
a hundred years. The reason was that they treated their subjects with moderation, and to a great extent observed the laws;
and in various ways gained the favour of the people by the care
which they took of them. Cleisthenes, in particular, was
respected for his military ability. If report may be believed,
he crowned the judge who decided against him in the games;
and, as some say, the sitting statue in the Agora of Sicyon is
the likeness of this person. (A similar story is told of Peisis-

tratus, who is said on one occasion to have allowed himself to be summoned and tried before the Areopagus.)

Next in duration to the tyranny of Orthagoras was that of the Cypselidae at Corinth, which lasted seventy-three years and six months: Cypselus reigned thirty years, Periander forty and a half, and Psammetichus the son of Gorgus three. Their continuance was due to similar causes: Cypselus was a popular man, who during the whole time of his rule never had a body-guard; and Periander, although he was a tyrant, was a great soldier. Third in duration was the rule of the Peisistratidae at Athens, but it was interrupted; for Peisistratus was twice driven out, so that out of thirty-three years he reigned only seventeen; and his sons reigned eighteen—altogether thirty-five years. Of other tyrannies, that of Hiero and Gelo at Syracuse was the most lasting. Even this, however, was short, not more than eighteen years in all; for Gelo continued tyrant for seven years, and died in the eighth; Hiero reigned for ten years, and Thrasybulus was driven out in the eleventh month. In fact, tyrannies generally have been of quite short duration.

I have now gone through almost all the causes by which constitutional governments and monarchies are either destroyed or preserved.

In the *Republic* of Plato, Socrates treats of revolutions, but not well, for he mentions no cause of change which peculiarly affects the first or perfect state. He only says that the cause is that nothing is abiding, but all things change in a certain cycle; and that the origin of the change consists in those numbers 'of which 4 and 3, married with 5, furnish two harmonies' (he means when the number of this figure becomes solid); he conceives that nature at certain times produces bad men who will not submit to education; in which latter particular he may very likely be not far wrong, for there may well be some men who cannot be educated and made virtuous. But why is such a cause of change peculiar to his ideal state, and not rather common to all states, or indeed, to everything which comes into being at all? And is it by the agency

of time, which, as he declares, makes all things change, that
15 things which did not begin together, change together? For
example, if something has come into being the day before
the completion of the cycle, will it change with things that
came into being before? Further, why should the perfect state
change into the Spartan? For governments more often take
an opposite form than one akin to them. The same remark
20 is applicable to the other changes; he says that the Spartan
constitution changes into an oligarchy, and this into a democracy, and this again into a tyranny. And yet the contrary
happens quite as often; for a democracy is even more likely
to change into an oligarchy than into a monarchy. Further,
25 he never says whether tyranny is, or is not, liable to revolutions, and if it is, what is the cause of them, or into what form
it changes. And the reason is, that he could not very well have
told: for there is no rule; according to him it should revert to
the first and best, and then there would be a complete cycle.
But in point of fact a tyranny often changes into a tyranny,
30 as that at Sicyon changed from the tyranny of Myron into
that of Cleisthenes; into oligarchy, as the tyranny of Antileon
did at Chalcis; into democracy, as that of Gelo's family did at
Syracuse; into aristocracy, as at Carthage, and the tyranny of
Charilaus in Lacedaemon. Often an oligarchy changes into a
35 tyranny, like most of the ancient oligarchies in Sicily; for example, the oligarchy at Leontini changed into the tyranny of
Panaetius; that at Gela into the tyranny of Cleander; that at
Rhegium into the tyranny of Anaxilaus; the same thing has
happened in many other states. And it is absurd to suppose
that the state changes into oligarchy merely because the rul-
1316^{b}1 ing class are lovers and makers of money, and not because
the very rich think it unfair that the very poor should have an
equal share in the government with themselves. Moreover,
in many oligarchies there are laws against making money in
5 trade. But at Carthage, which is a democracy, there is no such
prohibition; and yet to this day the Carthaginians have never
had a revolution. It is absurd too for him to say that an oligarchy is two cities, one of the rich, and the other of the poor. Is
not this just as much the case in the Spartan constitution, or

in any other in which either all do not possess equal property,   10
or all are not equally good men? Nobody need be any poorer
than he was before, and yet the oligarchy may change all the
same into a democracy, if the poor form the majority; and a
democracy may change into an oligarchy, if the wealthy class
are stronger than the people, and the one are energetic, the
other indifferent.

Once more, although the causes of the change are very   15
numerous, he mentions only one, which is, that the citizens
become poor through dissipation and debt, as though he
thought that all, or the majority of them, were originally rich.
This is not true: though it is true that when any of the leaders lose their property they are ripe for revolution; but, when
anybody else does, it is no great matter, and an oligarchy does   20
not even then more often pass into a democracy than into
any other form of government. Again, if men are deprived
of the honours of state, and are wronged, and insulted, they
make revolutions, and change forms of government, even
though they have not wasted their substance because they
might do what they like—of which extravagance he declares
excessive freedom to be the cause.

Finally, although there are many forms of oligarchies and   25
democracies, Socrates speaks of their revolutions as though
there were only one form of either of them.

BOOK VI

1 · We have now considered the varieties of the deliberative   30
or supreme power in states, and the various arrangements of
law-courts and state offices, and which of them are adapted
to different forms of government. We have also spoken of the   35
destruction and preservation of constitutions, how and from
what causes they arise.

Of democracy and all other forms of government there
are many kinds; and it will be well to assign to them severally
the modes of organization which are proper and advantageous to each, adding what remains to be said about them.

Moreover, we ought to consider the various combinations of these modes themselves; for such combinations make constitutions overlap one another, so that aristocracies have an oligarchical character, and constitutional governments incline to democracies.

1317ª1

When I speak of the combinations which remain to be considered, and thus far have not been considered by us, I mean such as these:—when the deliberative part of the government and the election of officers is constituted oligarchically, and the law-courts aristocratically, or when the courts and the deliberative part of the state are oligarchical, and the election of offices aristocratic, or when in any other way there is a want of harmony in the composition of a state.

I have shown already what forms of democracy are suited to particular cities, and what forms of oligarchy to particular peoples, and to whom each of the other forms of government is suited. Further, we must not only show which of these governments is the best for each state, but also briefly proceed to consider how these and other forms of government are to be established.

First of all let us speak of democracy, which will also bring to light the opposite form of government commonly called oligarchy. For the purposes of this inquiry we need to ascertain all the elements and characteristics of democracy, since from the combinations of these the varieties of democratic government arise. There are several of these differing from each other, and the difference is due to two causes. One has been already mentioned—differences of population; for the popular element may consist of farmers, or of artisans, or of labourers, and if the first of these is added to the second, or the third to the two others, not only does the democracy become better or worse, but its very nature is changed. A second cause remains to be mentioned: the various properties and characteristics of democracy, when variously combined, make a difference. For one democracy will have less and another will have more, and another will have all of these characteristics. There is an advantage in knowing them all, whether a man wishes to establish some new form of democracy, or only to remodel an existing one. Founders of states try to bring together all the elements which accord with the ideas of the several constitutions; but this is a mistake of theirs, as I have already remarked when speaking of the destruction and preservation of states. We will now set forth the principles, characteristics, and aims of such states.

2 • The basis of a democratic state is liberty; which, according to the common opinion of men, can only be enjoyed in such a state—this they affirm to be the great end of every democracy. One principle of liberty is for all to rule and be ruled in turn, and indeed democratic justice is the application of numerical not proportionate equality; whence it follows that the majority must be supreme, and that whatever the majority approve must be the end and the just. Every citizen, it is said, must have equality, and therefore in a democracy the poor have more power than the rich, because there are more of them, and the will of the majority is supreme. This, then, is one note of liberty which all democrats affirm to be the principle of their state. Another is that a man should live as he likes. This, they say, is the mark of liberty, since, on the other hand, not to live as a man likes is the mark of a slave. This is the second characteristic of democracy, whence has arisen the claim of men to be ruled by none, if possible, or, if this is impossible, to rule and be ruled in turns; and so it contributes to the freedom based upon equality.

Such being our foundation and such the principle from which we start, the characteristics of democracy are as follows:—the election of officers by all out of all; and that all should rule over each, and each in his turn over all; that the appointment to all offices, or to all but those which require experience and skill, should be made by lot; that no property qualification should be required for offices, or only a very low one; that a man should not hold the same office twice, or not often, or in the case of few except military offices; that the tenure of all offices, or of as many as possible, should be brief; that all men should sit in judgement, or that judges selected out of all should judge, in all matters, or in most and in the greatest and most important—such as the scrutiny of accounts, the constitution, and private contracts; that the assembly should be supreme over all causes, or at any rate over the most important, and the magistrates over none or only over a very few. Of all magistracies, a council is the most democratic when there is not the means of paying all the citizens, but when they are paid even this is robbed of its power; for the people then draw all cases to themselves, as I said in the previous discussion. The next characteristic of democracy is payment for services; assembly, law-courts, magistrates, everybody receives pay, when it is to be had; or when it is not to be had for all, then it is given to the law-courts and to the stated assemblies, to the council and to the magistrates, or at least to any of them who are compelled to have their meals together. [And whereas oligarchy is characterized by birth, wealth, and education, the marks of democracy appear to be the opposite of these—low birth, poverty, mean employment.][1] Another characteristic is that no magistracy is perpetual, but if any such have survived some ancient change in the constitution it should be stripped of its power, and the holders should be elected by lot and no longer by vote. These are the points common to all democracies; but democracy and demos in their truest form are based upon the recognized principle of democratic justice, that all should count equally; for equality implies that the poor should have no more share in the government than the rich, and should not be the only rulers, but that all should rule equally according to their numbers. And in this way men think that they will secure equality and freedom in their state.

3 • Next comes the question, how is this equality to be obtained? Are we to assign to a thousand poor men the property qualifications of five hundred rich men? and shall we give the thousand a power equal to that of the five hundred? or, if this is not to be the mode, ought we, still retaining the same ratio,

[1] Excised by Dreizehnter.

to take equal numbers from each and give them the control of the elections and of the courts?—Which, according to the democratic notion, is the juster form of the constitution— this or one based on numbers only? Democrats say that justice is that to which the majority agree, oligarchs that to which the wealthier class agree; in their opinion the decision should be given according to the amount of property. In both principles there is some inequality and injustice. For if justice is the will of the few, any one person who has more wealth than all the rest of the rich put together, ought, upon the oligarchical principle, to have the sole power—but this would be tyranny; or if justice is the will of the majority, as I was before saying, they will unjustly confiscate the property of the wealthy minority. To find a principle of equality in which they both agree we must inquire into their respective ideas of justice.

Now they agree in saying that whatever is decided by the majority of the citizens is to be deemed law. Granted, but not without some reserve; since there are two classes out of which a state is composed—the poor and the rich—that is to be deemed law, on which both or the greater part of both agree; and if they disagree, that which is approved by the greater number, and by those who have the higher qualification. For example, suppose that there are ten rich and twenty poor, and some measure is approved by six of the rich and is disapproved by fifteen of the poor, and the remaining four of the rich join with the party of the poor, and the remaining five of the poor with that of the rich; in such a case the will of those whose qualifications, when both sides are added up, are the greatest, should prevail. If they turn out to be equal, there is no greater difficulty than at present, when, if the assembly or the courts are divided, recourse is had to the lot, or to some similar expedient. But, although it may be difficult in theory to know what is just and equal, the practical difficulty of inducing those to forbear who can, if they like, encroach, is far greater, for the weaker are always asking for equality and justice, but the stronger care for none of these things.

4 • Of the four kinds of democracy, as was said in the previous discussion, the best is that which comes first in order; it is also the oldest of them all. I am speaking of them according to the natural classification of their inhabitants. For the best material of democracy is an agricultural population; there is no difficulty in forming a democracy where the mass
10 of the people live by agriculture or tending of cattle. Being poor, they have no leisure, and therefore do not often attend the assembly, and having the necessaries of life they are always at work, and do not covet the property of others. Indeed, they find their employment pleasanter than the cares of government or office where no great gains can be made
15 out of them, for the many are more desirous of gain than of honour. A proof is that even the ancient tyrannies were patiently endured by them, as they still endure oligarchies, if they are allowed to work and are not deprived of their prop-
20 erty; for some of them grow quickly rich and the others are well enough off. Moreover, they have the power of electing the magistrates and calling them to account; their ambition, if they have any, is thus satisfied; and in some democracies, although they do not all share in the appointment of offices, except through representatives elected in turn out of the whole people, as at Mantinea—yet, if they have the power
25 of deliberating, the many are contented. Even this form of government may be regarded as a democracy, and was such at Mantinea. Hence it is both expedient and customary in the afore-mentioned type of democracy that all should elect to offices, and conduct scrutinies, and sit in the law-courts,
30 but that the great offices should be filled up by election and from persons having a qualification; the greater requiring a greater qualification, or, if there are no offices for which a qualification is required, then those who are marked out by special ability should be appointed. Under such a form of government the citizens are sure to be governed well (for the offices will always be held by the best persons; the people are willing enough to elect them and are not jealous of the good).
35 The good and the notables will then be satisfied, for they will not be governed by men who are their inferiors, and the per-

sons elected will rule justly, because others will call them to account. Every man should be responsible to others, nor should anyone be allowed to do just as he pleases; for where absolute freedom is allowed there is nothing to restrain the evil which is inherent in every man. But the principle of responsibility secures that which is the greatest good in states; the right persons rule and are prevented from doing wrong, and the people have their due. It is evident that this is the best kind of democracy—and why? because the people are drawn from a certain class. Some of the ancient laws of most states were useful with a view to making the people husbandmen. They provided either that no one should possess more than a certain quantity of land, or that, if he did, the land should not be within a certain distance from the town or the acropolis.

Formerly in many states there was a law forbidding anyone to sell his original allotment of land. There is a similar law attributed to Oxylus, which is to the effect that there should be a certain portion of every man's land on which he could not borrow money. A useful corrective to the evil of which I am speaking would be the law of the Aphytaeans, who, although they are numerous, and do not possess much land, are all of them farmers. For their properties are reckoned in the census, not entire, but only in such small portions that even the poor may have more than the amount required.

Next best to an agricultural, and in many respects similar, are a pastoral people, who live by their flocks; they are the best trained of any for war, robust in body and able to camp out. The people of whom other democracies consist are far inferior to them, for their life is inferior; there is no room for excellence in any of their employments, whether they be artisans or traders or labourers. Besides, people of this class can readily come to the assembly, because they are continually moving about in the city and in the agora; whereas farmers are scattered over the country and do not meet or feel the same need of assembling together. Where the territory also happens to extend to a distance from the city, there is no difficulty in making an excellent democracy or constitutional government; for the people are compelled to settle in the

1319ᵃ1

5

10

15

20

25

30

35

country, and even if there is a town population the assembly ought not to meet, in democracies, when the country people cannot come. We have thus explained how the first and best form of democracy should be constituted; it is clear that the other or inferior sorts will deviate in a regular order, and the population which is excluded will at each stage be of a lower kind.

The last form of democracy, that in which all share alike, is one which cannot be borne by all states, and will not last long unless well regulated by laws and customs. The more general causes which tend to destroy this or other kinds of government have been pretty fully considered. In order to constitute such a democracy and strengthen the people, the leaders have been in the habit of including as many as they can, and making citizens not only of those who are legitimate, but even of the illegitimate, and of those who have only one parent a citizen, whether father or mother; for nothing of this sort comes amiss to such a democracy. This is the way in which demagogues proceed. Whereas the right thing would be to make no more additions when the number of the commonalty exceeds that of the notables and of the middle class and not to go beyond this. When in excess of this point, the constitution becomes disorderly, and the notables grow excited and impatient of the democracy, as in the insurrection at Cyrene; for no notice is taken of a little evil, but when it increases it strikes the eye. Measures like those which Cleisthenes passed when he wanted to increase the power of the democracy at Athens, or such as were taken by the founders of popular government at Cyrene, are useful in the extreme form of democracy. Fresh tribes and brotherhoods should be established; the private rites of families should be restricted and converted into public ones; in short, every contrivance should be adopted which will mingle the citizens with one another and get rid of old connexions. Again, the measures which are taken by tyrants appear all of them to be democratic; such, for instance, as the licence permitted to slaves (which may be to a certain extent advantageous) and also to women and children, and the allowing everybody to live as he likes. Such a government will have many supporters, for most persons would rather live in a disorderly than in a sober manner.

5 • The mere establishment of a democracy is not the only or principal business of the legislator, or of those who wish to create such a state, for any state, however badly constituted, may last one, two, or three days; a far greater difficulty is the preservation of it. The legislator should therefore endeavour to have a firm foundation according to the principles already laid down concerning the preservation and destruction of states; he should guard against the destructive elements, and should make laws, whether written or unwritten, which will contain all the preservatives of states. He must not think the truly democratic or oligarchical measure to be that which will give the greatest amount of democracy or oligarchy, but that which will make them last longest. The demagogues of our own day often get property confiscated in the law-courts in order to please the people. Hence those who have the welfare of the state at heart should counteract them, and make a law that the property of the condemned should not be public and go into the treasury but be sacred. Thus offenders will be as much afraid, for they will be punished all the same, and the people, having nothing to gain, will not be so ready to condemn the accused. Care should also be taken that state trials are as few as possible, and heavy penalties should be inflicted on those who bring groundless accusations; for it is the practice to indict, not members of the popular party, but the notables, although the citizens ought to be all attached to the constitution as well, or at any rate should not regard their rulers as enemies.

Now, since in the last form of democracy the citizens are very numerous, and can hardly be made to assemble unless they are paid, and to pay them when there are no revenues presses hardly upon the notables (for the money must be obtained by a property-tax and confiscations and corrupt practices of the courts, things which have before now overthrown many democracies); where, I say, there are no revenues, the

35

1320^a1

5

10

15

20

government should hold few assemblies, and the law-courts should consist of many persons, but sit for a few days only. This system has two advantages: first, the rich do not fear the

25 expense, even though they are unpaid themselves when the poor are paid; and secondly, cases are better tried, for wealthy persons, although they do not like to be long absent from their own affairs, do not mind going for a few days to the law-courts. Where there are revenues the demagogues should not be allowed after their manner to distribute the surplus;

30 the poor are always receiving and always wanting more and more, for such help is like water poured into a leaky cask. Yet the true friend of the people should see that they are not too poor, for extreme poverty lowers the character of the de-

35 mocracy; measures therefore should be taken which will give them lasting prosperity; and as this is equally the interest of all classes, the proceeds of the public revenues should be accumulated and distributed among its poor, if possible, in such quantities as may enable them to purchase a little farm,

1320^{b}1 or, at any rate, make a beginning in trade or farming. And if this benevolence cannot be extended to all, money should be distributed in turn according to tribes or other divisions, and in the meantime the rich should pay the fee for the attendance of the poor at the necessary assemblies; and should in return be excused from useless public services. By administering the

5 state in this spirit the Carthaginians retain the affections of the people; their policy is from time to time to send some of them into their dependent towns, where they grow rich. It is also worthy of a generous and sensible nobility to divide the poor amongst them, and give them the means of going

10 to work. The example of the people of Tarentum is also well deserving of imitation, for, by sharing the use of their own property with the poor, they gain their good will. Moreover, they divide all their offices into two classes, some of them being elected by vote, the others by lot; the latter, so that the people may participate in them, and the former, so that the state may be better administered. A like result may be gained

15 by dividing the same offices, so as to have two classes of magistrates, one chosen by vote, the other by lot.

Enough has been said of the manner in which democracies ought to be constituted.

6 • From these considerations there will be no difficulty in seeing what should be the constitution of oligarchies. We 20
have only to reason from opposites and compare each form of oligarchy with the corresponding form of democracy.

The first and best balanced of oligarchies is akin to a constitutional government. In this there ought to be two standards of qualification; the one high, the other low—the lower qualifying for the humbler yet indispensable offices and the higher for the superior ones. He who acquires the prescribed 25
qualification should have the rights of citizenship. The number of those admitted should be such as will make the entire governing body stronger than those who are excluded, and the new citizen should be always taken out of the better class of the people. The principle, narrowed a little, gives another 30
form of oligarchy; until at length we reach the most cliquish and tyrannical of them all, answering to the extreme democracy, which, being the worst, requires vigilance in proportion to its badness. For as healthy bodies and ships well provided 35
with sailors may undergo many mishaps and survive them, whereas sickly constitutions and rotten ill-manned ships are ruined by the very least mistake, so do the worst forms of government require the greatest care.

The populousness of democracies generally preserves them 1321ª1
(for number is to democracy in the place of justice based on merit); whereas the preservation of an oligarchy clearly depends on an opposite principle, viz. good order.

7 • As there are four chief divisions of the common people, 5
farmers, artisans, traders, labourers; so also there are four kinds of military forces—the cavalry, the heavy infantry, the light-armed troops, the navy. When the country is adapted for cavalry, then a strong oligarchy is likely to be established. For the security of the inhabitants depends upon a force of 10
this sort, and only rich men can afford to keep horses. The second form of oligarchy prevails when the country is adapted to

heavy infantry; for this service is better suited to the rich than to the poor. But the light-armed and the naval element are wholly democratic; and nowadays, where they are numerous, if the two parties quarrel, the oligarchy are often worsted by them in the struggle. A remedy for this state of things may be found in the practice of generals who combine a proper contingent of light-armed troops with cavalry and heavy-armed. And this is the way in which the poor get the better of the rich in civil contests; being lightly armed, they fight with advantage against cavalry and heavy infantry. An oligarchy which raises such a force out of the lower classes raises a power against itself. And therefore, since the ages of the citizens vary and some are older and some younger, the fathers should have their own sons, while they are still young, taught the agile movements of light-armed troops; and these, when they have been taken out of the ranks of the youth, should become light-armed warriors in reality. The oligarchy should also yield a share in the government to the people, either, as I said before, to those who have a property qualification, or, as in the case of Thebes, to those who have abstained for a certain number of years from mean employments, or, as at Massalia, to men of merit who are selected for their worthiness, whether previously citizens or not. The magistracies of the highest rank, which ought to be in the hands of the governing body, should have expensive duties attached to them, and then the people will not desire them and will take no offence at the privileges of their rulers when they see that they pay a heavy fine for their dignity. It is fitting also that the magistrates on entering office should offer magnificent sacrifices or erect some public edifice, and then the people who participate in the entertainments, and see the city decorated with votive offerings and buildings, will not desire an alteration in the government, and the notables will have memorials of their munificence. This, however, is anything but the fashion of our modern oligarchs, who are as covetous of gain as they are of honour; oligarchies like theirs may be well described as petty democracies. Enough of the manner in which democracies and oligarchies should be organized.

8 · Next in order follows the right distribution of offices, their number, their nature, their duties, of which indeed we have already spoken. No state can exist not having the necessary offices, and no state can be well administered not having the offices which tend to preserve harmony and good order. In small states, as we have already remarked, there must not be many of them, but in larger states there must be a larger number, and we should carefully consider which offices may properly be united and which separated.

First among necessary offices is that which has the care of the market; a magistrate should be appointed to inspect contracts and to maintain order. For in every state there must inevitably be buyers and sellers who will supply one another's wants; this is the readiest way to make a state self-sufficient and so fulfil the purpose for which men come together into one state. A second office of a similar kind undertakes the supervision and embellishment of public and private buildings, the maintaining and repairing of houses and roads, the prevention of disputes about boundaries, and other concerns of a like nature. This is commonly called the office of City-warden, and has various departments, which, in more populous towns, are shared among different persons, one, for example, taking charge of the walls, another of the fountains, a third of harbours. There is another equally necessary office, and of a similar kind, having to do with the same matters outside the walls and in the country—the magistrates who hold this office are called Wardens of the country, or Inspectors of the woods. Besides these three there is a fourth office of receivers of taxes, who have under their charge the revenue which is distributed among the various departments; these are called Receivers or Treasurers. Another officer registers all private contracts, and decisions of the courts, all public indictments, and also all preliminary proceedings. This office again is sometimes subdivided; but in some places a single officer is responsible for all these matters.

These officers are called Recorders or Sacred Recorders, Presidents, and the like.

Next to these comes an office of which the duties are the most necessary and also the most difficult, viz. that to which is committed the execution of punishments, or the exaction of fines from those who are posted up according to the registers; and also the custody of prisoners. The difficulty of this office arises out of the odium which is attached to it; no one will undertake it unless great profits are to be made, and anyone who does is loath to execute the law. Still the office is necessary; for judicial decisions are useless if they take no effect; and if society cannot exist without them, neither can it exist without the execution of them. It is an office which, being so unpopular, should not be entrusted to one person, but divided among several taken from different courts. In like manner an effort should be made to distribute among different persons the writing up of those who are on the register of public debtors. Some sentences should be executed by the magistrates also, and in particular penalties due to the outgoing magistrates should be exacted by the incoming ones; and as regards those due to magistrates already in office, when one court has given judgement, another should exact the penalty; for example, the wardens of the city should exact the fines imposed by the wardens of the agora, and others again should exact the fines imposed by them. For penalties are more likely to be exacted when less odium attaches to the exaction of them; but a double odium is incurred when the judges who have passed also execute the sentence, and if they are always the executioners, they will be the enemies of all.

In many places, while one magistracy executes the sentence, another has the custody of the prisoners, as, for example, 'the Eleven' at Athens. It is well to separate off the jailorship also, and try by some device to render the office less unpopular. For it is quite as necessary as that of the executioners; but good men do all they can to avoid it, and worthless persons cannot safely be trusted with it; for they themselves require a guard, and are not fit to guard others. There ought not therefore to be a single or permanent officer set apart for this duty; but it should be entrusted to the young,

wherever they are organized into a band or guard, and different magistrates acting in turn should take charge of it.

There are the indispensable officers, and should be ranked
first—next in order follow others, equally necessary, but of   30
higher rank, and requiring great experience and trustworthi-
ness. Such are the offices to which are committed the guard of
the city, and other military functions. Not only in time of war
but of peace their duty will be to defend the walls and gates,   35
and to muster and marshal the citizens. In some states there
are many such offices; in others there are a few only, while
small states are content with one; these officers are called
generals or commanders. Again, if a state has cavalry or light-
armed troops or archers or a naval force, it will sometimes   1322ᵇ1
happen that each of these departments has separate officers,
who are called admirals, or generals of cavalry or of light-
armed troops. And there are subordinate officers called naval
captains, and captains of light-armed troops and of horse,
having others under them—all these are included in the de-
partment of war. Thus much of military command.   5

But since some, not to say all, of these offices handle the
public money, there must of necessity be another office which
examines and audits them, and has no other functions. Such
officers are called by various names—Scrutineers, Auditors,   10
Accountants, Controllers. Besides all these offices there is another which is supreme over them; for the same office often
deals with rates and taxes, or presides, in a democracy, over
the assembly. For there must be a body which convenes the   15
supreme authority in the state. In some places they are called
'probuli', because they hold previous deliberations, but in a
democracy more commonly 'councillors'. These are the chief
political offices.

Another set of officers is concerned with the maintenance
of religion; priests and guardians see to the preservation and
repair of the temples of the gods and to other matters of reli-   20
gion. One office of this sort may be enough in small places, but
in larger ones there are a great many besides the priesthood;
for example superintendents of public worship, guardians

25 of shrines, treasurers of the sacred revenues. Nearly connected with these there are also the officers appointed for the performance of the public sacrifices, except any which the law assigns to the priests; such sacrifices derive their dignity from the public hearth of the city. They are sometimes called archons, sometimes kings, and sometimes prytanes.

These, then, are the necessary offices, which may be
30 summed up as follows: offices concerned with matters of religion, with war, with the revenue and expenditure, with the market, with the city, with the harbours, with the country; also with the courts of law, with the records of contracts, with
35 execution of sentences, with custody of prisoners, with audits and scrutinies and accounts of magistrates; lastly, there are those which preside over the public deliberations of the state. There are likewise magistracies characteristic of states which are peaceful and prosperous, and at the same time have a regard to good order: such as the offices of guardians of women, guardians of the laws, guardians of children, and directors of gymnastics; also superintendents of gymnastic
1323ᵃ1 and Dionysiac contests, and of other similar spectacles. Some of these are clearly not democratic offices; for example, the guardianships of women and children—the poor, not having any slaves, must employ both their women and children
5 as servants.

Once more: there are three offices according to whose directions the highest magistrates are chosen in certain states—guardians of the law, probuli, councillors—of these, the guardians of the law are an aristocratic, the probuli an oligarchical,
10 the council a democratic, institution. Enough, in outline, of the different kinds of offices.

BOOK VII

1 • He who would duly inquire about the best form of a state
15 ought first to determine which is the most eligible life; while this remains uncertain the best form of the state must also be uncertain; for, in the natural order of things, those men

may be expected to lead the best life who are governed in the best manner of which their circumstances admit. We ought therefore to ascertain, first of all, which is the most generally eligible life, and then whether the same life is or is not best for the state and for individuals.

Assuming that enough has been already said in discussions outside the school concerning the best life, we will now only repeat what is contained in them. Certainly no one will dispute the propriety of that partition of goods which separates them into three classes, viz. external goods, goods of the body, and goods of the soul, or deny that the happy man must have all three. For no one would maintain that he is happy who has not in him a particle of courage or temperance or justice or practical wisdom, who is afraid of every insect which flutters past him, and will commit any crime, however great, in order to gratify his lust for meat or drink, who will sacrifice his dearest friend for the sake of half a farthing, and is as feeble and false in mind as a child or a madman. These propositions are almost universally acknowledged as soon as they are uttered, but men differ about the degree or relative superiority of this or that good. Some think that a very moderate amount of excellence is enough, but set no limit to their desires for wealth, property, power, reputation, and the like. To them we shall reply by an appeal to facts, which easily prove that mankind does not acquire or preserve the excellences by the help of external goods, but external goods by the help of the excellences, and that happiness, whether consisting in pleasure or excellence, or both, is more often found with those who are most highly cultivated in their mind and in their character, and have only a moderate share of external goods, than among those who possess external goods to a useless extent but are deficient in higher qualities; and this is not only a matter of experience, but, if reflected upon, will easily appear to be in accordance with reason. For, whereas external goods have a limit, like any other instrument, and all things useful are useful for a purpose, and where there is too much of them they must either do harm, or at any rate be of no use, to their possessors, every good of the soul, the greater it is, is also of greater use, if the epithet useful as well as noble is appropriate to such subjects. No proof is required to show that the best state of one thing in relation to another corresponds in degree of excellence to the interval between the natures of which we say that these very states are states:

15 so that, if the soul is more noble than our possessions or our bodies, both absolutely and in relation to us, it must be admitted that the best state of either has a similar ratio to the other. Again, it is for the sake of the soul that goods external and goods of the body are desirable at all, and all wise men ought to choose them for the sake of the soul, and not the soul for the sake of them.

20 Let us acknowledge then that each one has just so much of happiness as he has of excellence and wisdom, and of excellent and wise action. The gods are a witness to us of this truth, for they are happy and blessed, not by reason of any external

25 good, but in themselves and by reason of their own nature. And herein of necessity lies the difference between good fortune and happiness; for external goods come of themselves, and chance is the author of them, but no one is just or temperate by or through chance. In like manner, and by a similar

30 train of argument, the happy state may be shown to be that which is best and which acts rightly; and it cannot act rightly without doing right actions, and neither individual nor state can do right actions without excellence and wisdom. Thus the courage, justice, and wisdom of a state have the same form

35 and nature as the qualities which give the individual who possesses them the name of just, wise or temperate.

Thus much may suffice by way of preface: for I could not avoid touching upon these questions, neither could I go through all the arguments affecting them; these are the business of another science.

Let us assume then that the best life, both for individuals and states, is the life of excellence, when excellence has ex-

1324ᵃ1 ternal goods enough for the performance of good actions. If there are any who dispute our assertion, we will in this treatise pass them over, and consider their objections hereafter.

2 • There remains to be discussed the question, whether the happiness of the individual is the same as that of the state, or different. Here again there can be no doubt—no one denies that they are the same. For those who hold that the well-being of the individual consists in his wealth, also think that riches make the happiness of the whole state, and those who value most highly the life of a tyrant deem that city the happiest which rules over the greatest number; while they who approve an individual for his excellence say that the more excellent a city is, the happier it is. Two points here present themselves for consideration: first, which is the more desirable life, that of a citizen who is a member of a state, or that of an alien who has no political ties; and again, which is the best form of constitution or the best condition of a state, either on the supposition that political privileges are desirable for all, or for a majority only? Since the good of the state and not of the individual is the proper subject of political thought and speculation, and we are engaged in a political discussion, while the first of these two points has a secondary interest for us, the latter will be the main subject of our inquiry.

Now it is evident that that form of government is best in which every man, whoever he is, can act best and live happily. But even those who agree in thinking that the life of excellence is the most desirable raise a question, whether the life of business and politics is or is not more desirable than one which is wholly independent of external goods, I mean than a contemplative life, which by some is maintained to be the only one worthy of a philosopher. For these two lives—the life of the philosopher and the life of the statesman—appear to have been preferred by those who have been most keen in the pursuit of excellence, both in our own and in other ages. Which is the better is a question of no small moment; for the wise man, like the wise state, will necessarily regulate his life according to the best end. There are some who think that while a despotic rule over others is the greatest injustice, to exercise a constitutional rule over them, even though not unjust, is a great impediment to a man's individual well-being.

Others take an opposite view; they maintain that the true life of man is the practical and political, and that every excellence admits of being practised, quite as much by statesmen and rulers as by private individuals. Others, again, are of the opinion that arbitrary and tyrannical rule alone makes for happiness; indeed, in some states the entire aim both of the laws and of the constitution is to give men despotic power over their neighbours.

And, therefore, although in most cities the laws may be said generally to be in a chaotic state, still, if they aim at anything, they aim at the maintenance of power: thus in Lacedaemon and Crete the system of education and the greater part of the laws are framed with a view to war. And in all nations which are able to gratify their ambition military power is held in esteem, for example among the Scythians and Persians and Thracians and Celts. In some nations there are even laws tending to stimulate the warlike virtues, as at Carthage, where we are told that men obtain the honour of wearing as many armlets as they have served campaigns. There was once a law in Macedonia that he who had not killed an enemy should wear a halter, and among the Scythians no one who had not slain his man was allowed to drink out of the cup which was handed round at a certain feast. Among the Iberians, a warlike nation, the number of enemies whom a man has slain is indicated by the number of obelisks which are fixed in the earth round his tomb; and there are numerous practices among other nations of a like kind, some of them established by law and others by custom. Yet to a reflecting mind it must appear very strange that the statesman should be always considering how he can dominate and tyrannize over others, whether they are willing or not. How can that which is not even lawful be the business of the statesman or the legislator? Unlawful it certainly is to rule without regard to justice, for there may be might where there is no right. The other arts and sciences offer no parallel; a physician is not expected to persuade or coerce his patients, nor a pilot the passengers in his ship. Yet most men appear to think that the art of despotic government is statesmanship, and what men

affirm to be unjust and inexpedient in their own case they are
not ashamed of practising towards others; they demand just   35
rule for themselves, but where other men are concerned they
care nothing about it. Such behaviour is irrational; unless
the one party is, and the other is not, born to serve, in which
case men have a right to command, not indeed all their fel-
lows, but only those who are intended to be subjects; just as
we ought not to hunt men, whether for food or sacrifice, but   40
only those animals which may be hunted for food or sacrifice, that is to say, such wild animals as are eatable. And surely
there may be a city happy in isolation, which we will assume   1325ᵃ1
to be well-governed (for it is quite possible that a city thus
isolated might be well-administered and have good laws);
but such a city would not be constituted with any view to war
or the conquest of enemies—all that sort of thing must be
excluded.

Hence we see very plainly that warlike pursuits, although   5
generally to be deemed honourable, are not the supreme end
of all things, but only means. And the good lawgiver should
inquire how states and races of men and communities may
participate in a good life, and in the happiness which is attainable by them. His enactments will not be always the same;   10
and where there are neighbours he will have to see what sort
of studies should be practised in relation to their several
characters, or how the measures appropriate in relation to
each are to be adopted. The end at which the best form of government should aim may be properly made a matter of future   15
consideration.

3 • Let us now address those who, while they agree that the
life of excellence is the most desirable, differ about the manner of practising it. For some renounce political power, and
think that the life of the freeman is different from the life of
the statesman and the best of all; but others think the life of   20
the statesman best. The argument of the latter is that he who
does nothing cannot do well, and that acting well is identical with happiness. To both we say: 'you are partly right and
partly wrong'. The first class are right in affirming that the life

of the freeman is better than the life of the despot; for there
is nothing noble in having the use of a slave, in so far as he is
a slave; or in issuing commands about necessary things. But
it is an error to suppose that every sort of rule is despotic like
that of a master over slaves, for there is as great a difference
between rule over freemen and rule over slaves as there is between slavery by nature and freedom by nature, about which
I have said enough at the commencement of this treatise.
And it is equally a mistake to place inactivity above action, for
happiness is activity, and the actions of the just and wise are
the realization of much that is noble.

But perhaps someone, accepting these premises, may still
maintain that supreme power is the best of all things, because
the possessors of it are able to perform the greatest number
of noble actions. If so, the man who is able to rule, instead
of giving up anything to his neighbour, ought rather to take
away his power; and the father should care nothing for his
son, nor the son for his father, nor friend for friend; they
should not bestow a thought on one another in comparison
with this higher object, for the best is the most desirable and
'acting well' is the best. There might be some truth in such
a view if we assume that robbers and plunderers attain the
chief good. But this can never be; their hypothesis is false.
For the actions of a ruler cannot really be honourable, unless
he is as much superior to other men as a man is to a woman,
or a father to his children, or a master to his slaves. And
therefore he who violates the law can never recover by any
success, however great, what he has already lost in depart-
ing from excellence. For equals the honourable and the just
consist in sharing alike, as is just and equal. But that the unequal should be given to equals, and the unlike to those who
are like, is contrary to nature, and nothing which is contrary
to nature is good. If, therefore, there is anyone superior in
excellence and in the power of performing the best actions,
he is the man we ought to follow and obey, but he must have
the capacity for action as well as excellence. If we are right
in our view, and happiness is assumed to be acting well, the
active life will be the best, both for every city collectively, and

for individuals. Not that a life of action must necessarily have relation to others, as some persons think, nor are those ideas only to be regarded as practical which are pursued for the sake of practical results, but much more the thoughts and contemplations which are independent and complete in themselves; since acting well, and therefore a certain kind of action, is an end, and even in the case of external actions the directing mind is most truly said to act. Neither, again, is it necessary that states which are cut off from others and choose to live alone should be inactive; for activity, as well as other things, may take place by sections; there are many ways in which the sections of a state act upon one another. The same thing is equally true of every individual. If this were otherwise, the gods and the universe, who have no external actions over and above their own energies, would be far enough from perfection. Hence it is evident that the same life is best for each individual, and for states and for mankind collectively.

4 • Thus far by way of introduction, in what has preceded I have discussed other forms of government; in what remains the first point to be considered is what should be the conditions of the ideal or perfect state; for the perfect state cannot exist without a due supply of the means of life. And therefore we must presuppose many purely imaginary conditions, but nothing impossible. There will be a certain number of citizens, a country in which to place them, and the like. As the weaver or shipbuilder or any other artisan must have the material proper for his work (and in proportion as this is better prepared, so will the result of his art be nobler), so the statesman or legislator must also have the materials suited to him.

First among the materials required by the statesman is population: he will consider what should be the number and character of the citizens, and then what should be the size and character of the country. Most persons think that a state in order to be happy ought to be large; but even if they are right, they have no idea what is a large and what a small state. For they judge of the size of the city by the number of the inhabitants; whereas they ought to regard, not their number,

but their power. A city too, like an individual, has a work to do; and that city which is best adapted to the fulfilment of its
15 work is to be deemed greatest, in the same sense of the word great in which Hippocrates might be called greater, not as a man, but as a physician, than some one else who was taller. And even if we reckon greatness by numbers, we ought not to include everybody, for there must always be in cities a mul-
20 titude of slaves and resident aliens and foreigners; but we should include those only who are members of the state, and who form an essential part of it. The number of the latter is a proof of the greatness of a city; but a city which produces numerous artisans and comparatively few soldiers cannot
25 be great, for a great city is not the same as a populous one. Moreover, experience shows that a very populous city can rarely, if ever, be well governed; since all cities which have a reputation for good government have a limit of population. We may argue on grounds of reason, and the same result will follow. For law is order, and good law is good order; but a
30 very great multitude cannot be orderly: to introduce order into the unlimited is the work of a divine power—of such a power as holds together the universe. Beauty is realized in number and magnitude, and the state which combines magnitude with good order must necessarily be the most beauti-
35 ful. To the size of states there is a limit, as there is to other things, plants, animals, implements; for none of these retain their natural power when they are too large or too small, but they either wholly lose their nature, or are spoiled. For example, a ship which is only a span long will not be a ship at all, nor a ship a quarter of a mile long; yet there may be a ship of
1326ᵇ1 a certain size, either too large or too small, which will still be a ship, but bad for sailing. In like manner a state when composed of too few is not, as a state ought to be, self-sufficient; when of too many, though self-sufficient in all mere necessaries, as a nation may be, it is not a state, being almost incapable of constitutional government. For who can be the
5 general of such a vast multitude, or who the herald, unless he have the voice of a Stentor?

A state, then, only begins to exist when it has attained a population sufficient for a good life in the political community: it may indeed, if it somewhat exceeds this number, be a greater state. But, as I was saying, there must be a limit. What the limit should be will be easily ascertained by experience. For both governors and governed have duties to perform; the special functions of a governor are to command and to judge. But if the citizens of a state are to judge and to distribute offices according to merit, then they must know each other's characters; where they do not possess this knowledge, both the election to offices and the decision of lawsuits will go wrong. When the population is very large they are manifestly settled at haphazard, which clearly ought not to be. Besides, in an over-populous state foreigners and resident aliens will readily acquire the rights of citizens, for who will find them out? Clearly then the best limit of the population of a state is the largest number which suffices for the purposes of life, and can be taken in at a single view. Enough concerning the size of a state.

5 • Much the same principle will apply to the territory of the state: everyone would agree in praising the territory which is most self-sufficient; and that must be the territory which can produce everything necessary, for to have all things and to want nothing is sufficiency. In size and extent it should be such as may enable the inhabitants to live at once temperately and liberally in the enjoyment of leisure. Whether we are right or wrong in laying down this limit we will inquire more precisely hereafter, when we have occasion to consider what is the right use of property and wealth—a matter which is much disputed, because men are inclined to rush into one of two extremes, some into meanness, others into luxury.

It is not difficult to determine the general character of the territory which is required (there are, however, some points on which military authorities should be heard); it should be difficult of access to the enemy, and easy of egress to the inhabitants. Further, we require that the land as well as the

inhabitants of whom we were just now speaking should be
taken in at a single view, for a country which is easily seen can
be easily protected. As to the position of the city, if we could
5   have what we wish, it should be well situated in regard both
to sea and land. This then is one principle, that it should be
a convenient centre for the protection of the whole country:
the other is, that it should be suitable for receiving the fruits
of the soil, and also for the bringing in of timber and any
10   other products that are easily transported.

6 • Whether a communication with the sea is beneficial to
a well-ordered state or not is a question which has often been
asked. It is argued that the introduction of strangers brought
15   up under other laws, and the increase of population, will be
adverse to good order; the increase arises from their using
the sea and having a crowd of merchants coming and going,
and is inimical to good government. Apart from these considerations, it would be undoubtedly better, both with a view
to safety and to the provision of necessaries, that the city and
20   territory should be connected with the sea; the defenders of
a country, if they are to maintain themselves against an enemy,
should be easily relieved both by land and by sea; and even if
they are not able to attack by sea and land at once, they will
25   have less difficulty in doing mischief to their assailants on
one element, if they themselves can use both. Moreover, it
is necessary that they should import from abroad what is not
found in their own country, and that they should export what
they have in excess; for a city ought to be a market, not indeed for others, but for herself.

Those who make themselves a market for the world only
30   do so for the sake of revenue, and if a state ought not to desire
profit of this kind it ought not to have such an emporium.
Nowadays we often see in countries and cities dockyards and
harbours very conveniently placed outside the city, but not
35   too far off; and they are kept in dependence by walls and similar fortifications. Cities thus situated manifestly reap the benefit of intercourse with their ports; and any harm which is
likely to accrue may be easily guarded against by the laws,

which will pronounce and determine who may hold communication with one another, and who may not.

There can be no doubt that the possession of a moderate naval force is advantageous to a city; the city should be formidable not only to its own citizens but to some of its neighbours, or, if necessary, able to assist them by sea as well as by land. The proper number or magnitude of this naval force is relative to the character of the state; for if her function is to take a leading part in politics, her naval power should be commensurate with the scale of her enterprises. The population of the state need not be much increased, since there is no necessity that the sailors should be citizens: the marines who have the control and command will be freemen, and belong also to the infantry; and wherever there is a dense population of country people and farmers, there will always be sailors more than enough. Of this we see instances at the present day. The city of Heraclea, for example, although small in comparison with many others, can man a considerable fleet. Such are our conclusions respecting the territory of the state, its harbours, its towns, its relations to the sea, and its maritime power.

7 · Having spoken of the number of the citizens, we will proceed to speak of what should be their character. This is a subject which can be easily understood by anyone who casts his eye on the more celebrated states of Greece, and generally on the distribution of races in the habitable world. Those who live in a cold climate and in Europe are full of spirit, but wanting in intelligence and skill; and therefore they retain comparative freedom, but have no political organization, and are incapable of ruling over others. Whereas the natives of Asia are intelligent and inventive, but they are wanting in spirit, and therefore they are always in a state of subjection and slavery. But the Hellenic race, which is situated between them, is likewise intermediate in character, being high-spirited and also intelligent. Hence it continues free, and is the best-governed of any nation, and, if it could be formed into one state, would be able to rule the world. There are also

1327ᵇ1

5

10

15

20

25

30

similar differences in the different tribes of Greece; for some
of them are of a one-sided nature, and are intelligent or courageous only, while in others there is a happy combination
of both qualities. And clearly those whom the legislator will
most easily lead to excellence may be expected to be both intelligent and courageous. Some say that the guardians should
be friendly towards those whom they know, fierce towards
those whom they do not know. Now, passion is the quality of
the soul which begets friendship and enables us to love; notably the spirit within us is more stirred against our friends
and acquaintances than against those who are unknown to
us, when we think that we are despised by them; for which
reason Archilochus, complaining of his friends, very naturally addresses his spirit in these words, 'For surely thou are
plagued on account of friends'.

The power of command and the love of freedom are in all
men based upon this quality, for passion is commanding and
invincible. Nor is it right to say that the guardians should be
fierce towards those whom they do not know, for we ought
not to be out of temper with anyone; and a lofty spirit is not
fierce by nature, but only when excited against evil-doers.
And this, as I was saying before, is a feeling which men show
most strongly towards their friends if they think they have
received a wrong at their hands: as indeed is reasonable; for,
besides the actual injury, they seem to be deprived of a benefit
by those who owe them one. Hence the saying, 'Cruel is the
strife of brethren', and again, 'They who love in excess also
hate in excess'.

Thus we have nearly determined the number and character of the citizens of our state, and also the size and nature of
their territory. I say 'nearly', for we ought not to require the
same accuracy in theory as in the facts given by perception.

8 • As in other natural compounds the conditions of a composite whole are not necessarily organic parts of it, so in a
state or in any other combination forming a unity not everything is a part which is a necessary condition. The members
of an association have necessarily some one thing the same

and common to all, in which they share equally or unequally; for example, food or land or any other thing. But where there are two things of which one exists for the sake of the other, they have nothing in common except that the one receives what the other produces. Such, for example, is the relation in which workmen and tools stand to their work; the house and the builder have nothing in common, but the art of the builder is for the sake of the house. And so states require property, but property, even though living beings are included in it, is no part of a state; for a state is a community of equals, aiming at the best life possible. Now, whereas happiness is the highest good, being a realization and perfect practice of excellence, which some can attain, while others have little or none of it, the various qualities of men are clearly the reason why there are various kinds of states and many forms of government; for different men seek after happiness in different ways and by different means, and so make for themselves different modes of life and forms of government. We must see also how many things are indispensable to the existence of a state, for what we call the parts of a state will be found among the indispensable things. Let us then enumerate the functions of a state, and we shall easily elicit what we want.

First, there must be food; secondly, arts, for life requires many instruments; thirdly, there must be arms, for the members of a community have need of them, and in their own hands, too, in order to maintain authority both against disobedient subjects and against external assailants; fourthly, there must be a certain amount of revenue, both for internal needs, and for the purposes of war; fifthly, or rather first, there must be a care of religion, which is commonly called worship; sixthly, and most necessary of all, there must be a power of deciding what is for the public interest, and what is just in men's dealings with one another.

These are the services which every state may be said to need. For a state is not a mere aggregate of persons, but, as we say, a union of them sufficing for the purposes of life; and if any of these things is wanting, it is impossible that the community can be absolutely self-sufficient. A state then

20 should be framed with a view to the fulfilment of these functions. There must be farmers to procure food, and artisans,
and a warlike and a wealthy class, and priests, and judges to
decide what is necessary and expedient.

9 · Having determined these points, we have in the next
25 place to consider whether all ought to share in every sort of
occupation. Shall every man be at once farmer, artisan, coun-
cillor, judge, or shall we suppose the several occupations just
mentioned assigned to different persons? or, thirdly, shall some
employments be assigned to individuals and others com-
30 mon to all? The same arrangement, however, does not occur
in every constitution; as we were saying, all may be shared by
all, or not all by all, but only some by some; and hence arise
the differences of constitutions, for in democracies all share
in all, in oligarchies the opposite practice prevails. Now, since
35 we are here speaking of the best form of government, i.e. that
under which the state will be most happy (and happiness, as
has been already said, cannot exist without excellence), it
clearly follows that in the state which is best governed and
possesses men who are just absolutely, and not merely relatively to the principle of the constitution, the citizens must
not lead the life of artisans or tradesmen, for such a life is ig-
noble and inimical to excellence. Neither must they be farmers, since leisure is necessary both for the development of ex-
1329ª1 cellence and the performance of political duties.
Again, there is in a state a class of warriors, and another of
councillors, who advise about the expedient and determine
matters of law, and these seem in an especial manner parts
5 of a state. Now, should these two classes be distinguished, or
are both functions to be assigned to the same persons? Here
again there is no difficulty in seeing that both functions will
in one way belong to the same, in another, to different persons. To different persons in so far as these employments are
suited to different primes of life, for the one requires wisdom
and the other strength. But on the other hand, since it is an
impossible thing that those who are able to use or to resist
10 force should be willing to remain always in subjection, from

this point of view the persons are the same; for those who carry arms can always determine the fate of the constitution. It remains therefore that both functions should be entrusted by the ideal constitution to the same persons, not, however, at the same time, but in the order prescribed by nature, who has given to young men strength and to older men wisdom. Such a distribution of duties will be expedient and also just, and is founded upon a principle of conformity to merit. Besides, the ruling class should be the owners of property, for they are citizens, and the citizens of a state should be in good circumstances; whereas artisans or any other class which is not a producer of excellence have no share in the state. This follows from our first principle, for happiness cannot exist without excellence, and a city is not to be termed happy in regard to a portion of the citizens, but in regard to them all. And clearly property should be in their hands, since the farmers will of necessity be slaves or barbarian country people.

Of the classes enumerated there remain only the priests, and the manner in which their office is to be regulated is obvious. No farmer or artisan should be appointed to it; for the gods should receive honour from the citizens only. Now since the body of the citizens is divided into two classes, the warriors and the councillors, and it is fitting that the worship of the gods should be duly performed, and also a rest provided in their service for those who from age have given up active life, to the old men of these two classes should be assigned the duties of the priesthood.

We have shown what are the necessary conditions, and what the parts of a state: farmers, artisans, and labourers of all kinds are necessary to the existence of states, but the parts of the state are the warriors and councillors. And these are distinguished severally from one another, the distinction being in some cases permanent, in others not.

10 • It is no new or recent discovery of political philosophers that the state ought to be divided into classes, and that the warriors should be separated from the farmers. The system has continued in Egypt and in Crete to this day, and was

established, as tradition says, by a law of Sesostris in Egypt and of Minos in Crete.

5 The institution of common tables also appears to be of ancient date, being in Crete as old as the reign of Minos, and in Italy far older. The Italian historians say that there was a

10 certain Italus king of Oenotria, from whom the Oenotrians were called Italians, and who gave the name of Italy to the promontory of Europe lying within the Scylletic and Lametic Gulfs, which are distant from one another only half a day's

15 journey. They say that this Italus converted the Oenotrians from shepherds into farmers, and besides other laws which he gave them, was the founder of their common meals; even in our day some who are derived from him retain this institution and certain other laws of his. On the side of Italy towards

20 Tyrrhenia dwelt the Opici, who are now, as of old, called Ausones; and on the side towards Iapygia and the Ionian Gulf, in the district called Siritis, the Chones, who are likewise of Oenotrian race. From this part of the world originally came the institution of common tables; the separation into castes

25 from Egypt, for the reign of Sesostris is of far greater antiquity than that of Minos. It is true indeed that these and many other things have been invented several times over in the course of ages, or rather times without number; for necessity may be supposed to have taught men the inventions which were absolutely required, and when these were provided, it was natural that other things which would adorn and enrich

30 life should grow up by degrees. And we may infer that in political institutions the same rule holds. Egypt witnesses to the antiquity of all these things, for the Egyptians appear to be of all people the most ancient; and they have laws and a regular constitution existing from time immemorial. We should therefore make the best use of what has been already

35 discovered, and try to supply defects.

I have already remarked that the land ought to belong to those who possess arms and have a share in the government, and that the farmers ought to be a class distinct from them; and I have determined what should be the extent and nature of the territory. Let me proceed to discuss the distribution of the land, and the character of the agricultural class; for I do not think that property ought to be common, as some maintain, but only that by friendly consent there should be a common use of it; and that no citizen should be in want of subsistence.

1330ª1

As to common meals, there is a general agreement that a well-ordered city should have them; and we will hereafter explain what are our own reasons for taking this view. They ought, however, to be open to all the citizens. And yet it is not easy for the poor to contribute the requisite sum out of their private means, and to provide also for their household. The expense of religious worship should likewise be a public charge. The land must therefore be divided into two parts, one public and the other private, and each part should be subdivided, part of the public land being appropriated to the service of the gods, and the other part used to defray the cost of the common meals; while of the private land, part should be near the border, and the other near the city, so that, each citizen having two lots, they may all of them have land in both places; there is justice and fairness in such a division and it tends to inspire unanimity among the people in their border wars. Where there is not this arrangement, some of them are too ready to come to blows with their neighbours, while others are so cautious that they quite lose the sense of honour. For this reason there is a law in some places which forbids those who dwell near the border to take part in public deliberations about wars with neighbours, on the ground that their interests will pervert their judgement. For the reasons already mentioned, then, the land should be divided in the manner described. The very best thing of all would be that the farmers should be slaves taken from among men who are not all of the same race and not spirited, for if they have no spirit they will be better suited for their work, and there will be no danger of their making a revolution. The next best thing would be that they should be barbarian country people, and of a like inferior nature; some of them should be the slaves of individuals, and employed on the private estates of men of property, the remainder should be the property of the state

5

10

15

20

25

30

and employed on the common land. I will hereafter explain what is the proper treatment of slaves, and why it is expedient that liberty should be always held out to them as the reward of their services.

11 • We have already said that the city should be open to the land and to the sea, and to the whole country as far as possible. In respect of the place itself our wish would be that its situation should be fortunate in four things. The first, health—this is a necessity: cities which lie towards the east, and are blown upon by winds coming from the east, are the healthiest; next in healthiness are those which are sheltered from the north wind, for they have a milder winter. The site of the city should likewise be convenient both for political administration and for war. With a view to the latter it should afford easy egress to the citizens, and at the same time be inaccessible and difficult of capture to enemies. There should be a natural abundance of springs and fountains in the town, or, if there is a deficiency of them, great reservoirs may be established for the collection of rain-water, such as will not fail when the inhabitants are cut off from the country by war. Special care should be taken of the health of the inhabitants, which will depend chiefly on the healthiness of the locality and of the quarter to which they are exposed, and secondly, on the use of pure water; this latter point is by no means a secondary consideration. For the elements which we use most and oftenest for the support of the body contribute most to health, and among these are water and air. For this reason, in all wise states, if there is a want of pure water, and the supply is not all equally good, the drinking water ought to be separated from that which is used for other purposes.

As to strongholds, what is suitable to different forms of government varies: thus an acropolis is suited to an oligarchy or a monarchy, but a plain to a democracy; neither to an aristocracy, but rather a number of strong places. The arrangement of private houses is considered to be more agreeable and generally more convenient if the streets are regularly laid out after the modern fashion which Hippodamus intro-

duced, but for security in war the antiquated mode of building, which made it difficult for strangers to get out of a town 25
and for assailants to find their way in, is preferable. A city
should therefore adopt both plans of building: it is possible
to arrange the houses irregularly, as farmers plant their vines
in what are called 'clumps'. The whole town should not be laid
out in straight lines, but only certain quarters and regions; 30
thus security and beauty will be combined.

As to walls, those who say that cities making any pretension to military virtue should not have them, are quite out
of date in their notions; and they may see the cities which
prided themselves on this fancy confuted by facts. True, there
is little courage shown in seeking for safety behind a rampart 35
when an enemy is similar in character and not much superior
in number; but the superiority of the besiegers may be and
often is too much both for ordinary human valour and for
that which is found only in a few; and if they are to be saved
and to escape defeat and outrage, the strongest wall will be
the truest soldierly precaution, more especially now that mis- 1331^a1
siles and siege engines have been brought to such perfection.
To have no walls would be as foolish as to choose a site for
a town in an exposed country, and to level the heights; or 5
as if an individual were to leave his house unwalled, lest the
inmates should become cowards. Nor must we forget that
those who have their cities surrounded by walls may either
take advantage of them or not, but cities which are unwalled 10
have no choice.

If our conclusions are just, not only should cities have
walls, but care should be taken to make them ornamental,
as well as useful for warlike purposes, and adapted to resist
modern inventions. For as the assailants of a city do all they
can to gain an advantage, so the defenders should make use 15
of any means of defence which have been already discovered,
and should devise and invent others, for when men are well
prepared no enemy even thinks of attacking them.

12 · As the walls are to be divided by guard-houses and
towers built at suitable intervals, and the body of citizens 20

must be distributed at common tables, the idea will naturally occur that we should establish some of the common tables in the guard-houses. These might be arranged as has been suggested; while the principal common tables of the magistrates will occupy a suitable place, and there also will be the buildings appropriated to religious worship except in the case of those rites which the law or the Pythian oracle has restricted to a special locality. The site should be a spot seen far and wide, which gives due elevation to excellence[1] and towers over the neighbourhood. Below this spot should be established an agora, such as that which the Thessalians call the 'freemen's agora'; from this all trade should be excluded, and no artisan, farmer, or any such person allowed to enter, unless he be summoned by the magistrates. It would be a pleasing use of the place, if the gymnastic exercises of the elder men were performed there. For in this noble practice different ages should be separated, and some of the magistrates should stay with the boys, while the grown-up men remain with the magistrates; for the presence of the magistrates is the best mode of inspiring true modesty and ingenuous fear. There should also be a traders' agora, distinct and apart from the other, in a situation which is convenient for the reception of goods both by sea and land. But we must not forget another section of the citizens, viz. the priests, for whom public tables should likewise be provided in their proper place near the temples. The magistrates who deal with contracts, indictments, summonses, and the like, and those who have the care of the agora and of the city respectively, ought to be established near an agora and some public place of meeting; the neighbourhood of the traders' agora will be a suitable spot; the upper agora we devote to the life of leisure, the other is intended for the necessities of trade.

The same order should prevail in the country, for there too the magistrates, called by some 'Inspectors of Forests'

---

[1]Text uncertain.

and by others 'Wardens of the Country', must have guard-   15
houses and common tables while they are on duty; temples
should also be scattered throughout the country, dedicated
some to gods and some to heroes.

But it would be a waste of time for us to linger over details
like these. The difficulty is not in imagining but in carrying
them out. We may talk about them as much as we like, but the   20
execution of them will depend upon fortune. Therefore let us
say no more about these matters for the present.

13 • Returning to the constitution itself, let us seek to
determine out of what and what sort of elements the state
which is to be happy and well-governed should be composed.   25
There are two things in which all well-being consists: one of
them is the choice of a right end and aim of action, and the
other the discovery of the actions which contribute towards
it; for the means and the end may agree or disagree.

Sometimes the right end is set before men, but in practice   30
they fail to attain it; in other cases they are successful in all
the contributory factors, but they propose to themselves a
bad end; and sometimes they fail in both. Take, for example,
the art of medicine; physicians do not always understand the
nature of health, and also the means which they use may not   35
effect the desired end. In all arts and sciences both the end
and the means should be equally within our control.

The happiness and well-being which all men manifestly
desire, some have the power of attaining, but to others, from
some accident or defect of nature, the attainment of them is
not granted; for a good life requires a supply of external goods,   1332ᵃ1
in a less degree when men are in a good state, in a greater degree when they are in a lower state. Others again, who possess
the conditions of happiness, go utterly wrong from the first
in the pursuit of it. But since our object is to discover the best
form of government, that, namely, under which a city will be
best governed, and since the city is best governed which has   5
the greatest opportunity of obtaining happiness, it is evident
that we must clearly ascertain the nature of happiness.

We maintain, and have said in the *Ethics*, if the arguments
there adduced are of any value, that happiness is the realization and perfect exercise of excellence, and this not conditional, but absolute. And I use the term 'conditional' to express that which is indispensable, and 'absolute' to express
that which is good in itself. Take the case of just actions; just
punishments and chastisements do indeed spring from a good
principle, but they are good only because we cannot do without
them—it would be better that neither individuals nor states
should need anything of the sort—but actions which aim at
honour and advantage are absolutely the best. The conditional action is only the choice of a lesser evil; whereas these
are the foundation and creation of good. A good man may
make the best even of poverty and disease, and the other ills
of life; but he can only attain happiness under the opposite
conditions (for this also has been determined in the *Ethics*,
that the good man is he for whom, because he is excellent, the
things that are absolutely good are good; it is also plain that
his use of these goods must be excellent and in the absolute
sense good). This makes men fancy that external goods are
the cause of happiness, yet we might as well say that a brilliant
performance on the lyre was to be attributed to the instrument and not to the skill of the performer.

It follows then from what has been said that some things
the legislator must find ready to his hand in a state, others
he must provide. And therefore we can only say: may our
state be constituted in such a manner as to be blessed with
the goods of which fortune disposes (for we acknowledge her
power): whereas excellence and goodness in the state are not
a matter of chance but the result of knowledge and choice. A
city can be excellent only when the citizens who have a share
in the government are excellent, and in our state all the citizens share in the government; let us then inquire how a man
becomes excellent. For even if we could suppose the citizen
body to be excellent, without each of them being so, yet the
latter would be better, for in the excellence of each the excellence of all is involved.

There are three things which make men good and excellent; these are nature, habit, reason. In the first place, every one must be born a man and not some other animal; so, too, he must have a certain character, both of body and soul. But some qualities there is no use in having at birth, for they are altered by habit, and there are some gifts which by nature are made to be turned by habit to good or bad. Animals lead for the most part a life of nature, although in lesser particulars some are influenced by habit as well. Man has reason, in addition, and man only. For this reason nature, habit, reason must be in harmony with one another; for they do not always agree; men do many things against habit and nature, if reason persuades them that they ought. We have already determined what natures are likely to be most easily moulded by the hands of the legislator. All else is the work of education; we learn some things by habit and some by instruction.

14 • Since every political society is composed of rulers and subjects, let us consider whether the relations of one to the other should interchange or be permanent. For the education of the citizens will necessarily vary with the answer given to this question. Now, if some men excelled others in the same degree in which gods and heroes are supposed to excel mankind in general (having in the first place a great advantage even in their bodies, and secondly in their minds), so that the superiority of the governors was undisputed and patent to their subjects, it would clearly be better that once for all the one class should rule and the others serve. But since this is unattainable, and kings have no marked superiority over their subjects, such as Scylax affirms to be found among the Indians, it is obviously necessary on many grounds that all the citizens alike should take their turn of governing and being governed. Equality consists in the same treatment of similar persons, and no government can stand which is not founded upon justice. For if the government is unjust everyone in the country unites with the governed in the desire to have a revolution, and it is an impossibility that the members

40

1332^{b}1

5

10

15

20

25

30

of the government can be so numerous as to be stronger than all their enemies put together. Yet that governors should be better than their subjects is undeniable. How all this is to be effected, and in what way they will respectively share in the government, the legislator has to consider. The subject has been already mentioned. Nature herself has provided the distinction when she made a difference between old and young within the same species, of whom she fitted the one to govern and the other to be governed. No one takes offence at being governed when he is young, nor does he think himself better than his governors, especially if he will enjoy the same privilege when he reaches the required age.

We conclude that from one point of view governors and governed are identical, and from another different. And therefore their education must be the same and also different. For he who would learn to command well must, as men say, first of all learn to obey. As I observed in the first part of this treatise, there is one rule which is for the sake of the rulers and another rule which is for the sake of the ruled; the former is a despotic, the latter a free government. Some commands differ not in the thing commanded, but in the intention with which they are imposed. That is why many apparently menial offices are an honour to the free youth by whom they are performed; for actions do not differ as honourable or dishonourable in themselves so much as in the end and intention of them. But since we say that the excellence of the citizen and ruler is the same as that of the good man, and that the same person must first be a subject and then a ruler, the legislator has to see that they become good men, and by what means this may be accomplished, and what is the end of the perfect life.

Now the soul of man is divided into two parts, one of which has a rational principle in itself, and the other, not having a rational principle in itself, is able to obey such a principle. And we call a man in any way good because he has the excellences of these two parts. In which of them the end is more likely to be found is no matter of doubt to those who adopt our division; for in the world both of nature and of art the inferior always exists for the sake of the superior, and the superior is that which has a rational principle. This principle, too, in our ordinary way of making the division, is divided into two kinds, for there is a practical and a specu- 25 lative principle. This part, then, must evidently be similarly divided. And there must be a corresponding division of actions; the actions of the naturally better part are to be preferred by those who have it in their power to attain to two out of the three or to all, for that is always to everyone the most desirable which is the highest attainable by him. The whole 30 of life is further divided into two parts, business and leisure, war and peace, and of actions some aim at what is necessary and useful, and some at what is honourable. And the preference given to one or the other class of actions must necessarily be like the preference given to one or other part of the soul and its actions over the other; there must be war for the sake of peace, business for the sake of leisure, things useful and 35 necessary for the sake of things honourable. All these points the statesman should keep in view when he frames his laws; he should consider the parts of the soul and their functions, and above all the better and the end; he should also remember the diversities of human lives and actions. For men must 1333ᵇ1 be able to engage in business and go to war, but leisure and peace are better; they must do what is necessary and indeed what is useful, but what is honourable is better. On such principles children and persons of every age which requires education should be trained. Whereas even the Greeks of the 5 present day who are reputed to be best governed, and the legislators who gave them their constitutions, do not appear to have framed their governments with a regard to the best end, or to have given them laws and education with a view to all the excellences, but in a vulgar spirit have fallen back 10 on those which promised to be more useful and profitable. Many modern writers have taken a similar view: they commend the Lacedaemonian constitution, and praise the legislator for making conquest and war his sole aim, a doctrine which may be refuted by argument and has long ago been 15

refuted by facts. For most men desire empire in the hope of accumulating the goods of fortune; and on this ground Thi-
20 bron and all those who have written about the Lacedaemonian constitution have praised their legislator, because the Lacedaemonians, by being trained to meet dangers, gained great power. But surely they are not a happy people now that their empire has passed away, nor was their legislator right. How ridiculous is the result, if, while they are continuing in
25 the observance of his laws and no one interferes with them, they have lost the better part of life! These writers further err about the sort of government which the legislator should approve, for the government of freemen is nobler and implies more excellence than despotic government. Neither is
30 a city to be deemed happy or a legislator to be praised because he trains his citizens to conquer and obtain dominion over their neighbours, for there is great harm in this. On a similar principle any citizen who could, should obviously try to obtain the power in his own state—the crime which the Lace-
35 daemonians accuse king Pausanias of attempting, although he had such great honour already. No such principle and no law having this object is either statesmanlike or useful or right. For the same things are best both for individuals and for states, and these are the things which the legislator ought to implant in the minds of his citizens. Neither should men
40 study war with a view to the enslavement of those who do not deserve to be enslaved; but first of all they should provide against their own enslavement, and in the second place
1334ª1 obtain empire for the good of the governed, and not for the sake of exercising a general despotism, and in the third place they should seek to be masters only over those who deserve to be slaves. Facts, as well as arguments, prove that the legis-
5 lator should direct all his military and other measures to the provision of leisure and the establishment of peace. For most of these military states are safe only while they are at war, but fall when they have acquired their empire; like unused iron they lose their edge in time of peace. And for this the legislator is to blame, he never having taught them how to lead the
10 life of peace.

15 • Since the end of individuals and of states is the same, the end of the best man and of the best constitution must also be the same; it is therefore evident that there ought to exist in both of them the excellences of leisure; for peace, as has been often repeated, is the end of war, and leisure of toil. But leisure and cultivation may be promoted not only by those excellences which are practised in leisure, but also by some of those which are useful to business. For many necessaries of life have to be supplied before we can have leisure. Therefore a city must be temperate and brave, and able to endure: for truly, as the proverb says, 'There is no leisure for slaves', and those who cannot face danger like men are the slaves of any invader. Courage and endurance are required for business and philosophy for leisure, temperance and justice for both, and more especially in times of peace and leisure, for war compels men to be just and temperate, whereas the enjoyment of good fortune and the leisure which comes with peace tend to make them insolent. Those then who seem to be the best-off and to be in the possession of every good, have special need of justice and temperance—for example, those (if such there be, as the poets say) who dwell in the Islands of the Blest; they above all will need philosophy and temperance and justice, and all the more the more leisure they have, living in the midst of abundance. There is no difficulty in seeing why the state that would be happy and good ought to have these excellences. If it is disgraceful in men not to be able to use the goods of life, it is peculiarly disgraceful not to be able to use them in time of leisure—to show excellent qualities in action and war, and when they have peace and leisure to be no better than slaves. That is why we should not practice excellence after the manner of the Lacedaemonians. For they, while agreeing with other men in their conception of the highest goods, differ from the rest of mankind in thinking that they are to be obtained by the practice of a single excellence. And since these goods and the enjoyment of them are greater than the enjoyment derived from the excellences . . .[2]

15

20

25

30

35

40

1334ᵇ1

[2] Dreizehnter marks a lacuna.

and that for its own sake, is evident from what has been said; we must now consider how and by what means it is to be attained.

We have already determined that nature and habit and reason are required, and, of these, the proper nature of the citizens has also been defined by us. But we have still to consider whether the training of early life is to be that of reason or habit, for these two must accord, and when in accord they will then form the best of harmonies. Reason may be mistaken and fail in attaining the highest ideal of life, and there may be a like influence of habit. Thus much is clear in the first place, that, as in all other things, birth implies an antecedent beginning, and that there are beginnings whose end is relative to a further end. Now, in men reason and mind are the end towards which nature strives, so that the birth and training in custom of the citizens ought to be ordered with a view to them. In the second place, as the soul and body are two, we see also that there are two parts of the soul, the rational and the irrational, and two corresponding states—reason and appetite. And as the body is prior in order of generation to the soul, so the irrational is prior to the rational. The proof is that anger and wishing and desire are implanted in children from their very birth, but reason and understanding are developed as they grow older. For this reason, the care of the body ought to precede that of the soul, and the training of the appetitive part should follow: none the less our care of it must be for the sake of the reason, and our care of the body for the sake of the soul.

16 • Since the legislator should begin by considering how the bodies of the children whom he is rearing may be as good as possible, his first care will be about marriage—at what age should his citizens marry, and who are fit to marry? In legislating on this subject he ought to consider the persons and the length of their life, that their procreative life may terminate at the same period, and that they may not differ in their bodily powers, as will be the case if the man is still able

to beget children while the woman is unable to bear them,
or the woman able to bear while the man is unable to beget,
for from these causes arise quarrels and differences between
married persons. Secondly, he must consider the time at
which the children will succeed to their parents; there ought
not to be too great an interval of age, for then the parents will   1335ᵃ1
be too old to derive any pleasure from their affection, or to
be of any use to them. Nor ought they to be too nearly of an
age; to youthful marriages there are many objections—the
children will be lacking in respect for the parents, who will
seem to be their contemporaries, and disputes will arise in
the management of the household. Thirdly, and this is the
point from which we digressed, the legislator must mould to   5
his will the bodies of newly-born children. Almost all these
objects may be secured by attention to one point. Since the
time of generation is commonly limited within the age of
seventy years in the case of a man, and of fifty in the case of a   10
woman, the commencement of the union should conform to
these periods. The union of male and female when too young
is bad for the procreation of children; in all other animals the
offspring of the young are small and ill-developed, and with
a tendency to produce female children, and therefore also
in man, as is proved by the fact that in those cities in which   15
men and women are accustomed to marry young, the people
are small and weak; in childbirth also younger women suffer
more, and more of them die; some persons say that this was
the meaning of the response once given to the Troezenians—   20
the oracle really meant that many died because they married
too young; it had nothing to do with the gathering of the harvest. It also conduces to temperance not to marry too soon;
for women who marry early are apt to be wanton; and in men
too the bodily frame is stunted if they marry while the seed is   25
growing (for there is a time when the growth of the seed, also,
ceases, or continues to but a slight extent). Women should
marry when they are about eighteen years of age, and men at
thirty-seven; then they are in the prime of life, and the decline
in the powers of both will coincide. Further, the children, if   30

their birth takes place soon, as may reasonably be expected, will succeed in the beginning of their prime, when the fathers
35 are already in the decline of life, and have nearly reached their term of three-score years and ten.

Thus much of the age proper for marriage: the season of the year should also be considered; according to our present custom, people generally limit marriage to the season of winter, and they are right. The precepts of physicians and natural
40 philosophers about generation should also be studied by the parents themselves; the physicians give good advice about
1335ᵇ1 the favourable conditions of the body, and the natural philosophers about the winds; of which they prefer the north to the south.

What constitution in the parent is most advantageous to the offspring is a subject which we will consider more carefully when we speak of the education of children, and we will
5 only make a few general remarks at present. The constitution of an athlete is not suited to the life of a citizen, or to health, or to the procreation of children, any more than the valetudinarian or exhausted constitution, but one which is in a mean between them. A man's constitution should be inured to labour, but not to labour which is excessive or of one sort
10 only, such as is practised by athletes; he should be capable of all the actions of a freeman. These remarks apply equally to both parents.

Women who are with child should take care of themselves; they should take exercise and have a nourishing diet. The first of these prescriptions the legislator will easily carry into effect
15 by requiring that they shall take a walk daily to some temple, where they can worship the gods who preside over birth. Their minds, however, unlike their bodies, they ought to keep quiet, for the offspring derive their natures from their mothers as plants do from the earth.

As to the exposure and rearing of children, let there be a
20 law that no deformed child shall live. But as to an excess in the number of children, if the established customs of the state forbid the exposure of any children who are born, let a limit

be set to the number of children a couple may have; and if couples have children in excess, let abortion be procured before sense and life have begun; what may or may not be lawfully done in these cases depends on the question of life and   25
sensation.

And now, having determined at what ages men and women are to begin their union, let us also determine how long they shall continue to beget and bear offspring for the state; men who are too old, like men who are too young, produce children who are defective in body and mind; the children of very   30
old men are weakly. The limit, then, should be the age which is the prime of their intelligence, and this in most persons, according to the notion of some poets who measure life by periods of seven years, is about fifty; at four or five years later, they should cease from having families; and from that time   35
forward only cohabit with one another for the sake of health, or for some similar reason.

As to adultery, let it be held disgraceful, in general, for any man or woman to be found in any way unfaithful when they are married, and called husband and wife. If during the time of bearing children anything of the sort occur, let the guilty person be punished with a loss of privileges in proportion to   1336ᵃ1
the offence.

17 • After the children have been born, the manner of rearing them may be supposed to have a great effect on their bodily strength. It would appear from the example of animals, and of those nations who desire to create the military   5
habit, that the food which has most milk in it is best suited to human beings; but the less wine the better, if they would escape diseases. Also all the motions to which children can be subjected at their early age are very useful. But in order to preserve their tender limbs from distortion, some nations have   10
had recourse to mechanical appliances which straighten their bodies. To accustom children to the cold from their earliest years is also an excellent practice, which greatly conduces to health, and hardens them for military service. Hence many

15 barbarians have a custom of plunging their children at birth into a cold stream; others, like the Celts, clothe them in a light wrapper only. For human nature should be early habituated to endure all which by habit it can be made to endure; but the process must be gradual.

20 And children, from their natural warmth, may be easily trained to bear cold. Such care should attend them in the first stage of life.

The next period lasts to the age of five; during this no de-
25 mand should be made upon the child for study or labour, lest its growth be impeded; and there should be sufficient motion to prevent the limbs from being inactive. This can be secured, among other ways, by play, but the play should not be vulgar or tiring or effeminate.

30 The Directors of Education, as they are termed, should be careful what tales or stories the children hear, for all such things are designed to prepare the way for the business of later life, and should be for the most part imitations of the occupations which they will hereafter pursue in earnest. Those
35 are wrong who in their *Laws* attempt to check the loud crying and screaming of children, for these contribute towards their growth, and, in a manner, exercise their bodies. Straining the voice has a strengthening effect similar to that produced by the retention of the breath in violent exertions. The
40 Directors of Education should have an eye to their bringing up, and in particular should take care that they are left as little as
1336ᵇ1 possible with slaves. For until they are seven years old they must live at home; and therefore, even at this early age, it is to be expected that they should acquire a taint of meanness from what they hear and see. Indeed, there is nothing which the legislator should be more careful to drive away than in-
5 decency of speech; for the light utterance of shameful words leads soon to shameful actions. The young especially should never be allowed to repeat or hear anything of the sort. A freeman who is found saying or doing what is forbidden, if he be too young as yet to have the privilege of reclining
10 at the public tables, should be disgraced and beaten, and an elder person degraded as his slavish conduct deserves. And

since we do not allow improper language, clearly we should also banish pictures or speeches from the stage which are indecent. Let the rulers take care that there be no image or picture representing unseemly actions, except in the temples of those gods at whose festivals the law permits even ribaldry, and whom the law also permits to be worshipped by persons of mature age on behalf of themselves, their children, and their wives. But the legislator should not allow youth to be spectators of iambi or of comedy until they are of an age to sit at the public tables and to drink strong wine; by that time education will have armed them against the evil influences of such representations.

We have made these remarks in a cursory manner—they are enough for the present occasion; but hereafter we will return to the subject and after a fuller discussion determine whether such liberty should or should not be granted, and in what way granted, if at all. Theodorus, the tragic actor, was quite right in saying that he would not allow any other actor, not even if he were quite second-rate, to enter before himself, because the spectators grew fond of the voices which they first heard. And the same principle applies universally to association with things as well as with persons, for we always like best whatever comes first. And therefore youth should be kept strangers to all that is bad, and especially to things which suggest vice or hate. When the five years have passed away, during the two following years they must look on at the pursuits which they are hereafter to learn. There are two periods of life with reference to which education has to be divided, from seven to the age of puberty, and onwards to the age of twenty-one. The poets who divide ages by sevens are in the main right: but we should observe the divisions actually made by nature; for the deficiencies of nature are what art and education seek to fill up.

Let us then first inquire if any regulations are to be laid down about children, and secondly, whether the care of them should be the concern of the state or of private individuals, which latter is in our own day the common custom, and in the third place, what these regulations should be.

BOOK VIII

1 • No one will doubt that the legislator should direct his at-
10   tention above all to the education of youth; for the neglect of
education does harm to the constitution. The citizen should
be moulded to suit the form of government under which he
lives. For each government has a peculiar character which
originally formed and which continues to preserve it. The
15   character of democracy creates democracy, and the character
of oligarchy creates oligarchy; and always the better the character, the better the government.

Again, for the exercise of any faculty or art a previous
training and habituation are required; clearly therefore for
20   the practice of excellence. And since the whole city has one
end, it is manifest that education should be one and the same
for all, and that it should be public, and not private—not as
at present, when everyone looks after his own children sepa-
25   rately, and gives them separate instruction of the sort which
he thinks best; the training in things which are of common
interest should be the same for all. Neither must we suppose
that anyone of the citizens belongs to himself, for they all
belong to the state, and are each of them a part of the state,
and the care of each part is inseparable from the care of the
30   whole. In this particular as in some others the Lacedaemonians are to be praised, for they take the greatest pains about
their children, and make education the business of the state.

2 • That education should be regulated by law and should
be an affair of state is not to be denied, but what should be
the character of this public education, and how young persons should be educated, are questions which remain to be
35   considered. As things are, there is disagreement about the
subjects. For men are by no means agreed about the things
to be taught, whether we look to excellence or the best life.
Neither is it clear whether education is more concerned with
intellectual or with moral excellence. The existing practice
40   is perplexing; no one knows on what principle we should
proceed—should the useful in life, or should excellence, or

should the higher knowledge, be the aim of our training?—
all three opinions have been entertained. Again, about the
means there is no agreement; for different persons, starting
with different ideas about the nature of excellence, naturally
disagree about the practice of it. There can be no doubt that
children should be taught those useful things which are really
necessary, but not all useful things; for occupations are divided into liberal and illiberal; and to young children should
be imparted only such kinds of knowledge as will be useful to
them without making mechanics of them. And any occupation, art, or science, which makes the body or soul or mind of
the freeman less fit for the practice or exercise of excellence,
is mechanical; wherefore we call those arts mechanical which
tend to deform the body, and likewise all paid employments,
for they absorb and degrade the mind.

There are also some liberal arts quite proper for a freeman
to acquire, but only in a certain degree, and if he attends to
them too closely, in order to attain perfection in them, the
same harmful effects will follow. The object also which a man
sets before him makes a great difference; if he does or learns
anything for his own sake or for the sake of his friends, or
with a view to excellence, the action will not appear illiberal;
but if done for the sake of others, the very same action will be
thought menial and servile. The received subjects of instruction, as I have already remarked, are partly of a liberal and
partly of an illiberal character.

3 • The customary branches of education are in number
four; they are—reading and writing, gymnastic exercises,
and music, to which is sometimes added drawing. Of these,
reading and writing and drawing are regarded as useful for the
purposes of life in a variety of ways, and gymnastic exercises
are thought to infuse courage. Concerning music a doubt
may be raised—in our own day most men cultivate it for the
sake of pleasure, but originally it was included in education,
because nature herself, as has been often said, requires that
we should be able, not only to work well, but to use leisure
well; for, as I must repeat once again, the first principle of all

action is leisure. Both are required, but leisure is better than occupation and is its end; and therefore the question must be
35 asked, what ought we to do when at leisure? Clearly we ought not to be playing, for then play would be the end of life. But if this is inconceivable, and play is needed more amid serious occupations than at other times (for he who is hard at work has need of relaxation, and play gives relaxation, whereas oc-
40 cupation is always accompanied with exertion and effort), we should introduce amusements only at suitable times, and they should be our medicines, for the emotion which they
1338ª1 create in the soul is a relaxation, and from the pleasure we obtain rest. But leisure of itself gives pleasure and happiness and enjoyment of life, which are experienced, not by the busy man, but by those who have leisure. For he who is occupied has in
5 view some end which he has not attained; but happiness is an end, since all men deem it to be accompanied with pleasure and not with pain. This pleasure, however, is regarded differently by different persons, and varies according to the habit of individuals; the pleasure of the best man is the best, and
10 springs from the noblest sources. It is clear then that there are branches of learning and education which we must study merely with a view to leisure spent in intellectual activity, and these are to be valued for their own sake; whereas those kinds of knowledge which are useful in business are to be deemed necessary, and exist for the sake of other things. And therefore our fathers admitted music into education, not on
15 the ground either of its necessity or utility, for it is not necessary, nor indeed useful in the same manner as reading and writing, which are useful in money-making, in the management of a household, in the acquisition of knowledge and in political life, nor like drawing, useful for a more correct judgement of the works of artists, nor again like gymnastics, which gives health and strength; for neither of these is to be
20 gained from music. There remains, then, the use of music for intellectual enjoyment in leisure; which is in fact evidently the reason of its introduction, this being one of the ways in which it is thought that a freeman should pass his leisure; as Homer says—

But he who alone should be called to the pleasant feast,   25

and afterwards he speaks of others whom he describes as inviting

The bard who would delight them all.

And in another place Odysseus says there is no better way of passing life than when men's hearts are merry and

The banqueters in the hall, sitting in order, hear the voice of   30
the minstrel.

It is evident, then, that there is a sort of education in which parents should train their sons, not as being useful or necessary, but because it is liberal or noble. Whether this is of one kind only, or of more than one, and if so, what they are, and how they are to be imparted, must hereafter be determined. Thus much we are already in a position to say; for the ancients bear witness to us—their opinion may be gath-   35
ered from the fact that music is one of the received and traditional branches of education. Further, it is clear that children should be instructed in some useful things—for example, in reading and writing—not only for their usefulness, but also because many other sorts of knowledge are acquired through them. With a like view they may be taught drawing, not to   40
prevent their making mistakes in their own purchases, or in order that they may not be imposed upon in the buying or selling of articles, but perhaps rather because it makes them   1338ᵇ1
judges of the beauty of the human form. To be always seeking after the useful does not become free and exalted souls. Now it is clear that in education practice must be used before theory, and the body be trained before the mind; and there-   5
fore boys should be handed over to the trainer, who creates in them the proper habit of body, and to the wrestling-master, who teaches them their exercises.

4 • Of those states which in our own day seem to take the greatest care of children, some aim at producing in them an athletic habit, but they only injure their bodies and stunt   10

their growth. Although the Lacedaemonians have not fallen into this mistake, yet they brutalize their children by laborious exercises which they think will make them courageous. But in truth, as we have often repeated, education should not
15 be exclusively, or principally, directed to this end. And even if we suppose the Lacedaemonians to be right in their end, they do not attain it. For among barbarians and among animals courage is found associated, not with the greatest ferocity, but with a gentle and lion-like temper. There are many
20 races who are ready enough to kill and eat men, such as the Achaeans and Heniochi, who both live about the Black Sea; and there are other mainland tribes, as bad or worse, who all live by plunder, but have no courage. It is notorious that
25 the Lacedaemonians themselves, while they alone were assiduous in their laborious drill, were superior to others, but now they are beaten both in war and gymnastic exercises. For their ancient superiority did not depend on their mode of training their youth, but only on the circumstance that
30 they trained them when their only rivals did not. Hence we may infer that what is noble, not what is brutal, should have the first place; no wolf or other wild animal will face a really noble danger; such dangers are for the brave man. And parents who devote their children to gymnastics while they neglect their necessary education, in reality make them me-
35 chanics; for they make them useful to the art of statesmanship in one quality only, and even in this the argument proves them to be inferior to others. We should judge the Lacedaemonians not from what they have been, but from what they are; for now they have rivals who compete with their education; formerly they had none.

It is an admitted principle that gymnastic exercises should
40 be employed in education, and that for children they should be of a lighter kind, avoiding severe diet or painful toil, lest the growth of the body be impaired. The evil of excessive
1339ª1 training in early years is strikingly proved by the example of the Olympic victors; for not more than two or three of them have gained a prize both as boys and as men; their early training and severe gymnastic exercises exhausted their constitu-

tions. When boyhood is over, three years should be spent in other studies; the period of life which follows may then be devoted to hard exercise and strict diet. Men ought not to labour at the same time with their minds and with their bodies; for the two kinds of labour are opposed to one another; the labour of the body impedes the mind, and the labour of the mind the body.

5 • Concerning music there are some questions which we have already raised; these we may now resume and carry further; and our remarks will serve as a prelude to this or any other discussion of the subject. It is not easy to determine the nature of music, or why anyone should have a knowledge of it. Shall we say, for the sake of amusement and relaxation, like sleep or drinking, which are not good in themselves, but are pleasant, and at the same time 'make care to cease', as Euripides says? And for this end men also appoint music, and make use of all three alike—sleep, drinking, music—to which some add dancing. Or shall we argue that music conduces to excellence, on the ground that it can form our minds and habituate us to true pleasures as our bodies are made by gymnastic to be of a certain character? Or shall we say that it contributes to the enjoyment of leisure and mental cultivation, which is a third alternative? Now obviously youths are not to be instructed with a view to their amusement, for learning is no amusement, but is accompanied with pain. Neither is intellectual enjoyment suitable to boys of that age, for it is the end, and that which is imperfect cannot attain the end. But perhaps it may be said that boys learn music for the sake of the amusement which they will have when they are grown up. If so, why should they learn themselves, and not, like the Persian and Median kings, enjoy the pleasure and instruction which is derived from hearing others? (for surely persons who have made music the business and profession of their lives will be better performers than those who practise only long enough to learn). If they must learn music, on the same principle they should learn cookery, which is absurd. And even granting that music may form the character, the

objection still holds: why should we learn ourselves? Why cannot we attain true pleasure and form a correct judgement from hearing others, as the Lacedaemonians do?—for they, without learning music, nevertheless can correctly judge, as they say, of good and bad melodies. Or again, if music should be used to promote cheerfulness and refined intellectual enjoyment, the objection still remains—why should we learn ourselves instead of enjoying the performances of others? We may illustrate what we are saying by our conception of the gods; for in the poets Zeus does not himself sing or play on the lyre. Indeed we call professional performers artisans; no freeman would play or sing unless he were intoxicated or in jest. But these matters may be left for the present.

The first question is whether music is or is not to be a part of education. Of the three things mentioned in our discussion, which does it produce—education or amusement or intellectual enjoyment?—for it may be reckoned under all three, and seems to share in the nature of all of them. Amusement is for the sake of relaxation, and relaxation is of necessity sweet, for it is the remedy of pain caused by toil; and intellectual enjoyment is universally acknowledged to contain an element not only of the noble but of the pleasant, for happiness is made up of both. All men agree that music is one of the pleasantest things, whether with or without song; as Musaeus says,

Song is to mortals of all things the sweetest.

Hence and with good reason it is introduced into social gatherings and entertainments, because it makes the hearts of men glad: so that on this ground alone we may assume that the young ought to be trained in it. For innocent pleasures are not only in harmony with the end of life, but they also provide relaxation. And whereas men rarely attain the end, but often rest by the way and amuse themselves, not only with a view to a further end, but also for the pleasure's sake, it may be well at times to let them find a refreshment in music. It sometimes happens that men make amusement the end, for the end probably contains some element of plea-

sure, though not any ordinary pleasure; but they mistake the
lower for the higher, and in seeking for the one find the other,
since every pleasure has a likeness to the end of action. For
the end is not desirable for the sake of any future good, nor   35
do the pleasures which we have described exist for the sake of
any future good but of the past, that is to say, they are the alleviation of past toils and pains. And we may infer this to be the
reason why men seek happiness from these pleasures. But
music is pursued, not only as an alleviation of past toil, but   40
also as providing recreation. And who can say whether, having this use, it may not also have a nobler one? In addition to
this common pleasure, felt and shared in by all (for the plea-   1340ᵃ1
sure given by music is natural, and therefore adapted to all
ages and characters), may it not have also some influence over   5
the character and the soul? It must have such an influence if
characters are affected by it. And that they are so affected is
proved in many ways, and not least by the power which the
songs of Olympus exercise; for beyond question they inspire   10
enthusiasm, and enthusiasm is an emotion of the character
of the soul. Besides, when men hear imitations, even apart
from the rhythms and tunes themselves, their feelings move
in sympathy. Since then music is a pleasure, and excellence   15
consists in rejoicing and loving and hating rightly, there is
clearly nothing which we are so much concerned to acquire
and to cultivate as the power of forming right judgements,
and of taking delight in good dispositions and noble actions.
Rhythm and melody supply imitations of anger and gentle-
ness, and also of courage and temperance, and of all the quali-   20
ties contrary to these, and of the other qualities of character,
which hardly fall short of the actual affections, as we know
from our own experience, for in listening to such strains our
souls undergo a change. The habit of feeling pleasure or pain
at mere representations is not far removed from the same
feeling about realities; for example, if any one delights in the   25
sight of a statue for its beauty only, it necessarily follows that
the sight of the original will be pleasant to him. The objects of
no other sense, such as taste or touch, have any resemblance   30
to moral qualities; in visible objects there is only a little, for

there are figures which are of a moral character, but only to a slight extent, and all do not participate in the feeling about them. Again, figures and colours are not imitations, but signs, of character, indications which the body gives of states of
35 feeling. The connexion of them with morals is slight, but in so far as there is any, young men should be taught to look, not at the works of Pauson, but at those of Polygnotus, or any other painter or sculptor who expresses character. On the
40 other hand, even in mere melodies there is an imitation of character, for the musical modes differ essentially from one another, and those who hear them are differently affected
1340^b1 by each. Some of them make men sad and grave, like the so-called Mixolydian, others enfeeble the mind, like the relaxed modes, another, again, produces a moderate and settled temper, which appears to be the peculiar effect of the Dorian; the
5 Phrygian inspires enthusiasm. The whole subject has been well treated by philosophical writers on this branch of education, and they confirm their arguments by facts. The same principles apply to rhythms; some have a character of rest,
10 others of motion, and of these latter again, some have a more vulgar, others a nobler movement. Enough has been said to show that music has a power of forming the character, and should therefore be introduced into the education of the
15 young. The study is suited to the stage of youth, for young persons will not, if they can help, endure anything which is not sweetened by pleasure, and music has a natural sweetness. There seems to be in us a sort of affinity to musical modes and rhythms, which makes some philosophers say that the soul is a harmony, others, that it possesses harmony.

20   6 • And now we have to determine the question which has been already raised, whether children should be themselves taught to sing and play or not. Clearly there is a considerable difference made in the character by the actual practice of the art. It is difficult, if not impossible, for those who do
25 not perform to be good judges of the performance of others. Besides, children should have something to do, and the rattle of Archytas, which people give to their children in order to

amuse them and prevent them from breaking anything in the house, was a capital invention, for a young thing cannot be quiet. The rattle is a toy suited to the infant mind, and education is a rattle or toy for children of a larger growth. We conclude then that they should be taught music in such a way as to become not only critics but performers.

The question what is or is not suitable for different ages may be easily answered; nor is there any difficulty in meeting the objection of those who say that the study of music is mechanical. We reply in the first place, that they who are to be judges must also be performers, and that they should begin to practise early, although when they are older they may be spared the execution; they must have learned to appreciate what is good and to delight in it, thanks to the knowledge which they acquired in their youth. As to the vulgarizing effect which music is supposed to exercise, this is a question which we shall have no difficulty in determining when we have considered to what extent freemen who are being trained to political excellence should pursue the art, what melodies and what rhythms they should be allowed to use, and what instruments should be employed in teaching them to play; for even the instrument makes a difference. The answer to the objection turns upon these distinctions; for it is quite possible that certain methods of teaching and learning music do really have a degrading effect. It is evident then that the learning of music ought not to impede the business of riper years, or to degrade the body or render it unfit for civil or military training, whether for bodily exercises at the time or for later studies.

The right measure will be attained if students of music stop short of the arts which are practised in professional contests, and do not seek to acquire those fantastic marvels of execution which are now the fashion in such contests, and from these have passed into education. Let the young practise even such music as we have prescribed, only until they are able to feel delight in noble melodies and rhythms, and not merely in that common part of music in which every slave or child and even some animals find pleasure.

From these principles we may also infer what instruments should be used. The flute, or any other instrument which requires great skill, as for example the harp, ought not to be admitted into education, but only such as will make men intelligent students of music or of the other parts of education.
20 Besides, the flute is not an instrument which is expressive of character; it is too exciting. The proper time for using it is when the performance aims not at instruction, but at the relief of the passions. And there is a further objection; the impediment which the flute presents to the use of the voice detracts from its educational value. The ancients therefore
25 were right in forbidding the flute to youths and freemen, although they had once allowed it. For when their wealth gave them a greater inclination to leisure, and they had loftier notions of excellence, being also elated with their success, both
30 before and after the Persian War, with more zeal than discernment they pursued every kind of knowledge, and so they introduced the flute into education. In Lacedaemon there was a choragus who led the chorus with a flute, and at Athens the instrument became so popular that most freemen could
35 play upon it. The popularity is shown by the tablet which Thrasippus dedicated when he furnished the chorus to Ecphantides. Later experience enabled men to judge what was or was not really conducive to excellence, and they rejected both the flute and several other old-fashioned instruments, such as the Lydian harp, the many-stringed lyre, the 'heptagon',
1341^{b}1 'triangle', 'sambuca', and the like—which are intended only to give pleasure to the hearer, and require extraordinary skill of hand. There is a meaning also in the myth of the ancients, which tells how Athene invented the flute and then threw it away. It was not a bad idea of theirs that the Goddess disliked
5 the instrument because it made the face ugly; but with still more reason may we say that she rejected it because the acquirement of flute-playing contributes nothing to the mind, since to Athene we ascribe both knowledge and art. Thus then we reject the professional instruments and also the pro-
10 fessional mode of education in music (and by professional we mean that which is adopted in contests), for in this the

performer practises the art, not for the sake of his own improvement, but in order to give pleasure, and that of a vulgar sort, to his hearers. For this reason the execution of such music is not the part of a freeman but of a paid performer, and the result is that the performers are vulgarized, for the end at which they aim is bad. The vulgarity of the spectator tends to lower the character of the music and therefore of the performers; they look to him—he makes them what they are, and fashions even their bodies by the movements which he expects them to exhibit.

7 • We have also to consider rhythms and modes, and their use in education. Shall we use them all or make a distinction? and shall the same distinction be made for those who practise music with a view to education, or shall it be some other? Now we see that music is produced by melody and rhythm, and we ought to know what influence these have respectively on education, and whether we should prefer excellence in melody or excellence in rhythm. But as the subject has been very well treated by many musicians of the present day, and also by philosophers who have had considerable experience of musical education, to these we would refer the more exact student of the subject; we shall only speak of it now after the manner of the legislator, stating the general principles.

We accept the division of melodies proposed by certain philosophers into melodies of character, melodies of action, and passionate or inspiring melodies, each having, as they say, a mode corresponding to it. But we maintain further that music should be studied, not for the sake of one, but of many benefits, that is to say, with a view to education, or purgation (the word 'purgation' we use at present without explanation, but when hereafter we speak of poetry, we will treat the subject with more precision); music may also serve for intellectual enjoyment, for relaxation and for recreation after exertion. It is clear, therefore, that all the modes must be employed by us, but not all of them in the same manner. In education the modes most expressive of character are to be preferred, but in listening to the performances of others

we may admit the modes of action and passion also. For feelings such as pity and fear, or, again, enthusiasm, exist very
strongly in some souls, and have more or less influence over
all. Some persons fall into a religious frenzy, and we see them
restored as a result of the sacred melodies—when they have
used the melodies that excite the soul to mystic frenzy—as
though they had found healing and purgation. Those who
are influenced by pity or fear, and every emotional nature,
must have a like experience, and others in so far as each is
susceptible to such emotions, and all are in a manner purged
and their souls lightened and delighted. The melodies which
purge the passions likewise give an innocent pleasure to mankind. Such are the modes and the melodies in which those
who perform music at the theatre should be invited to compete. But since the spectators are of two kinds—the one free
and educated, and the other a vulgar crowd composed of artisans, labourers, and the like—there ought to be contests and
exhibitions instituted for the relaxation of the second class
also. And the music will correspond to their minds; for as
their minds are perverted from the natural state, so there are
perverted modes and highly strung and unnaturally coloured
melodies. A man receives pleasure from what is natural to
him, and therefore professional musicians may be allowed
to practise this lower sort of music before an audience of a
lower type. But, for the purposes of education, as I have already said, those modes and melodies should be employed
which are expressive of character, such as the Dorian, as we
said before; though we may include any others which are approved by philosophers who have had a musical education.
The Socrates of the *Republic* is wrong in retaining only the
Phrygian mode along with the Dorian, and the more so because he rejects the flute; for the Phrygian is to the modes
what the flute is to musical instruments—both of them are
exciting and emotional. Poetry proves this, for Bacchic frenzy
and all similar emotions are most suitably expressed by the
flute, and are better set to the Phrygian than to any other
mode. The dithyramb, for example, is acknowledged to be
Phrygian, a fact of which the connoisseurs of music offer

many proofs, saying, among other things, that Philoxenus, having attempted to compose his *Mysians* as a dithyramb in the Dorian mode, found it impossible, and fell back by the 10 very nature of things into the more appropriate Phrygian. All men agree that the Dorian music is the gravest and manliest. And whereas we say that the extremes should be avoided and the mean followed, and whereas the Dorian is a mean be- 15 tween the other modes, it is evident that our youth should be taught the Dorian music.

Two principles have to be kept in view, what is possible, and what is becoming: at these every man ought to aim. But even these are relative to age; the old, who have lost their powers, 20 cannot very well sing the high-strung modes, and nature herself seems to suggest that their songs should be of the more relaxed kind. That is why the musicians too blame Socrates, and with justice, for rejecting the relaxed modes in education under the idea that they are intoxicating, not in the ordinary 25 sense of intoxication (for wine rather tends to excite men), but because they have no strength in them. And so, with a view also to the time of life when men begin to grow old, they ought to practise the gentler modes and melodies as well as the others, and, further, any mode, such as the Lydian above all others ap- 30 pears to be, which is suited to children of tender age, and possesses the elements both of order and of education. Thus it is clear that education should be based upon three principles— the mean, the possible, the becoming, these three.

ECONOMICS *

E. S. Forster

(Book III by G. C. Armstrong)

BOOK I

1343ª1 1 • THE SCIENCES OF POLITICS AND ECONOMICS differ not only as widely as a household and a city (the subject-matter with which they severally deal), but also in the fact that the science of politics involves a number of rulers, whereas the sphere of economics is a monarchy.

5 Now certain of the arts fall into sub-divisions, and it does not pertain to the same art to manufacture and to use the article manufactured, for instance, a lyre or pipes; but the function of political science is both to constitute a city in the beginning and also when it has come into being to make a right use of it. It is clear, therefore, that it must be the function of economic science too both to found a household and also to make use of it.

10 Now a city is an aggregate made up of households and land and property, self-sufficient with regard to a good life. This is clear from the fact that, if men cannot attain this end, the community is dissolved. Further, it is for this end that they associate together; and that for the sake of which any particular thing exists and has come into being is its substance. It is evi-15 dent, therefore, that economics is prior in origin to politics; for its function is prior, since a household is part of a city. We must therefore examine economics and see what its function is.

2 • The parts of a household are man and property. But since the nature of any given thing is most quickly seen by 20 taking its smallest parts, this would apply also to a household. So, according to Hesiod, it would be necessary that there should be

---

*The traditional *Corpus Aristotelicum* contains several works probably not written by Aristotle. The authenticity of the title of this work has been doubted.

First and foremost a house, a woman, and an ox for the plough ... ,[1]

for the first point concerns subsistence, the second free men. We should have, therefore, to organize properly the association of husband and wife; and this involves providing what sort of a woman she ought to be. In regard to property the first care is that which comes naturally. Now in the course of nature the art of agriculture is prior, and next come those arts which extract the products of the earth, mining and the like. Agriculture ranks first because of its justice; for it does not take anything away from men, either with their consent, as do retail trading and the mercenary arts, or against their will, as do the warlike arts. Further, agriculture is natural; for by nature all derive their sustenance from their mother, and so men derive it from the earth. In addition to this it also conduces greatly to bravery; for it does not make men's bodies unserviceable, as do the illiberal arts, but it renders them able to lead an open-air life and work hard; furthermore it makes them adventurous against the foe, for husbandmen are the only citizens whose property lies outside the fortifications.

3 · As regards the human part of the household, the first care is concerning a wife; for a common life is above all things natural to the female and to the male. For we have elsewhere laid down the principle that nature aims at producing many such forms of association, just as also it produces the various kinds of animals. But it is impossible for the female to accomplish this without the male or the male without the female, so that their common life has necessarily arisen. Now in the other animals this intercourse is not based on reason, but depends on the amount of natural instinct which they possess and is entirely for the purpose of procreation. But in the civilized and more intelligent animals the bond of unity is more complex (for in them we see more mutual help and goodwill and co-operation), above all in the case

TEXT: B. A. van Groningen and A. Wartelle, Budé, Paris, 1968
[1] *Works and Days*, 405.

of man, because the female and the male co-operate to ensure not merely existence but a good life. And the production of children is not only a way of serving nature but also
of securing advantage; for the trouble which parents bestow
upon their helpless children when they are themselves vig-
orous is repaid to them in old age when they are helpless by
their children, who are then in their full vigour. At the same
time also nature thus periodically provides for the perpetu-
ation of mankind as a species, since she cannot do so individually. Thus the nature both of the man and of the woman
has been preordained by the will of heaven to live a common
life. For they are distinguished in that the powers which they
possess are not applicable to purposes in all cases identical,
but in some respects their functions are opposed to one another though they all tend to the same end. For nature has
made the one sex stronger, the other weaker, that the latter
through fear may be the more cautious, while the former by
its courage is better able to ward off attacks; and that the one
may acquire possessions outside the house, the other preserve those within. In the performance of work, she made
one sex able to lead a sedentary life and not strong enough
to endure exposure, the other less adapted for quiet pursuits
but well constituted for outdoor activities; and in relation to
offspring she has made both share in the procreation of children, but each render its peculiar service towards them, the
woman by nurturing, the man by educating them.

4 • First, then, he must not do her any wrong; for thus a
man is less likely himself to be wronged. This is inculcated
by the general law, as the Pythagoreans say, that one least of
all should injure a wife as being 'a suppliant and taken from
her hearth'. Now wrong inflicted by a husband is the formation of connexions outside his own house. As regards association, she ought not to need him when he is present or be
incapacitated in his absence, but should be accustomed to
be competent whether he is present or not. The saying of
Hesiod is a good one:

A man should marry a maiden, that habits discreet he may teach her.[2]

For dissimilarity of habits tends more than anything to destroy affection. As regards adornment, husband and wife ought not to approach one another with false affectation in their person any more than in their manners; for if the society of husband and wife requires such embellishment, it is no better than play-acting on the tragic stage.

5 • Of possessions, that which is the best and the worthiest subject of economics comes first and is most essential—I mean, man. It is necessary therefore first to provide oneself with good slaves. Now slaves are of two kinds, the overseer and the worker. And since we see that methods of education produce a certain character in the young, it is necessary when one has procured slaves to bring up carefully those to whom the higher duties are to be entrusted. The intercourse of a master with his slaves should be such as to allow them to be neither insolent nor uncontrolled. To the higher class of slaves he ought to give some share of honour, and to the workers abundance of nourishment. And since the drinking of wine makes even freemen insolent, and many nations even of freemen abstain therefrom (the Carthaginians, for instance, when they are on military service), it is clear that wine ought never to be given to slaves, or at any rate very seldom. Three things make up the life of a slave, work, punishment, and food. To give them food but no punishment and no work makes them insolent; and that they should have work and punishment but no food is tyrannical and destroys their efficiency. It remains therefore to give them work and sufficient food; for it is impossible to rule without offering rewards, and a slave's reward is his food. And just as all other men become worse when they get no advantage by being better and there are no rewards for virtue and vice, so also is it

[2] *Works and Days*, 699.

with servants. Therefore we must take careful notice and bestow or withhold everything, whether food or clothing or leisure or punishments, according to merit, in word and deed
10 following the practice adopted by physicians in the matter
of medicine, remembering at the same time that food is not
medicine because it must be given continually.

The slave who is best suited for his work is the kind that
is neither too cowardly nor too courageous. Slaves who have
either of these characteristics are injurious to their owners;
those who are too cowardly lack endurance, while the high-
15 spirited are not easy to control. All ought to have a definite
end in view; for it is just and beneficial to offer slaves their
freedom as a prize, for they are willing to work when a prize
is set before them and a limit of time is defined. One ought to
bind slaves to one's service by letting them have children, and
not to have many persons of the same race in a household,
any more than in a state. One ought to provide sacrifices and
pleasures more for the sake of slaves than for freemen; for in
20 the case of the former there are present more of the reasons
why such things have been instituted.

6 • The householder has four roles in relation to wealth.
He ought to be able to acquire it, and to guard it; otherwise
there is no advantage in acquiring it, but it is a case of drawing
25 water with a sieve, or the proverbial jar with a hole in it. Further, he ought to be able to order his possessions aright and
make a proper use of them; for it is for these purposes that we
require wealth. The various kinds of property ought to be distinguished, and those which are productive ought to be more
numerous than the unproductive, and the sources of income
ought to be so distributed that they may not run a risk with
all their possessions at the same time. For the preservation of
30 wealth it is best to follow both the Persian and the Laconian
methods. The Attic system of economy is also useful; for they
sell their produce and buy what they want, and thus there is
not the need of a storehouse in the smaller establishments.
The Persian system was that everything should be organized
and that the master should superintend everything person-

ally, as Dio said of Dionysius; for no one looks after the prop- 35
erty of others as well as he looks after his own, so that, as far
as possible, a man ought to attend to everything himself. The 1345ᵃ1
sayings of the Persian and the Libyan may not come amiss;
the former of whom, when asked what was the best thing to
fatten a horse, replied, 'His master's eye', while the Libyan,
when asked what was the best manure, answered, 'The master's foot-prints'. Some things should be attended to by the 5
master, others by his wife, according to the sphere allotted to
each in the economy of the household. Inspections need only
be made occasionally in small establishments, but should be
frequent where overseers are employed. For good imitation is
impossible unless a good example is set, especially when trust 10
is delegated to others; for unless the master is careful, it is impossible for his overseers to be careful. And since it is good for
the formation of character and useful in the interests of economy, masters ought to rise earlier than their slaves and retire
to rest later, and a house should never be left unguarded any
more than a city, and when anything needs doing it ought not
to be left undone, whether it be day or night. There are occa- 15
sions when a master should rise while it is still night; for this
helps to make a man healthy and wealthy and wise. On small
estates the Attic system of disposing of the produce is a useful
one; but on large estates, where a distinction is made between
yearly and monthly expenditure and likewise between the 20
daily and the occasional use of household appliances, such
matters must be entrusted to overseers. Furthermore, a peri-
odical inspection should be made, in order to ascertain what
is still existing and what is lacking.

The house must be arranged both with a view to one's possessions and for the health and well-being of its inhabitants. 25
By possessions I mean the consideration of what is suitable
for produce and clothing, and in the case of produce what is
suitable for dry and what for moist produce, and amongst
other possessions what is suitable for property whether animate or inanimate, for slaves and freemen, women and men, 30
strangers and citizens. With a view to well-being and health,
the house ought to be airy in summer and sunny in winter.

This would be best secured if it faces north and is not as wide as it is long. In large establishments a man who is no use for other purposes seems to be usefully employed as a doorkeeper to safeguard what is brought into and out of the house. For the ready use of household appliances the Laconian method is a good one; for everything ought to have its own proper place and so be ready for use and not require to be searched for.

BOOK II

1 • He who intends to practise economy aright ought to be fully acquainted with the places in which his labour lies and to be naturally endowed with good parts and by choice industrious and upright; for if he is lacking in any of these respects, he will make many mistakes in the business which he takes in hand.

Now there are four kinds of economy, that of the king, that of the provincial governor, that of the city, and that of the individual. This is a broad method of division; and we shall find that the other forms of economy fall within it.

Of these that of the king is the most important and the simplest, . . . ,[1] that of the city is the most varied and the easiest, that of the individual the least important and the most varied. They must necessarily have most of their characteristics in common; but it is the points which are peculiar to each kind that we must consider. Let us therefore examine royal economy first. It is universal in its scope, but has four special departments—the coinage, exports, imports, and expenditure. To take each of these separately: in regard to the coinage, I mean the question as to what coin should be struck and when; in the matter of exports and imports, what commodities it will be advantageous to receive from the satraps in tax and dispose of and when; in regard to expenditure, what expenses ought to be curtailed and when, and whether

___

[1]van Groningen and Wartelle mark a lacuna here.

one should pay what is expended in coin or in commodities which have an equivalent value.

Let us next take satrapic economy. Here we find six kinds of revenue—[from land, from the peculiar products of the district, from merchandise, from taxes, from cattle, and from all other sources].[2] Of these the first and most important is that which comes from land (which some call tax on land-produce, others tithe); next in importance is the revenue from peculiar products, from gold, or silver, or copper, or anything else which is found in a particular locality; thirdly comes that derived from merchandise; fourthly, the revenue from the cultivation of the soil and from market-dues; fifthly, that which comes from cattle, which is called tax on animal produce or tithe; and sixthly, that which is derived from men, which is called the poll-tax or tax on artisans.

Thirdly, let us examine the economy of the city. Here the most important source of revenue is from the peculiar products of the country, next comes that derived from merchandise and customs, and lastly that which comes from the ordinary taxes.

Fourthly and lastly, let us take individual economy. Here we find wide divergences, because economy is not necessarily always practised with one aim in view. It is the least important kind of economy, because the incomings and expenses are small. Here the main source of revenue is the land, next other kinds of regular activity, and thirdly investments of money.

Further, there is a consideration which is common to all branches of economy and which calls for the most careful attention, especially in individual economy, namely, that the expenditure must not exceed the income.

Now that we have mentioned the divisions of the subject, we must next consider whether the satrapy or city with which we are dealing can produce all, or the most important revenues which we have just distinguished; if it can, it should use them. Next we must consider which sources of revenue do

[2] Excised by van Groningen and Wartelle.

not exist at all but can be introduced, or are at present small but can be augmented; and which of the expenses at present incurred, and to what amount, can be dispensed with without doing any harm to the whole.

25 We have now mentioned the various kinds of economy and their constituent parts. We have further made a collection of all the methods that we conceived to be worth mentioning, which men of former days have employed or cunningly devised in order to provide themselves with money. For we conceived that this information also might be useful; for

30 a man will be able to apply some of these instances to such business as he himself takes in hand.

2 • Cypselus, the Corinthian, having vowed to Zeus that, if he made himself master of the city, he would dedicate to him all the property of the Corinthians, ordered them to draw up

1346ᵇ1 a list of their possessions. When they had done so, he took a tenth part from each citizen and told them to trade with the remainder. As each year came round, he did the same thing again, with the result that in ten years he had all that he had consecrated to the god, while the Corinthians had acquired

5 other property.

Lygdamis, the Naxian, having driven certain men into exile, when no one was willing to buy their possessions except at a low price, sold them to the exiles themselves. And offer-

10 ings belonging to them which were lying half finished in certain workshops he sold to the exiles and any one else who wished to buy them, allowing the name of the purchaser to be inscribed upon them.

The Byzantines being in need of money sold the sacred enclosures belonging to the state. Those which were fertile they sold on lease, and those which were unproductive in perpetuity. They treated in the same way the enclosures which belonged to associations and clans and all which were sit-

15 uated on private estates; for the owners of the rest of the property bought them at a high price. To the associations they sold other lands, viz. the public lands round the gymna-

20 sium, or the market-place, or the harbour; and they sold the

places where markets were held at which various commodities were sold, and the rights over the sea-fisheries and the sale of salt, and . . . [3] of jugglers, and soothsayers, and druggists, and other such persons plied their trades; but they ordered them to pay over a third of their profits. And they sold the right of changing money to a single bank, and no one else might either give money in exchange to anyone, or receive 25 it in exchange from anyone, under penalty of forfeiting the money. And whereas there was a law amongst them that no one should have political rights who was not born of parents who were both citizens, being in want of money they passed a decree that a man who was sprung from a citizen on one side only should become a citizen if he paid down thirty minae.

And as they were suffering from want of food and lack of 30 money, they made the ships from the Black Sea put in; but, as time went on, the merchants protested and so they paid them interest at ten per cent. and ordered those who purchased anything to pay the ten per cent. in addition to the price. And whereas certain resident aliens had lent money on security 1347ª1 of property, because these had not the right to hold property, they passed a decree that any one who wished could obtain a title to the property by paying a third of the loan to the state.

Hippias, the Athenian, put up for sale the parts of the upper rooms which projected into the public streets, and 5 the steps and fences in front of the houses, and the doors which opened outwards. The owners of the property therefore bought them, and a large sum was thus collected. He also declared the coinage then current in Athens to be base, and fixing a price for it ordered it to be brought to him; but when they met to consider the striking of a new type of coin, 10 he gave them back the same money again. And if anyone was about to equip a trireme or a division of cavalry or to provide a tragic chorus or incur expense on any other such state-service, he fixed a moderate fine and allowed him, if he liked, to pay this and be enrolled amongst those who had performed state services. He also ordered that a measure of

[3] van Groningen and Wartelle mark a lacuna.

barley, and another of wheat, and an obol should be brought
to the priestess of Athena-on-the-Acropolis on behalf of anyone who died, and that the same offering should be made by
anyone to whom a child was born.

The Athenians who dwell in Potidaea, being in need of
money to carry on war, ordered all the citizens to draw up a
list of their property, each man enrolling not his whole property collectively in his own deme, but each piece of property
separately in the place where it was situated, in order that the
poor might give in an assessment; anyone who possessed no
property was to assess his own person at two minae. On the
basis of this assessment they each contributed the amount
enjoined.

Sosipolis of Antissa, when the city was in want of money,
since the citizens were wont to celebrate the feast of Dionysus with great splendour and every year went to great expense
in providing, amongst other things, very costly victims, persuaded them, when the festival was near at hand, to vow to
Dionysus that they would give double offerings the next year
and collect and sell the dedications for the current year. Thus
a substantial sum was collected for the needs of the moment.

The people of Lampsacus, expecting a large fleet of triremes to come against them, ordered the dealers to sell a
medimnus of barley-meal, of which the market price was four
drachmae, at six *drachmae*, and a *chous* of oil, the price of which
was three *drachmae*, at four *drachmae* and a half, and likewise
wine and the other commodities. The individual seller thus
received the old price, while the city gained the surplus and
so was well provided with money.

The people of Heraclea, when they were sending forty
ships against the tyrants on the Bosporus, not being well provided with money, bought up from the merchants all their
corn and oil and wine and the rest of their stores, fixing a date
in the future at which they were to make the payment. Now
it suited the merchants better to sell their cargoes whole-
sale rather than retail. So the people of Heraclea, giving the
soldiers two months' pay, took the provisions with them on
board merchant-vessels and put an official in charge of each

of the ships. When they reached the enemies' territory, the soldiers bought up all the provisions from them. Thus money was collected before the generals had to pay the soldiers again, and so the same money was distributed time after time until they returned home.

When the Samians begged for money for their return home, the Lacedaemonians passed a decree that they would fast for one day, themselves and their domestics and their beasts of burden, and would give to the Samians the amount that each of them usually expended.

The Chalcedonians, having a large number of foreign mercenaries in their city, owed them pay which they could not give them. They therefore proclaimed that if any citizen or resident alien had any right of seizure against any state or individual and wished to exercise it, they should give in their names. When many did so, they seized the ships which sailed into the Black Sea on a plausible pretext, and appointed a time at which they promised to give an account of their captures. When a large sum of money had been collected they dismissed the soldiers and submitted themselves to trial for their reprisals, and the state out of its revenues made restitution to those who had been unjustly plundered.

When the people of Cyzicus were at variance and the popular party had gained the upper hand and the wealthy citizens had been imprisoned, they passed a decree, since they owed money to their soldiers, that they would not put their prisoners to death, but would exact money from them and send them into exile.

The Chians, who have a law that a public register of debts should be kept, being in want of money decreed that debtors should pay their debts to the state and that the state should disburse the interest from its revenues to the creditors until they should be able to restore the principal.

Mausolus, tyrant of Caria, when the king of Persia sent and ordered him to pay his tribute, collected together the richest men in the country and told them that the king was demanding the tribute, but he himself could not provide it. And certain men, who had been suborned to do so,

immediately promised to contribute and named the amount that each would give. Upon this the wealthier men, partly through shame and partly from fear, promised and actually
10 contributed far larger sums.

On another occasion when he was in need of money, he called together the Mylassians and told them that this city of his, though it was their mother-city, was unfortified and that the king of Persia was marching against him. He therefore ordered the Mylassians each to contribute as much money as
15 possible, saying that by what they paid now they would save the rest of their possessions. When a large contribution had been made, he kept the money and told them that at the moment the god would not allow them to build the wall.

Condalus, a governor under Mausolus, whenever during his passage through the country anyone brought him a
20 sheep or a pig or a calf, used to make a record of the donor and the date and order him to take it back home and keep it until he returned. When he thought that sufficient time had elapsed, he used to ask for the animal which was being kept for him, and reckoned up and demanded the produce-tax on it as well. And any trees which projected over or fell into the
25 royal roads he used to sell . . . the produce-taxes.[4] And if any soldier died, he demanded a drachma as a toll for the corpse passing the gates; and so he not only received money from this source, but also the officers could not deceive him as to the date of the soldier's death. Also, noticing that the Lycians were fond of wearing their hair long, he said that a dispatch
30 had come from the king of Persia ordering him to send hair to make false fringes and that he was therefore commanded by Mausolus to cut off their hair. He therefore said that, if they would pay him a fixed poll-tax, he would have hair sent from Greece. They gladly gave him what he asked, and a large sum of money was collected from a great number of them.

35 Aristotle, the Rhodian, who was governor of Phocaea, was in want of money. Perceiving therefore that there were
1348ᵇ1 two parties amongst the Phocaeans, he made secret over-

---

[4]van Groningen and Wartelle mark a lacuna.

tures to one party saying that the other faction was offering him money on condition that he would turn the scale in their favour, but that for his own part he would rather receive money from *them* and give the direction of affairs into their hands. When they heard this, those who were present immediately gave him the money, supplying him with all he asked for. He then went to the other party and showed them what he had received from their opponents; whereupon they also professed their willingness to give him an equal sum. So he took the money from both parties and reconciled them one with another. Also, noticing that there was much litigation among the citizens and that there were grievances of long standing among them owing to war, he established a court of law and proclaimed that unless they submitted their cases to judgement within a period which he appointed, there would be no further settlement of their former claims. Then getting control of a number of suits and of the cases which were subject to appeal with damages, and receiving money from both parties by other means, he collected a large sum.

The Clazomenians, when they were suffering from famine and were in want of money, decreed that private individuals who had any olive oil should lend it to the state, which would pay them interest. Now olives are abundant in this country. When the owners had lent them the oil, they hired ships and sent it to the marts from which their corn came, giving the value of the oil as a pledge. And when they owed pay to their soldiers to the amount of twenty talents and could not provide it, they paid the generals four talents a year as interest. But finding that they did not reduce the principal and that they were continually spending money to no purpose, they struck an iron coinage to represent a sum of twenty talents of silver, and then distributing it among the richest citizens in proportion to their wealth they received in exchange an equivalent sum in silver. Thus the individual citizens had money to disburse for their daily needs and the state was freed from debt. They then paid them interest out of their revenues and continually divided it up and distributed it in proper proportions, and called in the iron coinage.

The Selymbrians were once in need of money: they had a law which forbade the export of corn; when a famine oc-
35 curred and they had a supply of last season's corn, they passed a decree that private persons should hand over their corn to the state at a fixed price, each reserving a year's supply; they
1349ᵃ1 then allowed anyone who wished to export his supply, fixing a price which they thought would give them a profit.

The people of Abydos, when their land was untitled owing to political dissensions and the resident aliens were paying them nothing because they still owed them money, passed
5 a decree that anyone who was willing should lend money to the farmers in order that they might till the soil, providing that they should enjoy the first-fruits of the crop and that the others should have what remained.

The Ephesians, being in need of money, made a law that their women should not wear gold ornaments, but should
10 lend to the state what they already possessed; and fixing the amount which was to be paid they allowed the name of any one who presented that sum to be inscribed as that of the dedicator on certain of the pillars in the temple.

Dionysius of Syracuse, wishing to collect money, called to-
15 gether an assembly and declared that Demeter had appeared to him and bade him bring the ornaments of the women to her temple. He had therefore, he said, done so with the ornaments of the women of his own household; and he demanded that everyone else should do the same, lest ven-geance from the goddess should fall upon them. Anyone who
20 refused would, he said, be guilty of sacrilege. When all had brought what they possessed through fear of the goddess and dread of Dionysius, after dedicating the ornaments to the goddess he then appropriated them, saying that they were lent to him by her. And when some time had elapsed and the women began wearing ornaments again, he ordered that any women who wished to wear jewellery of gold should dedicate a fixed sum in the temple.

And when he was intending to build triremes, he knew
25 that he would be in want of money. He therefore called to-

gether an assembly and said that a certain city was to be betrayed to him and that he needed money for this purpose. He
therefore asked the citizens to contribute two staters each;
and they did so. He then let two or three days elapse, and
pretending that he had failed in his attempt, after commend-
ing their generosity he gave every man his contribution back   30
again. By this action he won the hearts of the citizens. And
so they again contributed, thinking that they would receive
their money back again; but he took the money and kept it
for building his ships.

And when he was in need of money he struck a coinage of
tin, and calling an assembly together he spoke at great length
in favour of the money which had been coined; and they, even   35
against their will, decreed that everyone should regard any
of it that he accepted as silver and not as tin.

On another occasion, being in want of money, he asked 1349^b1
the citizens to give him contributions; but they declared that
they had nothing to give. Accordingly he brought out his
own household goods and offered them for sale, as though
compelled to do so by poverty. When the Syracusans bought
them, he kept a record of what each had bought, and when   5
they had paid the price, he ordered each of them to bring back
the articles which he had bought.

And when the citizens owing to the taxes could not keep
cattle, he said that he had enough up to the present; those
therefore who acquired cattle should now be free from a tax
on them. But since many soon acquired a large number of cattle, thinking that they could keep them without paying a tax   10
on them, when he thought that a fitting moment had come
he gave orders that they should assess their value and then
imposed a tax. Accordingly the citizens, angry at having been
deceived, slew their cattle and sold them. And when, to prevent this, he ordered them to kill only as many as were needed
for daily use, they next devoted them for sacrifice to the gods.
Dionysius then forbade them to sacrifice any female beast.

On another occasion when he was in need of money,
he ordered all families of orphans to enrol themselves; and   15

when they[5] had done so, he enjoyed their property until each came of age.

And after he had captured Rhegium he called an assembly of the inhabitants together and informed them that he would be quite justified in enslaving them, but under the circumstances he would let them go free if he received the amount
20 which he had spent on the war and three *minae* a head from all of them. The Rhegians then brought to light the wealth which before had been hidden, and the poor borrowed from the richer citizens and from foreigners and provided the sum
25 which he demanded. When he had received it from them he nevertheless sold them all as slaves, and seized all the treasures which had before been hidden and were now brought to light.

Also having borrowed money from the citizens under promise of repayment, when they demanded it back he ordered them to bring him whatever money any of them possessed, threatening them with death as the penalty if they failed to do so.
30 When the money had been brought, he issued it again after stamping it afresh so that each *drachma* had the value of two *drachmae*, and paid back the original debt and the money which they brought him on this occasion.[6]

And when he sailed against Tyrrhenia with a hundred ships he took much gold and silver and a considerable quantity of
35 other ornaments of all kinds from the temple of Leucothea. And knowing that the sailors too were keeping many things for themselves, he made a proclamation that everyone should
1350ᵃ1 bring him the half of what he had and might retain the other half; and he threatened with death anyone who failed to deliver up the half. The sailors, supposing that if they gave up the half they would be allowed undisturbed possession of the rest, did so; but Dionysius, when he had received it, ordered
5 them to go back and bring him the other half.

---

[5] Omitting ἄλλων.
[6] Reading π ρότερον ἀπέδωκε καὶ ὃ νῦν ἀνήνεγκαν.

The Mendaeans used the proceeds of their harbour customs and their other dues for the administration of their city, but did not exact the taxes on land and houses; but they kept a register of property-owners, and whenever they needed money, they paid as though they owed taxes. They thus profited during the time which elapsed by having full use of the money without paying interest.

When they were at war with the Olynthians and needed money, seeing that they had slaves they decreed that a female and a male slave should be left to each citizen and the rest sold, so that private individuals might lend money to the state.

Callistratus the Athenian, when the harbour-dues in Macedonia were usually sold at twenty talents, made them fetch double that price. For, noticing that the richer men always bought them because it was necessary that the sureties provided for the twenty talents should be possessed of one talent, he proclaimed that anyone who liked could purchase them and that sureties should be provided for only a third or any other proportion which each could guarantee.

Timotheus, the Athenian, when he was at war with the Olynthians, and in need of money, struck a bronze coinage and distributed it to the soldiers. When they protested, he told them that the merchants and retailers would all sell their goods on the same terms as before. He then told the merchants, if they received any bronze money, to use it again to buy the commodities sent in for sale from the country and anything which was brought in as plunder, and said that, if they brought him any bronze money which they had left over, they should receive silver for it.

When he was making war in the neighbourhood of Corcyra and was in difficulties, and the soldiers were demanding their pay and refusing to obey him and threatening to go over to the enemy, he called together an assembly and told them that no money could reach him owing to the stormy weather—though he had, he declared, such an abundance of supplies that he offered them as a free gift the three months' rations which they had already received. They, supposing that

Timotheus would never have made such a valuable conces-   1350^{b}1
sion unless he really expected the money, kept silence about
the pay; and he meanwhile achieved the objects which he had
in view.

When he was besieging Samos he actually sold to the in-
5   habitants the fruits and the produce of their lands, and so
had abundance of money to pay his soldiers. And when there
was a shortage of provisions in the camp owing to the arrival
of newcomers, he forbade the sale of corn ready ground, and
of any smaller measure than a *medimnus*, and of any liquid in
10 a smaller quantity than a *metreta*. Accordingly the commanders of divisions and companies bought up provisions whole-
sale and distributed them to the soldiers, while the newcomers brought their own provisions with them and, when they
departed, sold anything that they had left. The result was that
15 the soldiers had an abundance of provisions.

Datames, the Persian, having soldiers under his command, could supply their daily needs from the enemy's country, but having no money to give them, and being requested
to pay them, when the time came at which it was due he
devised the following plan. He called together an assembly
20 and told them that he had no lack of money, but that it was
in a certain place which he named. He therefore moved his
camp and started to march thither. Then when he was near
the place, he went in advance to it and took from the temples
there all the embossed silver plate which they contained. He
then loaded his mules so that the silver plate was visible and
they looked as though they were carrying silver, and contin-
25 ued the march. The soldiers, when they saw it, thought that
the loads were all solid silver and were encouraged, thinking
that they would receive their pay. But Datames told them
that he must go to Amisus and have the silver minted. Now
the journey to Amisus was one of many days and exposed to
the weather. So all this time he made use of the army, merely
30 giving them their rations.

He kept in his personal service all the skilled artificers in
the army and the retailers who carried on traffic in any commodity; and no one else was permitted to do any of these

things. Chabrias, the Athenian, advised Taus, king of Egypt, when he was starting on an expedition and was in need of money, to say to the priests that owing to the expense some of the temples and the majority of the priests must be dispensed with.

When the priests heard this, each wishing to retain his   1351ª1
own temple and to remain a priest himself, they offered him money. And when Taus had accepted money from all of them, Chabrias advised him to order them to expend a tenth part of the amount which they formerly spent on their temple and themselves, and to lend the rest to him until the war against   5
the king of Persia should come to an end. And he advised him to fix the necessary amount and demand a contribution from each household and likewise from each individual; and that, when corn was sold, the buyer and the seller should give an obol for each *artabe* over and above the price; and that he should demand the payment of a tenth part of the profits derived from shipping and manufactures and any other form of   10
industry. And he advised him, when he was leaving the country on an expedition, to order that any unminted silver or gold which anyone possessed should be brought to him: and when most people brought it, he advised him to make use of   15
it and to commend the lenders to the provincial governors so that they might repay them out of the taxes.

Iphicrates, the Athenian, when Cotys had collected an army, provided him with money in the following way. He advised him to order the men under his command to sow land   20
for him with three *medimni* of corn. The result of this was that a great quantity of corn was collected. Accordingly he brought it down to the markets and sold it, and thus gained an abundance of money.

Cotys, the Thracian, tried to borrow money from the Peirinthians so that he might pay his soldiers; but the Peirinthi-   25
ans refused to give him any. He therefore begged them at any rate to grant him some men from among their citizens to act as a garrison for certain strongholds, in order that he might make full use of the soldiers who were at present on duty there. To this request they promptly acceded, thinking that

they would thus obtain possession of these strongholds. But
30 Cotys threw into prison those who were sent and ordered
the Peirinthians to recover them by sending him the money
which he wished to borrow from them.

Mentor, the Rhodian, having arrested Hermeias and
seized his estates, allowed the overseers whom Hermeias
had appointed to retain their positions. But when they all felt
35 secure and took steps to recover anything which had been
hidden or deposited for safety elsewhere, he arrested them
and deprived them of all they had.

1351ᵇ1 Memnon, the Rhodian, after making himself master of
Lampsacus, was in need of money. He therefore exacted a
heavy tribute from the richest citizens, telling them that they
could collect it from the rest of the citizens. But when the latter had contributed, he ordered them to lend him this sum
5 as well, fixing a period within which he would pay them back.

On another occasion when he was in need of money, he
demanded contributions from them, saying that they should
be repaid out of the revenues. They therefore contributed,
thinking that they would soon receive their money back. But
when the time was at hand for the payment of the revenues,
10 he told them that he needed these revenues as well, but would
repay them later with interest.

He also excused himself from paying the rations and
wages of those who were serving under him for six days in the
year, declaring that on these days they had no watch to keep,
no marching and no expenses, meaning the 'omitted' days.[7]
15 As he was already giving the soldiers their rations on the second day of the new month, he thus passed over three days in
the first month and five by the following month, and so on till
he reached a total of thirty days.

Charidemus of Orus, who held certain places in Aeolia,
20 when Artabazus was marching against him needed money to
pay his soldiers. At first, then, the citizens gave him contributions, but afterwards they declared that they had nothing left

---

[7] I.e. the six days 'omitted' from the year, one in each of the six 29-day
months.

to give. Charidemus then ordered the inhabitants of the place which he thought was richest to send away to another place any coin or other valuable treasure which they possessed, and he promised to give them an escort; at the same time it was clear that he himself was also removing his valuables. When they had obeyed him, he led them a little way outside the city and, after examining what they had, took all that he needed and sent them back again. He also made a proclamation in the cities over which he ruled that no one was to keep any arms in his house, the penalty for so doing being a fine which he specified. He then took no further action and paid no attention to the matter. The citizens, thinking that he had not meant the proclamation to be taken seriously, continued to keep the arms which they happened to possess. But Charidemus suddenly instituted a house to house search and exacted the fine from those in whose houses he found any arms.

A certain Philoxenus, a Macedonian who was satrap of Caria, being in need of money, said that he intended to celebrate the Dionysia, and he nominated the richest of the Carians to defray the cost of the choruses and gave directions as to what they had to supply. But seeing that they were annoyed, he sent to them secretly and asked them what they were willing to give to be released from serving. They declared their readiness to give considerably more than they thought it would cost them, in order to be freed from the trouble and the neglect of their private affairs which it would entail. Philoxenus accepted what they offered and put others on the list, until he had received even more than he had wanted ... [8]

Evaeses, the Syrian, being satrap of Egypt, discovering that the provincial governors were on the point of revolting from him, summoned them to the palace and hanged them all, and ordered that their relatives should be told that they were in prison. Their relatives therefore severally began to negotiate on their behalf and tried to buy the release of the captives. Evaeses made an agreement in each case and, after

[8] The text is corrupt here.

15 receiving the sums for which he had stipulated, restored them to their relatives—dead.

Cleomenes, an Alexandrian who was satrap of Egypt, when there was a severe famine everywhere else while Egypt was less seriously affected, forbade the export of corn, and when the provincial governors declared that they would not be able to pay the tribute because corn could not be exported, 20 he cancelled the prohibition, but put a heavy tax on the corn. The result was that, if he did not . . . [9] he received a large tax at the cost of a small exportation and the provincial governors lost their excuse.

As he was sailing through the district in which the crocodile is regarded as a deity, one of his slaves was carried off. 25 He therefore summoned the priests and told them that since he had been injured without provocation he intended to take vengeance on the crocodiles, and gave orders to hunt them. The priests, in order that their god might not be held in contempt, collected all the gold that they possessed and presented it to him, with the result that he desisted.

When king Alexander commanded him to found a city 30 near the Pharos and to establish there the mart which was formerly held at Canopus, he sailed to Canopus and told the priests and the owners of property there that he had come to transfer them. The priests and inhabitants collected and gave 35 him a sum of money to induce him to leave their mart undisturbed. This he accepted and for the moment left them alone, but afterwards, when he had the material for building ready, 1352b1 he sailed to Canopus and demanded an excessive amount of money from them, which he said represented the difference to him between having the mart near the Pharos and at Canopus. And when they said that they would not be able to give him the money he made them move their city.

And when he had sent someone to make a purchase and 5 discovered that his messenger had got what he wanted cheaply but intended to charge him an excessive price, he told the

[9]van Groningen and Wartelle mark a lacuna.

friends of the purchaser that he had heard that he had made his purchases at an excessive price and therefore he would go there himself; at the same time with assumed wrath he railed against his stupidity. When they heard this they told Cleomenes that he ought not to believe those who spoke against the messenger until he came himself and rendered his account. When the purchaser arrived they told him what Cleomenes had said; and he, wishing to make a good impression on them and on Cleomenes, submitted the prices at which he had actually bought the goods.

When corn was being sold in the country at ten *drachmae*, he summoned the dealers and asked them at what price they would do business with him. They named a lower price than that at which they were selling to the merchants. However, he ordered them to hand over their corn at the same price as they were selling to everyone else; and fixing the price of corn at thirty-two *drachmae* he then sold it himself.

He also called the priests together and told them that the expenditure on the temples in the country was excessive; consequently some of the temples and the majority of the priests must be abolished. The priests individually and collectively gave him the sacred treasures, thinking that he really intended to carry out his threat and because each wished that his own temple should be undisturbed and himself continue to be priest.

When Alexander was in the region of Babylon, Antimenes the Rhodian *hêmiolios* raised money in the following way. An ancient law existed in Babylonia that anything which was brought into the country should pay a duty of ten per cent., but no one ever enforced it. Antimenes, waiting till all the satraps and soldiers were expected and no small number of ambassadors and craftsmen . . . [10] and persons travelling on their own private affairs, and many gifts were being brought up, exacted the ten per cent. duty according to the existing law.

[10] The text is corrupt here.

On another occasion, when providing the slaves who were to look after the camp, he commanded that any owner who
35 wished should register the value which he put upon them, and they were to pay eight *drachmae* a year; if the slave ran away the owner was to receive the price which he had registered. Many slaves being registered, he amassed a considerable sum
1353ᵃ1 of money. And whenever any slave ran away he ordered the satrap of the country[11] in which the camp was situated to recover the runaway or else to pay the price to the owner.

5 Ophelas, the Olynthian, having appointed a superintendent over the province of Athribis, when the provincial governors of that district came to him and expressed their willingness to pay of their own accord a much larger sum and begged him to dismiss the superintendent whom he had just appointed, asked them if they would be able to pay what they promised; when they answered in the affirmative he left the
10 superintendent at his post and bade him exact the amount of tribute which they themselves had assessed. Thus he did not think it right either to degrade the official whom he had appointed or to impose a heavier tribute upon them than they themselves had fixed, but at the same time he himself received a far larger amount of money.

15 Pythocles, the Athenian, recommended to the Athenians that the state should take the lead from the mines at Laurium out of private hands at the market price of two *drachmae* and that they should then themselves fix the price at six *drachmae* and so sell it.

Chabrias, when crews had been enrolled for a hundred and
20 twenty ships and Taus only needed sixty, ordered the crews of the sixty ships which remained behind to supply those who sailed with two months' provisions, or else to sail themselves. They, wishing to attend to their own affairs, complied with his demand.

Antimenes ordered the satraps to keep the storehouses
25 along the royal roads filled according to the custom of the

[11] Reading τῆς γῆς.

country; but whenever an army or any other body of men unaccompanied by the king passed along, he used to send one
of his own men and sell the contents of the storehouses.

Cleomenes, when the first day of the month was approach-
ing and he had to give his soldiers their rations, purposely put
back into harbour, and as the new month advanced he put
out again and distributed the rations; he then left an interval
until the first day of the next month. The soldiers, therefore, 5
because they had recently received their rations, kept quiet;
and Cleomenes by passing over a month each year ... [12]

Stabelbius, the Mysian, when he owed his soldiers pay,
called the officers together[13] and told them that he had no
need of private soldiers but only of officers, and that, when 10
he did need soldiers, he would give each officer a sum of
money and send him out to collect mercenaries, and that he
would rather give the officers the pay which ought to go to
the soldiers. He therefore ordered them each to send away
their own levies out of the country. The officers, thinking that
it would be an opportunity to make money, dismissed the 15
soldiers in accordance with his commands. But after a short
interval he collected the officers together and told them that
just as a flute player was no use without a chorus, so too officers were useless without private soldiers; he therefore ordered them to leave the country.

Dionysius, when he was making a round of the temples, 20
whenever he saw a gold or silver table displayed, ordered that
a libation should be poured out 'to good luck' and that the
table should be carried off; and whenever he saw amongst
the statues one which held out a wine cup, he would say, 'I
accept your pledge', and order the statue to be carried away.
And he used to strip the gold from the statues, saying that he 25
would give them others lighter and more fragrant; he then
clad them with white garments and crowns of white poplar.

---

[12] The text is corrupt.
[13] Reading ὁ Μυσός, ὀφείλων στρατιώταις μισθόν, συγκαλέσας τούς ἡγέμονας.

BOOK III[1]

1 · A good wife should be the mistress of her home, having under her care all that is within it, according to the rules we have laid down. She should allow none to enter without her husband's knowledge, dreading above all things the gossip of gadding women, which tends to poison the soul. She alone should have knowledge of what happens within, whilst if any harm is wrought by those from without, her husband will bear the blame. She must exercise control of the money spent on such festivities as her husband has approved, keeping well within the limit set by law upon expenditure, dress, and ornament; and remembering that beauty depends not on costliness of raiment, nor does abundance of gold so conduce to the excellence of a woman as self-control in all that she does, and her inclination towards an honourable and well-ordered life. For such adornment as this both elevates the mind and is a far surer warrant for the payment, to the woman herself in her old age and to her children after her, of the due meed of praise.

This, then, is the province over which a woman should be minded to bear an orderly rule; for it seems not fitting that a man should know all that passes within the house. But in all other matters, let it be her aim to obey her husband; giving no heed to public affairs, nor desiring any part in arranging the marriages of her children. Rather, when the time shall come to give or receive in marriage sons or daughters, let her even then hearken to her husband in all respects, and agreeing with him obey his behest; considering that it is less unseemly for him to deal with a matter within the house than it is for her to pry into those outside its walls. It is fitting that a woman of well-ordered life should consider that her husband's uses are as laws appointed for her own life by divine will, along with the marriage state and the fortune she shares.

---

[1]This book survives only in Latin translation; it is not included in Bekker's edition, so that the customary Bekker-references are absent. The English translation is adapted from that of G. C. Armstrong.

If she endures them with patience and gentleness, she will rule her home with ease; otherwise, not so easily. Hence not only when her husband is in prosperity and good report does it beseem her to be in agreement with him, and to render him the service he wills, but also in times of adversity. If, through sickness or fault of judgement, his good fortune fails, then must she show her quality, encouraging him ever with words of cheer and yielding him obedience in all fitting ways; only let her do nothing base or unworthy of herself, or remember any wrong her husband may have done her through distress of mind. Let her refrain from all complaint, nor charge him with the wrong, but rather attribute everything of this kind to sickness or ignorance or accidental errors. For the more sedulous her service herein, the fuller will be his gratitude when he is restored, and freed from his sickness; and if she has failed to obey him when he commanded aught that is amiss, the deeper will be his recognition when health returns. Hence, whilst careful to avoid obedience in such circumstances, in other respects she will serve him more assiduously than if she had been a bondwoman bought and taken home. For he has indeed bought her with a great price—with partnership in his life and in the procreation of children; than which things nought could be greater or more sacred. And besides all this, the wife who had only lived in company with a fortunate husband would not have had the like opportunity to show her true quality. For though there is no small merit in a right and noble use of prosperity, still the right endurance of adversity justly receives an honour greater by far. For only a great soul can live in the midst of trouble and wrong without itself committing any base act. And so, while praying that her husband may be spared adversity, if trouble should come it beseems the wife to consider that here a good woman wins her highest praise. Let her bethink herself how Alcestis would never have attained such renown nor Penelope have deserved all the high praises bestowed on her had not their husbands known adversity; whereas the troubles of Admetus and Ulysses have obtained for their wives a reputation that shall never die. For because in time of distress they proved themselves faithful and dutiful to their husbands, the gods have bestowed on them the honour they deserved. To find partners in prosperity is easy enough; but only the best women are ready to share in adversity. For all these reasons it is fitting that a woman should pay her husband an honour greater by far, nor feel shame on his account even when, as Orpheus says, Holy health of soul, and wealth, the child of a brave spirit, companion him no more.

2 • Such then is the pattern of the rules and ways of living which a good wife will observe. And the rules which a good husband will follow in treatment of his wife will be similar; seeing that she has entered his home as the partner of his life and his children; and that the offspring she leaves behind her will bear the names of their parents, her name as well as his. And what could be more sacred than this, or more desired by a man of sound mind, than to beget by a noble and honoured wife children who, as shepherds of their old age, shall be the most loyal and discreet guardians of their father and mother, and the preservers of the whole house? Rightly reared by father and mother, children will grow up virtuous, as those who have treated them piously and righteously deserve that they should; but without such education they will be flawed. For unless parents have given their children an example of how to live, the children in their turn will be able to offer a fair and specious excuse. Such parents will risk being rejected by their offspring for their evil lives, and thus bringing destruction upon their own heads.

Hence his wife's training should be the object of a man's unstinting care; that so far as is possible their children may spring from the noblest of stock. For the tiller of the soil spares no pains to sow his seed in the most fertile and best cultivated land, looking thus to obtain the fairest fruits; and to save it from devastation he is ready, if such be his lot, to fall in conflict with his foes, a death which men crown with the highest of praise. Seeing, then, that such care is lavished on the body's food, surely every care should be taken on behalf of our own children's mother and nurse, in whom is implanted the seed from which there springs a living soul. For it is only by this means that each mortal, successively produced, participates in immortality; and that petitions and prayers continue to be offered to ancestral gods. So that he who thinks lightly of this would seem also to be slighting the gods. Thus it is on behalf of the gods, in whose presence he offered sacrifice, that he led his wife home, promising to honour her far above all others except his parents.

Now a virtuous wife is best honoured when she sees that her husband is faithful to her, and has no preference for another woman, but before all others loves and trusts her and holds her as his own. And so much the more will the woman seek to be what he accounts her, if she perceives that her husband's affection for her is faithful and righteous, and she too will be faithful and righteous towards him. Hence a man of sound mind ought not to forget what honours are proper to his parents or what fittingly belong to his wife and children; so that rendering to each and all their own, he may obey the law of men and of gods. For the deprivation we feel most of all is that of the special honour which is our due; nor will abundant gifts of what belongs to others be welcome to him who is dispossessed of his own. Now to a wife nothing is of more value, nothing more rightfully her own, than honoured and faithful partnership with her husband. Hence it befits not a man of sound mind to bestow his person promiscuously, or have random intercourse with women; for otherwise the base-born will share in the rights of his lawful children, and his wife will be robbed of her honour due, and shame be attached to his sons.

3 • To all these matters, therefore, a man should give heed. And it is fitting that he should approach his wife in an honourable way, full of self-restraint and awe; and in his conversation with her, should use only the words of a right-minded man, suggesting only such acts as are themselves lawful and honourable; treating her with much self-restraint and trust,

and passing over any trivial or unintentional errors she has committed. And if through ignorance she has done wrong, he should advise her of it without threatening, in a courteous and modest manner. Indifference and harsh reproof he must alike avoid. Between a courtesan and her lover, such tempers are allowed their course; between a free woman and her lawful spouse there should be a reverent and modest mingling of love and fear. For of fear there are two kinds. The fear which virtuous and honourable sons feel towards their fathers, and loyal citizens towards rightminded rulers, has for its companions reverence and modesty; but the other kind, felt by slaves for masters and by subjects for despots who treat them with injustice and wrong, is associated with hostility and hatred.

Reflecting on all this, a husband should choose the better course and secure the agreement, loyalty, and devotion of his wife, so that whether he himself is present or not, there may be no difference in her attitude towards him, since she realizes that they are alike guardians of the common interests; and so when he is away she may feel that to her no man is kinder or more virtuous or more truly hers than her own husband. And she will make this manifest from the beginning by her unfailing regard for the common welfare, novice though she may be in such matters. And if the husband learns first to master himself, he will thereby become his wife's best guide in all the affairs of life, and will teach her to follow his example. For Homer pays no honour either to affection or to fear where modesty is absent. Everywhere he bids affection be coupled with self-control and shame; whilst the fear he commends is such as Helen owns when she thus addresses Priam: "Beloved sire of my lord, it is fitting that I fear thee and dread thee and revere";[2] meaning that her love for him is mingled with fear and modest shame. And again, Ulysses speaks to Nausicaa in this manner: "Thou, lady, dost fill me

[2] *Iliad* III 172.

with wonder and with fear."[3] For Homer believes that this is
the feeling of a husband and wife for one another, and that
if they so feel, it will be well with them both. For no one ever
loves or admires or fears in this shamefaced way one of baser
character; but such are the feelings towards one another of
nobler souls and those by nature good; or of the inferior toward those they know to be their betters. Feeling thus toward
Penelope, Ulysses remained faithful to her in his wander-
ings; whereas Agamemnon did wrong to his wife for the sake
of Chryseis, declaring in open assembly that a base captive
woman, and of alien race besides, was in no way inferior to
Clytemnestra in womanly excellence. This was ill spoken of
the mother of his children; nor was his connexion with the
other a righteous one. How could it be, when he had but recently compelled her to be his concubine, and before he had
any experience of her behaviour to him? Ulysses on the other
hand, when the daughter of Atlas besought him to share her
bed and board, and promised him immortality, could not
bring himself even for the sake of immortality to betray the
kindness and love and loyalty of his wife, deeming immortality purchased by unrighteousness to be the worst of all punishments. For it was only to save his comrades that he yielded
his person to Circe; and in answer to her he even declared
that in his eyes nothing could be more lovely than his native
isle, rugged though it were; and prayed that he might die, if
only he might look upon his mortal wife and son. So firmly
did he keep troth with his wife; and received in return from
her the like loyalty.

4 • Once again, in the words addressed by Ulysses to Nausicaa the poet makes clear the great honour in which he holds
the virtuous companionship of man and wife in marriage.
There he prays the gods to grant her a husband and a home;
and between herself and her husband, precious unity of mind;
provided that such unity be for righteous ends. For, says he,

[3] *Odyssey* VI 168.

there is no greater blessing on earth than when husband and wife rule their home in harmony of mind and will. Moreover it is evident from this that the unity which the poet commends is no mutual subservience in each other's vices, but one that is rightfully allied with wisdom and understanding; for this is the meaning of the words "rule the house in harmony of mind." And he goes on to say that wherever such a love is found, it is a cause of sore distress to those who hate them and of delight to those that love them; while the truth of his words is most of all acknowledged by the happy pair. For when wife and husband are agreed about the best things in life, of necessity the friends of each will also be mutually agreed; and the strength which the pair gain will make them formidable to their enemies and helpful to their own. But when discord reigns between them, their friends too will disagree, while the pair themselves will realize most fully their weakness.

In all these precepts it is clear that the poet is teaching husband and wife to dissuade one another from whatever is evil and dishonourable, while unselfishly furthering to the best of their power one another's honourable and righteous aims. In the first place they will strive to perform all duty towards their parents, the husband towards those of his wife no less than towards his own, and she in her turn towards his. Their next duties are towards their children, their friends, their estate, and their entire household which they will treat as a common possession; each vying with the other in the effort to contribute most to the common welfare, and to excel in virtue and righteousness; laying aside arrogance, and ruling with justice in a kindly and unassuming spirit. And so at length, when they reach old age, and are freed from the duty of providing for others and from preoccupation with the pleasures and desires of youth, they will be able to give answer also to their children, if question arises which of them has contributed more good things to the common household store; and will be well assured that whatsoever of evil has befallen them is due to fortune, and whatsoever of good, to their own virtue. One who comes victorious through such question wins from heaven, as Pindar says, his chiefest reward; for "hope, and a soul filled with fair thoughts are supreme in the manifold mind of mortals"; and next, from his children the good fortune of being sustained by them in his old age. And therefore it behoves us to preserve throughout our lives a righteous attitude towards all gods and mortal men, to each individually, and to all in common; and not least towards our own wives and children and parents.

CONSTITUTION
OF ATHENS

F. G. Kenyon

1 • . . . . [THEY[1] WERE TRIED] BY A COURT empanelled from
among the noble families, and sworn upon the sacrifices. The
part of accuser was taken by Myron. They were found guilty
of the sacrilege, and their bodies were cast out of their graves
and their race banished for evermore. In view of this expia-
tion, Epimenides the Cretan performed a purification of the
city.

2 • After this event there was contention for a long time
between the upper classes and the populace. Not only was
the constitution at this time oligarchical in every respect, but
the poorer classes, men, women, and children, were the serfs
of the rich. They were known as Pelatae and also as Hecte-
mori, because they cultivated the lands of the rich at the rent
thus indicated. The whole country was in the hands of a few
persons, and if the tenants failed to pay their rent they were
liable to be haled into slavery, and their children with them.
All loans were secured upon the debtor's person up to the
time of Solon, who was the first to appear as the champion
of the people. But the hardest and bitterest part of the constitution in the eyes of the masses was their state of serfdom.
Not but what they were also discontented with every other
feature of their lot; for, to speak generally, they had no share
in anything.

TEXT: F. G. Kenyon, OCT, Oxford, 1920
[1]Sc. the Alcmeonidae. The papyrus begins in the middle of a sentence.

3 • Now the ancient constitution, as it existed before the time of Draco, was organized as follows. The magistrates were elected according to qualifications of birth and wealth. At first they governed for life, but subsequently for terms of ten years. The first magistrates, both in date and in importance, were the King, the Polemarch, and the Archon. The earliest of these offices was that of the King, which existed from ancestral antiquity. To this was added, secondly, the office of Polemarch, on account of some of the kings proving feeble in war; for it was on this account that Ion was invited to accept the post on an occasion of pressing need. The last of the three offices was that of the Archon, which most authorities state to have come into existence in the time of Medon. Others assign it to the time of Acastus, and adduce as proof the fact that the nine Archons swear to execute their oaths 'as in the days of Acastus', which seems to suggest that it was in his time that the descendants of Codrus retired from the kingship in return for the prerogatives conferred upon the Archon. Whichever way it be, the difference in date is small; but that it was the last of these magistracies to be created is also shown by the fact that the Archon has no part in the ancestral sacrifices, as the King and the Polemarch have, but exclusively in those of later origin. So it is only at a comparatively late date that the office of Archon has become of great importance, through the dignity conferred by these later additions. The Thesmothetae were appointed many years afterwards, when these offices had already become annual, with the object that they might publicly record all legal decisions, and act as guardians of them with a view to determining the issues between litigants. Accordingly their office, alone of those which have been mentioned, was never of more than annual duration.

Such, then, is the relative chronological precedence of these offices. At that time the nine Archons did not all live together. The King occupied the building now known as the Bucolium, near the Prytaneum, as may be seen from the fact that even to the present day the marriage of the King's wife to Dionysus and its consummation take place there. The Archon lived in the Prytaneum, the Polemarch in the Epilyceum. The latter building was formerly called the Polemarcheum, but after Epilycus, during his term of office as Polemarch, had rebuilt it and fitted it up, it was called the Epilyceum. The Thesmothetae occupied the Thesmotheteum. In the time of Solon, however, they all came together into the Thesmotheteum. They had power to decide cases finally on their own authority, not, as now, merely to hold a preliminary hearing. Such then was the arrangement of the magistracies. The Council of Areopagus had as its duty the protection of the laws; but in point of fact it administered the greater and most important part of the government of the state, and inflicted punishments and fines summarily upon all who misbehaved themselves. For the Archons were elected under qualifications of birth and wealth, and the Areopagus was composed of those who had served as Archons; for which reason the membership of the Areopagus is the only office which has continued to be a life-magistracy to the present day.

4 • Such was, in outline, the first constitution; but not very long after the events above recorded, in the archonship of Aristaechmus, Draco enacted his ordinances. Now his constitution had the following form. The franchise was given to all who could furnish themselves with a military equipment. The nine Archons and the Treasurers were elected by this body from persons possessing an unencumbered property of not less than ten minas, the less important officials from those who could furnish themselves with a military equipment, and the generals and commanders of the cavalry from those who could show an unencumbered property of not less than a hundred minas, and had children born in lawful wedlock over ten years of age. These officers were required to hold to bail the Prytanes, the generals, and the cavalry commanders of the preceding year until their accounts had been audited, taking four securities of the same class as that to which the generals and the cavalry commanders belonged. There was also to be a Council, consisting of four hundred and one members, cho-

sen by lot from among those who possessed the franchise. Both for this and for the other magistracies the lot was cast among those who were over thirty years of age; and no one might hold office twice until every one else had had his turn, after which they were to cast the lot afresh. If any member of the Council failed to attend when there was a sitting of the Council or of the Assembly, he paid a fine, to the amount of three drachmas if he was a Pentacosiomedimnus, two if he was a Knight, and one if he was a Zeugites. The Council of Areopagus was guardian of the laws, and kept watch over the magistrates to see that they executed their offices in accordance with the laws. Any person who felt himself wronged might lay an information before the Council of Areopagus, on declaring what law was broken by the wrong done to him. But, as has been said before, loans were secured upon the persons of the debtors, and the land was in the hands of a few.

5 • Since such, then, was the organization of the constitution, and the many were in slavery to the few, the people rose against the upper class. The strife was keen, and for a long time the two parties were ranged in hostile camps against one another, until, by common consent, they appointed Solon to be mediator and Archon, and committed the whole constitution to his hands—he had written the poem, which begins with the words:

> I behold, and within my heart deep sadness has claimed its
>   place,
> As I mark the oldest home of the ancient Ionian race
> Slain by the sword.

In this poem he fights and disputes on behalf of each party in turn against the other, and finally he advises them to come to terms and put an end to the quarrel existing between them. By birth and reputation Solon was one of the foremost men of the day, but in wealth and position he was of the middle class, as is generally agreed on other grounds, and is, indeed, established by his own evidence in these poems, where he exhorts the wealthy not to be grasping.

But ye who have store of good, who are sated and overflow,
Restrain your swelling soul, and still it and keep it low:
Let the heart that is great within you be trained a lowlier way;
Ye shall not have all at your will, and we will not for ever obey.

Indeed, he constantly fastens the blame for the conflict on the rich; and accordingly at the beginning of the poem he says that he fears 'the love of wealth and an overweening mind', evidently meaning that it was through these that the quarrel arose.

6 • As soon as he was at the head of affairs, Solon liberated the people once and for all, by prohibiting all loans on the security of the debtor's person; and in addition he made laws and cancelled all debts, public and private. This measure is commonly called the Seisachtheia[2] since thereby the people had their loads removed from them. In connexion with it some persons try to traduce the character of Solon. It so happened that, when he was about to enact the Seisachtheia, he communicated his intention to some members of the upper class, whereupon, as the partisans of the popular party say, his friends stole a march on him; while those who wish to attack his character maintain that he too had a share in the fraud himself. For these persons borrowed money and bought up a large amount of land, and so when, a short time afterwards, all debts were cancelled, they became wealthy; and this, they say, was the origin of the families which were afterwards looked on as having been wealthy from primeval times. However, the story of the popular party is more plausible. A man who was so moderate and public-spirited in all his other actions, that when it was within his power to put his fellow-citizens beneath his feet and establish himself as tyrant, he preferred instead to incur the hostility of both parties by placing his honour and the general welfare above his personal aggrandisement, is not likely to have consented to defile his hands by such a petty and palpable fraud. That he

---

[2] 'Removal of burdens'.

had this absolute power is indicated by the desperate condition of the country; moreover, he mentions it himself repeatedly in his poems, and it is universally admitted. We are therefore bound to consider this accusation to be false.

7 • Next Solon drew up a constitution and enacted new laws; and the ordinances of Draco ceased to be used, with the exception of those relating to murder. The laws were inscribed on the wooden stands, and set up in the King's Porch, and all swore to obey them; and the nine Archons made oath upon the stone, declaring that they would dedicate a golden statue if they should transgress any of them. This is the origin of the oath to that effect which they take to the present day. Solon ratified his laws for a hundred years; and the following was the fashion in which he organized the constitution. He divided the population according to property into four classes, just as it had been divided before, namely, Pentacosiomedimni, Knights, Zeugitae, and Thetes. The various magistracies, namely, the nine Archons, the Treasurers, the Commissioners for Public Contracts [Poletae], the Eleven, and the Exchequer Clerks [Colacretae], he assigned to the Pentacosiomedimni, the Knights, and the Zeugitae, giving offices to each class in proportion to the value of their property. To those who ranked among the Thetes he gave nothing but a place in the Assembly and in the juries. A man had to rank as a Pentacosiomedimnus if he made, from his own land, five hundred measures, whether liquid or solid. Those ranked as Knights who made three hundred measures, or, as some say, those who were able to maintain a horse. In support of the latter definition they adduce the name of the class, which may be supposed to be derived from this fact, and also some votive offerings of early times; for in the Acropolis there is a votive offering, a statue of Diphilus, bearing this inscription:

> The son of Diphilus, Anthemion hight,
> Raised from the Thetes and become a Knight,
> Did to the gods this sculptured charger bring,
> For his promotion a thank-offering.

And a horse stands in evidence beside the man, implying that this was what was meant by belonging to the rank of Knight. At the same time it seems more reasonable to suppose that this class, like the Pentacosiomedimni, was defined by the possession of an income of a certain number of measures. Those ranked as Zeugitae who made two hundred measures, liquid or solid; and the rest ranked as Thetes, and were not eligible for any office. Hence it is that even at the present day, when a candidate for any office is asked to what class he belongs, no one would think of saying that he belonged to the Thetes.

8 • The elections to the various offices Solon enacted should be by lot, out of candidates selected by each of the tribes. Each tribe selected ten candidates for the nine archonships, and among these the lot was cast. Hence it is still the custom for each tribe to choose ten candidates by lot, and then the lot is again cast among these. A sign that Solon regulated the elections to office according to the property classes may be found in the law still in force with regard to the Treasurers, which enacts that they shall be chosen from the Pentacosiomedimni. Such was Solon's legislation with respect to the nine Archons; whereas in early times the Council of Areopagus summoned suitable persons according to its own judgement and appointed them for the year to the several offices. There were four tribes, as before, and four tribe-kings. Each tribe was divided into three Trittyes, with twelve Naucraries in each; and the Naucraries had officers of their own, called Naucrari, whose duty it was to superintend the current receipts and expenditure. Hence, among the laws of Solon now obsolete, it is repeatedly written that the Naucrari are to receive and to spend out of the Naucraric fund. Solon also appointed a Council of four hundred, a hundred from each tribe; but he assigned to the Council of the Areopagus the duty of superintending the laws, acting as before as the guardian of the constitution in general. It kept watch over the affairs of the state in most of the more important matters, and corrected offend-

ers, with full powers to inflict either fines or punishment. The money received in fines it brought up into the Acropolis, without assigning the reason for the mulct. It also tried those who conspired for the overthrow of the state, Solon having enacted a process of impeachment to deal with such offenders. Further, since he saw the state often engaged in internal disputes, while many of the citizens from sheer indifference accepted whatever might turn up, he made a law with express reference to such persons, enacting that any one who, in a time of civil factions, did not take up arms with either party, should lose his rights as a citizen and cease to have any part in the state.

9 • Such, then, was his legislation concerning the magistracies. There are three points in the constitution of Solon which appear to be its most democratic features: first and most important, the prohibition of loans on the security of the debtor's person; secondly, the right of every person who so willed to claim redress on behalf of any one to whom wrong was being done; thirdly, the institution of the appeal to the jury-courts; and it is to this last, they say, that the masses have owed their strength most of all, since, when the people are master of the voting-power, it is master of the constitution. Moreover, since the laws were not drawn up in simple and explicit terms (but like the one concerning inheritances and wards of state), disputes inevitably occurred, and the courts had to decide in every matter, whether public or private. Some persons in fact believe that Solon deliberately made the laws indefinite, in order that the final decision might be in the hands of the people. This, however, is not probable, and the reason no doubt was that it is impossible to attain ideal perfection when framing a law in general terms; for we must judge of his intentions, not from the actual results in the present day, but from the rest of his legislation.

10 • These seem to be the democratic features of his laws; but in addition, before the period of his legislation, he carried through his abolition of debts, and after it his increase in the

standards of weights and measures, and of the currency. During his administration the measures were made larger than those of Pheidon, and the mina, which previously had a standard of seventy drachmas, was raised to the full hundred. The standard coin in earlier times was the two-drachma piece. He also made weights corresponding with the coinage, sixty-three minas going to the talent; and the odd three minas were distributed among the staters and the other values.

11 • When he had completed his organization of the constitution in the manner that has been described, he found himself beset by people coming to him and harassing him concerning his laws, criticizing here and questioning there, till, as he wished neither to alter what he had decided on nor yet to be an object of ill will by remaining in Athens, he set off on a journey to Egypt, with the combined objects of trade and travel, giving out that he should not return for ten years. He considered that it was not right for him to expound the laws personally, but that every one should obey them just as they were written. Moreover, many members of the upper class had been estranged from him on account of his abolition of debts, and both parties were alienated through their disappointment at the condition of things which he had created. The mass of the people had expected him to make a complete redistribution of all property, and the upper class hoped he would restore everything to its former position, or, at any rate, make but a small change. Solon, however, had resisted both classes. He might have made himself a despot by attaching himself to whichever party he chose, but he preferred to incur the enmity of both, by being the saviour of his country and the ideal lawgiver.

12 • The truth of this view of Solon's policy is established alike by common consent and by the mention he has himself made of the matter in his poems. Thus:

> I gave to the mass of the people such rank as befitted their need,
> I took not away their honour, and I granted naught to their greed;

While those who were rich in power, who in wealth were
    glorious and great,
I bethought me that naught should befall them unworthy their
    splendour and state;
So I stood with my shield outstretched, and both were safe in
    its sight,
And I would not that either should triumph, when the triumph
    was not with right.

Again he declares how the mass of the people ought to be treated:

But thus will the people best the voice of their leaders obey,
When neither too slack is the rein, nor violence holdeth the
    sway;
For indulgence breedeth a child, the presumption that spurns
    control,
When riches too great are poured upon men of unbalanced
    soul.

And again elsewhere he speaks about the persons who wished to redistribute the land:

So they came in search of plunder, and their cravings knew no
    bound,
Every one among them deeming endless wealth would here be
    found,
And that I with glozing smoothness hid a cruel mind within.
Fondly then and vainly dreamt they; now they raise an angry
    din,
And they glare askance in anger, and the light within their eyes
Burns with hostile flames upon me. Yet therein no justice lies.
All I promised, fully wrought I with the gods at hand to cheer,
Naught beyond in folly ventured. Never to my soul was dear
With a tyrant's force to govern, nor to see the good and base
Side by side in equal portion share the rich home of our race.

Once more he speaks of the abolition of debts and of those who before were in servitude, but were released owing to the Seisachtheia:

Of all the aims for which I summoned forth
The people, was there one I compassed not?
Thou, when slow time brings justice in its train,
O mighty mother of the Olympian gods,
Dark Earth, thou best canst witness, from whose breast
I swept the pillars broadcast planted there,
And made thee free, who hadst been slave of yore.
And many a man whom fraud or law had sold
Far from his god-built land, an outcast slave,
I brought again to Athens; yea, and some,
Exiles from home through debt's oppressive load,
Speaking no more the dear Athenian tongue,
But wandering far and wide, I brought again;
And those that here in vilest slavery
Crouched 'neath a master's frown, I set them free.
Thus might and right were yoked in harmony,
Since by the force of law I won my ends
And kept my promise. Equal laws I gave
To evil and to good, with even hand
Drawing straight justice for the lot of each.
But had another held the goad as I,
One in whose heart was guile and greediness,
He had not kept the people back from strife.
For had I granted, now what pleased the one,
Then what their foes devised in counterpoise,
Of many a man this state had been bereft.
Therefore I showed my might on every side,
Turning at bay like wolf among the hounds.

And again he reviles both parties for their grumblings in the
times that followed:

Nay, if one must lay blame where blame is due,
Were't not for me, the people ne'er had set
Their eyes upon these blessings e'en in dreams—
While greater men, the men of wealthier life,
Should praise me and should court me as their friend.

For had any other man, he says, received this exalted post,

He had not kept the people back, nor ceased
Till he had robbed the richness of the milk.
But I stood forth a landmark in the midst.
And barred the foes from battle.

13 • Such, then, were Solon's reasons for his departure
from the country. After his retirement the city was still torn
by divisions. For four years, indeed, they lived in peace; but in
the fifth year after Solon's government they were unable to
elect an Archon on account of their dissensions, and again
four years later they elected no Archon for the same reason.
Subsequently, after a similar period had elapsed, Damasias
was elected Archon; and he governed for two years and two
months, until he was forcibly expelled from his office. After
this it was agreed, as a compromise, to elect ten Archons, five
from the Eupatridae, three from the Agroeci, and two from
the Demiurgi; and they ruled for the year following Damasias. It is clear from this that the Archon was at the time the
magistrate who possessed the greatest power, since it is always in connexion with this office that conflicts are seen to
arise. But altogether they were in a continual state of internal disorder. Some found the cause and justification of their
discontent in the abolition of debts, because thereby they had
been reduced to poverty; others were dissatisfied with the political constitution, because it had undergone a revolutionary
change; while with others the motive was found in personal
rivalries among themselves. The parties at this time were
three in number. First there was the party of the Shore, led by
Megacles the son of Alcmeon, which was considered to aim at
a moderate form of government; then there were the men of
the Plain, who desired an oligarchy and were led by Lycurgus;
and thirdly there were the men of the Highlands, at the head
of whom was Pisistratus, who was looked on as an extreme
democrat. This party was reinforced by those who had been
deprived of the debts due to them, from motives of poverty,
and by those who were not of pure descent, from motives of
personal apprehension. A proof of this is seen in the fact that

after the tyranny was overthrown a revision was made of the citizen-roll, on the ground that many persons were partaking in the franchise without having a right to it. The names given to the respective parties were derived from the districts in which they held their lands.

14 • Pisistratus, who had the reputation of being an extreme democrat, and had also distinguished himself greatly in the war with Megara, wounded himself, and by representing that his injuries had been inflicted on him by his political rivals, he persuaded the people, through a motion proposed by Aristion, to grant him a bodyguard. After he had got these 'club-bearers', as they were called, he made an attack with them on the people and seized the Acropolis. This happened in the archonship of Corneas, thirty-one years after the legislation of Solon. It is related that, when Pisistratus asked for his bodyguard, Solon opposed the request, and declared that in so doing he proved himself wiser than half the people and braver than the rest—wiser than those who did not see that Pisistratus designed to make himself tyrant, and braver than those who saw it and kept silence. But when all his words availed nothing he carried forth his armour and set it up in front of his house, saying that he had helped his country so far as lay in his power (he was already a very old man), and that he called on all others to do the same. Solon's exhortations, however, proved fruitless, and Pisistratus assumed the sovereignty. His administration was more like a constitutional government than the rule of a tyrant; but before his power was firmly established, the adherents of Megacles and Lycurgus made a coalition and drove him out. This took place in the archonship of Hegesias, five years after the first establishment of his rule. Eleven years later Megacles, being in difficulties in a party struggle, again opened negotiations with Pisistratus, proposing that the latter should marry his daughter; and on these terms he brought him back to Athens, by a very primitive and simple-minded device. He first spread abroad a rumour that Athena was bringing back Pisistratus, and then, having found a woman of great stature and

beauty, named Phyë (according to Herodotus, of the deme of Paeania, but as others say a Thracian flower-seller of the deme of Collytus), he dressed her in a garb resembling that of the goddess and brought her into the city with Pisistratus. The latter drove in on a chariot with the woman beside him, and the inhabitants of the city, struck with awe, received him with adoration.

15 • In this manner did his first return take place. But later, about six years after his return, he was again expelled. For he did not hold power for long: he refused to treat the daughter of Megacles as his wife, and being afraid in consequence of a combination of the two opposing parties, he retired from the country. First he led a colony to a place called Rhaicelus, in the region of the Thermaic gulf; and thence he passed to the country in the neighbourhood of Mt. Pangaeus. Here he acquired wealth and hired mercenaries; and not till ten years had elapsed did he return to Eretria and make an attempt to recover the government by force. In this he had the assistance of many allies, notably the Thebans and Lygdamis of Naxos, and also the Knights who held the supreme power in the constitution of Eretria. After his victory in the battle at Pallene he captured Athens, and when he had disarmed the people he at last had his tyranny securely established, and was able to take Naxos and set up Lygdamis as ruler there. He effected the disarmament of the people in the following manner. He ordered a parade in full armour in the Theseum, and began to make a speech to the people. He spoke for a short time, until the people called out that they could not hear him, whereupon he bade them come up to the entrance of the Acropolis, in order that his voice might be better heard. Then, while he continued to speak to them at great length, men whom he had appointed for the purpose collected the arms and locked them up in the chambers of the Theseum hard by, and came and made a signal to him that it was done. Pisistratus accordingly, when he had finished the rest of what he had to say, told the people also what had happened to their arms; adding that they were not to be surprised or alarmed, but go home and

attend to their private affairs, while he would himself for the future manage all the business of the state.

16 • Such was the origin and such the vicissitudes of the tyranny of Pisistratus. His administration was temperate, as has been said before, and more like constitutional government than a tyranny. Not only was he in every respect humane and mild and ready to forgive those who offended, but, in addition, he advanced money to the poorer people to help them in their labours, so that they might make their living by agriculture. In this he had two objects, first that they might not spend their time in the city but might be scattered over all the country, and secondly that, being moderately well off and occupied with their own business, they might have neither the wish nor the time to attend to public affairs. At the same time his revenues were increased by the thorough cultivation of the country, since he imposed a tax of one tenth on all the produce. For the same reasons he instituted the local justices, and often made expeditions in person into the country to inspect it and to settle disputes between individuals, that they might not come into the city and neglect their farms. It was in one of the progresses that, as the story goes, Pisistratus had his adventure with the man of Hymettus, who was cultivating the spot afterwards known as 'Tax-free Farm'. He saw a man digging and working at a very stony piece of ground, and being surprised he sent his attendant to ask what he got out of this plot of land. 'Aches and pains', said the man; 'and that's what Pisistratus ought to have his tenth of'. The man spoke without knowing who his questioner was; but Pisistratus was so pleased with his frank speech and his industry that he granted him exemption from all taxes. And so in matters in general he burdened the people as little as possible with his government, but always cultivated peace and kept them in all quietness. Hence the tyranny of Pisistratus was often spoken of proverbially as 'the age of gold'; for when his sons succeeded him the government became much harsher. But most important of all in this respect was his popular and kindly disposition. In all things he was ac-

customed to observe the laws, without giving himself any exceptional privileges. Once he was summoned on a charge of homicide before the Areopagus, and he appeared in person to make his defence; but the prosecutor was afraid to present himself and abandoned the case. For these reasons he held power long, and whenever he was expelled he regained his position easily. The majority alike of the upper class and of the people were in his favour; the former he won by his social intercourse with them, the latter by the assistance which he gave to their private purses, and his nature fitted him to win the hearts of both. Moreover, the laws in reference to tyrants at that time in force at Athens were very mild, especially the one which applies more particularly to the establishment of a tyranny. The law ran as follows: 'These are the ancestral statutes of the Athenians; if any persons shall make an attempt to establish a tyranny, or if any person shall join in setting up a tyranny, he shall lose his civic rights, both himself and his whole house'.

17 • Thus did Pisistratus grow old in the possession of power, and he died of illness in the archonship of Philoneus, thirty-three years from the time at which he first established himself as tyrant, during nineteen of which he was in possession of power; the rest he spent in exile. It is evident from this that the story is mere gossip which states that Pisistratus was the youthful favourite of Solon and commanded in the war against Megara for the recovery of Salamis. It will not harmonize with their respective ages, as any one may see who will reckon up the years of the life of each of them, and the dates at which they died. After the death of Pisistratus his sons took up the government, and conducted it on the same system. He had two sons by his legitimate wife, Hippias and Hipparchus, and two by his Argive consort, Iophon and Hegesistratus, who was surnamed Thessalus. For Pisistratus took a wife from Argos, Timonassa, the daughter of a man of Argos, named Gorgilus; she had previously been the wife of Archius of Ambracia; one of the descendants of Cypselus. This was the origin of his friendship with the Argives, on account of

which a thousand of them were brought over by Hegesistratus and fought on his side in the battle at Pallene. Some authorities say that this marriage took place after his first expulsion from Athens, others while he was in possession of the government.

18 • Hippias and Hipparchus assumed the control of affairs on grounds alike of standing and of age; but Hippias, as being the elder and also naturally of a statesmanlike and shrewd disposition, was really the head of the government. Hipparchus was youthful in disposition, amorous, and fond of literature (it was he who invited to Athens Anacreon, Simonides, and the other poets), while Thessalus was much junior in age, and was violent and headstrong in his behaviour. It was from his character that all the evils arose which befell the house. He became enamoured of Harmodius, and, since he failed to win his affection, he lost all restraint upon his passion, and in addition to other exhibitions of rage he finally prevented the sister of Harmodius from taking the part of a basketbearer in the Panathenaic procession, slanderously alleging that Harmodius was a person of loose life. Thereupon, in a frenzy of wrath, Harmodius and Aristogeiton did their celebrated deed, in conjunction with a number of confederates. But while they were lying in wait for Hippias in the Acropolis at the time of the Panathenaea (Hippias, at this moment, was awaiting the arrival of the procession, while Hipparchus was organizing its dispatch) they saw one of the persons privy to the plot talking familiarly with him. Thinking that he was betraying them, and desiring to do something before they were arrested, they rushed down and made their attempt without waiting for the rest of their confederates. They succeeded in killing Hipparchus near the Leocoreum while he was engaged in arranging the procession, but ruined the design as a whole; of the two leaders, Harmodius was killed on the spot by the guards, while Aristogeiton was arrested, and perished later after suffering long tortures. While under the torture he accused many persons who belonged by birth to the most distin-

guished families and were also personal friends of the tyrants. At first the government could find no clue to the conspiracy; for the current story, that Hippias made all who were taking part in the procession leave their arms, and then detected those who were carrying secret daggers, cannot be true, since at that time they did not bear arms in the processions, this being a custom instituted at a later period by the democracy. According to the story of the popular party, Aristogeiton accused the friends of the tyrants with the deliberate intention that the latter might commit an impious act, and at the same time weaken themselves, by putting to death innocent men who were their own friends; others say that he told no falsehood, but was betraying the actual accomplices. At last, when for all his efforts he could not obtain release by death, he promised to give further information against a number of other persons; and, having induced Hippias to give him his hand to confirm his word, as soon as he had hold of it he reviled him for giving his hand to the murderer of his brother, till Hippias, in a frenzy of rage, lost control of himself and snatched out his dagger and dispatched him.

19 • After this event the tyranny became much harsher. In consequence of his vengeance for his brother, and of the execution and banishment of a large number of persons, Hippias became a distrusted and an embittered man. About three years after the death of Hipparchus, finding his position in the city insecure, he set about fortifying Munichia, with the intention of establishing himself there. While he was still engaged on this work, however, he was expelled by Cleomenes, king of Lacedaemon, in consequence of the Spartans being continually incited by oracles to overthrow the tyranny. These oracles were obtained in the following way. The Athenian exiles, headed by the Alcmeonidae, could not by their own power effect their return, but failed continually in their attempts. Among their other failures, they fortified a post in Attica, Lipsydrium, above Mt. Parnes, and were there joined by some partisans from the city; but they were besieged by

the tyrants and reduced to surrender. After this disaster the following became a popular drinking song:

> Ah! Lipsydrium, faithless friend!
> Lo, what heroes to death didst send,
> Nobly born and great in deed!
> Well did they prove themselves at need
> Of noble sires a noble seed.

Having failed, then, in every other method, they took the contract for rebuilding the temple at Delphi, thereby obtaining ample funds, which they employed to secure the help of the Lacedaemonians. All this time the Pythia kept continually enjoining on the Lacedaemonians who came to consult the oracle, that they must free Athens; till finally she succeeded in impelling the Spartans to that step, although the house of Pisistratus was connected with them by ties of hospitality. The resolution of the Lacedaemonians was, however, at least equally due to the friendship which had been formed between the house of Pisistratus and Argos. Accordingly they first sent Anchimolus by sea at the head of an army; but he was defeated and killed, through the arrival of Cineas of Thessaly in support with a force of a thousand horsemen. Then, being roused to anger by this disaster, they sent their king, Cleomenes, by land at the head of a larger force; and he, after defeating the Thessalian cavalry when they attempted to intercept his march into Attica, shut up Hippias within what was known as the Pelargic wall and blockaded him there with the assistance of the Athenians. While he was sitting down before the place, it so happened that the sons of the Pisistratidae were captured in an attempt to slip out; upon which the tyrants capitulated on condition of the safety of their children, and surrendered the Acropolis to the Athenians, five days being first allowed them to remove their effects. This took place in the archonship of Harpactides, after they had held the tyranny for about seventeen years since their father's death, or in all, including the period of their father's rule, for forty-nine years.

20 • After the overthrow of the tyranny, the rival leaders in the state were Isagoras son of Tisander, a partisan of the tyrants, and Cleisthenes, who belonged to the family of the Alcmeonidae. Cleisthenes, being beaten in the political clubs, called in the people by offering the franchise to the masses. Thereupon Isagoras, finding himself left inferior in power, invited Cleomenes, who was united to him by ties of hospitality, to return to Athens, and persuaded him to 'drive out the pollution', a plea derived from the fact that the Alcmeonidae were supposed to be under the curse of pollution. On this Cleisthenes retired from the country, and Cleomenes, entering Attica with a small force, expelled, as polluted, seven hundred Athenian families. Having effected this, he next attempted to dissolve the Council, and to set up Isagoras and three hundred of his partisans as the supreme power in the state. The Council, however, resisted, the populace flocked together, and Cleomenes and Isagoras, with their adherents, took refuge on the Acropolis. Here the people sat down and besieged them for two days; and on the third they agreed to let Cleomenes and all his followers depart, while they summoned Cleisthenes and the other exiles back to Athens. When the people had thus obtained the command of affairs, Cleisthenes was their chief and popular leader. For the Alcmeonidae were perhaps the chief cause of the expulsion of the tyrants, and for the greater part of their rule were at perpetual war with them. But even earlier than the attempts of the Alcmeonidae, Cedon made an attack on the tyrants; whence there came another popular drinking song, addressed to him:

> Pour a health yet again, boy, to Cedon; forget not this duty
>   to do,
> If a health is an honour befitting the name of a good man and
>   true.

21 • The people, therefore, had good reason to place confidence in Cleisthenes. Accordingly, now that he was the popular leader, three years after the expulsion of the tyrants, in

the archonship of Isagoras, his first step was to distribute the whole population into ten tribes in place of the existing four, with the object of intermixing the members of the different tribes, and so securing that more persons might have a share in the franchise. From this arose the saying 'Do not look at the tribes', addressed to those who wished to scrutinize the lists of the old families. Next he made the Council to consist of five hundred members instead of four hundred, each tribe now contributing fifty, whereas formerly each had sent a hundred. The reason why he did not organize the people into twelve tribes was that he might not have to use the existing division into trittyes; for the four tribes had twelve trittyes, so that he would not have achieved his object of redistributing the population in fresh combinations. Further, he divided the country into thirty groups of demes, ten from the districts about the city, ten from the coast, and ten from the interior. These he called trittyes; and he assigned three of them by lot to each tribe, in such a way that each should have one portion in each of these three localities. All who lived in any given deme he declared fellow-demesmen, to the end that the new citizens might not be exposed by the habitual use of family names, but that men might be officially described by the names of their demes; and accordingly it is by the names of their demes that the Athenians speak of one another. He also instituted Demarchs, who had the same duties as the previously existing Naucrari—the demes being made to take the place of the naucraries. He gave names to the demes, some from the localities to which they belonged, some from the persons who founded them, since some of the areas no longer corresponded to localities possessing names. On the other hand he allowed every one to retain his family and clan and religious rites according to ancestral custom. The names given to the tribes were the ten which the Pythia appointed out of the hundred selected national heroes.

22 • By these reforms the constitution became much more democratic than that of Solon. The laws of Solon had been obliterated by disuse during the period of the tyranny, while

Cleisthenes substituted new ones with the object of securing the goodwill of the masses. Among these was the law concerning ostracism. Four years after the establishment of this system, in the archonship of Hermocreon, they first imposed upon the Council of Five Hundred the oath which they take to the present day. Next they began to elect the generals by tribes, one from each tribe, while the Polemarch was the commander of the whole army. Then, eleven years later, in the archonship of Phaenippus they won the battle of Marathon; and two years after this victory, when the people had now gained self-confidence, they for the first time made use of the law of ostracism. This had originally been passed as a precaution against men in high office, because Pisistratus took advantage of his position as a popular leader and general to make himself tyrant; and the first person ostracized was one of his relatives, Hipparchus son of Charmus, of the deme of Collytus, the very person on whose account especially Cleisthenes had enacted the law, as he wished to get rid of him. (The Athenians, with the usual leniency of the democracy, allowed all the partisans of the tyrants, who had not joined in their evil deeds in the time of the troubles, to remain in the city; and the chief and leader of these was Hipparchus.) Then in the very next year, in the archonship of Telesinus, they for the first time since the tyranny elected, tribe by tribe, the nine Archons by lot out of the five hundred candidates selected by the demes, all the earlier ones having been elected by vote; and in the same year Megacles son of Hippocrates, of the deme of Alopece, was ostracized. Thus for three years they continued to ostracize the friends of the tyrants, on whose account the law had been passed; but in the following year they began to remove others as well who seemed to be more powerful than was expedient. The first person unconnected with the tyrants who was ostracized was Xanthippus son of Ariphron. Two years later, in the archonship of Nicodemus, the mines of Maroneia were discovered, and the state made a profit of a hundred talents from the working of them. Some persons advised the people to make a distribution of the money among themselves, but this was prevented by Themistocles. He refused to say on what he proposed to spend the money, but he bade them lend it to the hundred richest men in Athens, one talent to each, and then, if the manner in which it was employed pleased the people, the expenditure should be charged to the state, but otherwise the state should receive the sum back from those to whom it was lent. On these terms he received the money and with it he had a hundred triremes built, each of the hundred individuals building one; and it was with these ships that they fought the battle of Salamis against the barbarians. About this time Aristides the son of Lysimachus was ostracized. Three years later, however, in the archonship of Hypsichides, all the ostracized persons were recalled, on account of the advance of the army of Xerxes; and it was laid down for the future that persons under sentence of ostracism must not live between Geraestus and Scyllaeum, on pain of losing their civic rights irrevocably.

23 • So far, then, had the city progressed by this time, growing gradually with the growth of the democracy; but after the Persian wars the Council of Areopagus once more developed strength and assumed the control of the state. It did not acquire this supremacy by virtue of any formal decree, but because it had been the cause of the battle of Salamis being fought. When the generals were utterly at a loss how to meet the crisis and made proclamation that every one should see to his own safety, the Areopagus provided eight drachmas to each member of the ships' crews, and so prevailed on them to go on board. On these grounds people bowed to its prestige; and during this period Athens was well administered. At this time they devoted themselves to the prosecution of war and were in high repute among the Greeks, so that the command by sea was conferred upon them in spite of the opposition of the Lacedaemonians. The leaders of the people during this period were Aristides, son of Lysimachus, and Themistocles, son of Neocles, of whom the latter appeared to devote himself to the conduct of war, while the former had the reputation of being a clever statesman and the most upright man

of his time. Accordingly the one was usually employed as general, the other as political adviser. The rebuilding of the fortifications they conducted in combination, although they were political opponents; but it was Aristides who, seizing the opportunity afforded by the discredit brought upon the Lacedaemonians by Pausanias, guided the public policy in the matter of the defection of the Ionian states from the alliance with Sparta. It follows that it was he who made the first assessment of tribute from the various allied states, two years after the battle of Salamis, in the archonship of Timosthenes; and it was he who took the oath of offensive and defensive alliance with the Ionians, on which occasion they cast the masses of iron into the sea.

24 • After this, seeing the state growing in confidence and much wealth accumulated, he advised the people to lay hold of the leadership of the league, and to quit the country districts and settle in the city. He pointed out to them that all would be able to gain a living there, some by service in the army, others in the garrisons, others by taking a part in public affairs; and in this way they would secure the leadership. This advice was taken; and when the people had assumed the supreme control they proceeded to treat their allies in a more imperious fashion, with the exception of the Chians, Lesbians, and Samians. These they maintained to protect their empire, leaving their constitutions untouched, and allowing them to retain whatever dominion they then possessed. They also secured an ample maintenance for the mass of the population in the way which Aristides had pointed out to them. Out of the proceeds of the tributes and the taxes and the contributions of the allies more than twenty thousand persons were maintained. There were 6,000 jurymen, 1,600 bowmen, 1,200 Knights, 500 members of the Council, 500 guards of the dockyards, besides fifty guards in the Acropolis. There were some 700 magistrates at home, and some 700 abroad. Further, when they subsequently went to war, there were in addition 2,500 heavy-armed troops, twenty guardships, and other ships which collected the tributes, with crews

amounting to 2,000 men, selected by lot; and besides these there were the persons maintained by the Prytaneum, and orphans, and gaolers, since all these were supported by the state.

25 • Such was the way in which the people earned their livelihood. The supremacy of the Areopagus lasted for about seventeen years after the Persian wars, although gradually declining. But as the strength of the masses increased, Ephialtes, son of Sophonides, a man with a reputation for incorruptibility and public virtue, who had become the leader of the people, made an attack upon that Council. First of all he ruined many of its members by bringing actions against them with reference to their administration. Then, in the archonship of Conon, he stripped the Council of all the acquired prerogatives from which it derived its guardianship of the constitution, and assigned some of them to the Council of Five Hundred, and others to the Assembly and the law-courts. In this revolution he was assisted by Themistocles, who was himself a member of the Areopagus, but was expecting to be tried before it on a charge of treasonable dealings with Persia. This made him anxious that it should be overthrown, and accordingly he warned Ephialtes that the Council intended to arrest him, while at the same time he informed the Areopagites that he would reveal to them certain persons who were conspiring to subvert the constitution. He then conducted the representatives delegated by the Council to the residence of Ephialtes, promising to show them the conspirators who assembled there, and proceeded to converse with them in an earnest manner. Ephialtes, seeing this, was seized with alarm and took refuge in suppliant guise at the altar. Every one was astounded at the occurrence, and presently, when the Council of Five Hundred met, Ephialtes and Themistocles together proceeded to denounce the Areopagus to them. This they repeated in similar fashion in the Assembly, until they succeeded in depriving it of its power. Not long afterwards, however, Ephialtes was assassinated by Aristodicus of Tanagra. In this way was the Council of Areopagus deprived of its guardianship of the state.

26 • After this the administration of the state became more and more lax, in consequence of the eager rivalry of candidates for popular favour. During this period the moderate party, as it happened, had no real chief, their leader being Cimon son of Miltiades, who was a comparatively young man, and had been late in entering public life; and at the same time the general populace suffered great losses by war. The soldiers for active service were selected at that time from the roll of citizens, and as the generals were men of no military experience, who owned their position solely to their family standing, it continually happened that some two or three thousand of the troops perished on an expedition; and in this way the best men alike of the lower and the upper classes were exhausted. Consequently in most matters of administration less heed was paid to the laws than had formerly been the case. No alteration, however, was made in the method of election of the nine Archons, except that five years after the death of Ephialtes it was decided that the candidates to be submitted to the lot for that office might be selected from the Zeugitae as well. The first Archon from that class was Mnesitheides. Up to this time all the Archons had been taken from the Pentacosiomedimni and Knights, while the Zeugitae were confined to the ordinary magistracies, save where an evasion of the law was overlooked. Four years later, in the archonship of Lysicrates, the thirty 'local justices', as they were called, were re-established; and two years afterwards, in the archonship of Antidotus, in consequence of the great increase in the number of citizens, it was resolved, on the motion of Pericles, that no one should be admitted to the franchise who was not of citizen birth by both parents.

27 • After this Pericles came forward as popular leader, having first distinguished himself while still a young man by prosecuting Cimon on the audit of his official accounts as general. Under his auspices the constitution became still more democratic. He took away some of the privileges of the Areopagus, and, above all, he turned the policy of the state in the direction of sea power, which caused the masses to acquire confidence in themselves and consequently to take

the constitution more and more into their own hands. Moreover, forty-eight years after the battle of Salamis, in the archonship of Pythodorus, the Peloponnesian war broke out, during which the populace was shut up in the city and became accustomed to gain its livelihood by military service, and so, partly voluntarily and partly involuntarily, determined to assume the administration of the state itself. Pericles was also the first to institute pay for service in the law-courts, as a bid for popular favour to counterbalance the wealth of Cimon. The latter, having private possessions on a regal scale, not only performed the regular public services magnificently, but also maintained a large number of his fellow-demesmen. Any member of the deme of Laciadae could go every day to Cimon's house and there receive a reasonable provision; while his estate was guarded by no fences, so that any one who liked might help himself to the fruit from it. Pericles' private property was quite unequal to this magnificence and accordingly he took the advice of Damonides of Oea (who was commonly supposed to be the person who prompted Pericles in most of his measures, and was therefore subsequently ostracized), which was that, as he was beaten in the matter of private possessions, he should make gifts to the people from their own property; and accordingly he instituted pay for the members of the juries. Some critics accuse him of thereby causing a deterioration in the character of the juries, since it was always the common people who put themselves forward for selection as jurors, rather than the men of better position. Moreover, bribery came into existence after this, the first person to introduce it being Anytus, after his command at Pylos. He was prosecuted by certain individuals on account of his loss of Pylos, but escaped by bribing the jury.

28 • So long as Pericles was leader of the people, things went tolerably well with the state; but when he was dead there was a great change for the worse. Then for the first time did the people choose a leader who was of no reputation among men of good standing, whereas up to this time such men had always been found as leaders of the democracy.

The first leader of the people, in the very beginning of things, was Solon, and the second was Pisistratus, both of them men of birth and position. After the overthrow of the tyrants there was Cleisthenes, a member of the house of the Alcmeonidae; and he had no rival opposed to him after the expulsion of the party of Isagoras. After this Xanthippus was the leader of the people, and Miltiades of the upper class. Then came Themistocles and Aristides, and after them Ephialtes as leader of the people, and Cimon son of Miltiades of the wealthier class. Pericles followed as leader of the people, and Thucydides, who was connected by marriage with Cimon, of the opposition. After the death of Pericles, Nicias, who subsequently fell in Sicily, appeared as leader of the aristocracy, and Cleon son of Cleaenetus of the people. The latter seems, more than any one else, to have been the cause of the corruption of the democracy by his wild undertakings; and he was the first to use unseemly shouting and coarse abuse on the Bema, and to harangue the people with his cloak girt up short about him, whereas all his predecessors had spoken decently and in order. These were succeeded by Theramenes son of Hagnon as leader of the one party, and the lyre-maker Cleophon of the people. It was Cleophon who first granted the two-obol donation and for some time it continued to be given; but then Callicrates of Paeania ousted him by promising to add a third obol to the sum. Both of these persons were subsequently condemned to death; for the people, even if they are deceived for a time, in the end generally come to detest those who have beguiled them into any unworthy action. After Cleophon the popular leadership was occupied successively by the men who chose to talk the biggest and pander the most to the tastes of the majority, with their eyes fixed only on the interests of the moment. The best statesmen at Athens, after those of early times, seem to have been Nicias, Thucydides, and Theramenes. As to Nicias and Thucydides, nearly every one agrees that they were not merely men of birth and character, but also statesmen, and that they ruled the state with paternal care. On the merits of Theramenes opinion is divided, because it so happened that in his time public affairs were in a very stormy state. But those who give their opinion deliberately find him, not, as his critics falsely assert, overthrowing every kind of constitution, but supporting every kind so long as it did not transgress the laws; thus showing that he was able, as every good citizen should be, to live under any form of constitution, while he refused to countenance illegality and was its constant enemy.

29 • So long as the fortune of the war continued even, the Athenians preserved the democracy; but after the disaster in Sicily, when the Lacedaemonians had gained the upper hand through their alliance with the king of Persia, they were compelled to abolish the democracy and establish in its place the constitution of the Four Hundred. The speech recommending this course before the vote was made by Melobius, and the motion was proposed by Pythodorus of Anaphlystus; but the real argument which persuaded the majority was the belief that the king of Persia was more likely to form an alliance with them if the constitution were on an oligarchical basis. The motion of Pythodorus was to the following effect. The popular Assembly was to elect twenty persons from among those over forty years of age, who, in conjunction with the existing ten members of the Committee of Public Safety, after taking an oath that they would frame such measures as they thought best for the state, should then prepare proposals for the public safety. In addition, any other person might make proposals, so that of all the schemes before them the people might choose the best. Cleitophon concurred with the motion of Pythodorus, but moved that the committee should also investigate the ancient laws enacted by Cleisthenes when he created the democracy, in order that they might have these too before them and so be in a position to decide wisely; his suggestion being that the constitution of Cleisthenes was not really democratic, but closely akin to that of Solon. When the committee was elected, their first proposal was that the Prytanes should be completed to put to the vote any motion that was offered on behalf of the public safety. Next they abolished all indictments for il-

legal proposals, all impeachments and public prosecutions, in order that every Athenian should be free to give his counsel on the situation, if he chose; and they decreed that if any person imposed a fine on any other for his acts in this respect, or prosecuted him or summoned him before the courts, he should, on an information being laid against him, be brought before the generals, who should deliver him to the Eleven to be put to death. After these preliminary measures, they drew up the constitution in the following manner. The revenues of the state were not to be spent on any purpose except the war. All magistrates should serve without remuneration for the period of the war, except the nine Archons and the Prytanes for the time being, who should each receive three obols a day. The whole of the rest of the administration was to be committed, for the period of the war, to those Athenians who were most capable of serving the state personally or pecuniarily, to the number of not less than five thousand. This body was to have full powers, to the extent even of making treaties with whomsoever they willed; and ten representatives, over forty years of age, were to be elected from each tribe to draw up the list of the Five Thousand, after taking an oath on a full and perfect sacrifice.

30 • These were the recommendations of the committee; and when they had been ratified the Five Thousand elected from their own number a hundred commissioners to draw up the constitution. They, on their appointment, drew up and produced the following recommendations. There should be a Council, holding office for a year, consisting of men over thirty years of age, serving without pay. To this body should belong the Generals, the nine Archons, the Amphictyonic Registrar [Hieromnemon], the Taxiarchs, the Hipparchs, the Phylarchs, the commanders of garrisons, the Treasurers of Athena and the other gods, ten in number, the Hellenic Treasurers [Hellenotamiae], the Treasurers of the other non-sacred moneys, to the number of twenty, the ten Commissioners of Sacrifices [Hieropoei], and the ten Superintendents of the mysteries.

All these were to be appointed by the Council from a larger number of selected candidates, chosen from its members for the time being. The other offices were all to be filled by lot, and not from the members of the Council. The Hellenic Treasurers who actually administered the funds should not sit with the Council. As regards the future, four Councils were to be created, of men of the age already mentioned, and one of these was to be chosen by lot to take office at once, while the others were to receive it in turn, in the order decided by the lot. For this purpose the hundred commissioners were to distribute themselves and all the rest as equally as possible into four parts, and cast lots for precedence, and the selected body should hold office for a year. They were to administer that office as seemed to them best, both with reference to the safe custody and due expenditure of the finances, and generally with regard to all other matters to the best of their ability. If they desired to take a larger number of persons into counsel, each member might call in one assistant of his own choice, subject to the same qualification of age. The Council was to sit once every five days, unless there was any special need for more frequent sittings. The casting of the lot for the Council was to be held by the nine Archons; votes on divisions were to be counted by five tellers chosen by lot from the members of the Council, and of these one was to be selected by lot every day to act as president. These five persons were to cast lots for precedence between the parties wishing to appear before the Council, giving the first place to sacred matters, the second to heralds, the third to embassies, and the fourth to all other subjects; but matters concerning the war might be dealt with, on the motion of the generals, whenever there was need, without balloting. Any member of the Council who did not enter the Council-house at the time named should be fined a drachma for each day, unless he was away on leave of absence from the Council.

31 • Such was the constitution which they drew up for the time to come, but for the immediate present they devised the following scheme. There should be a Council of Four Hun-

dred, as in the ancient constitution, forty from each tribe, chosen out of candidates of more than thirty years of age, selected by the members of the tribes. This Council should appoint the magistrates and draw up the form of oath which they were to take; and in all that concerned the laws, in the examination of official accounts, and in other matters generally, they might act according to their discretion. They must, however, observe the laws that might be enacted with reference to the constitution of the state, and had no power to alter them nor to pass others. The generals should be provisionally elected from the whole body of the Five Thousand, but so soon as the Council came into existence it was to hold an examination of military equipments, and thereon elect ten persons, together with a secretary, and the persons thus elected should hold office during the coming year with full powers, and should have the right, whenever they desired it, of joining in the deliberations of the Council. They were also to elect a single Hipparch and ten Phylarchs; but for the future the Council was to elect these officers according to the regulations above laid down. No office, except those of member of the Council and of general, might be held more than once, either by the first occupants or by their successors. With reference to the future distribution of the Four Hundred into the four successive sections, the hundred commissioners must divide them whenever the time came for the citizens to join in the Council along with the rest.

32 • The hundred commissioners appointed by the Five Thousand drew up the constitution as just stated; and after it had been ratified by the people, under the presidency of Aristomachus, the existing Council, that of the year of Callias, was dissolved before it had completed its term of office. It was dissolved on the fourteenth day of the month Thargelion, and the Four Hundred entered into office on the twenty-first; whereas the regular Council, elected by lot, ought to have entered into office on the fourteenth of Scirophorion. Thus was the oligarchy established, in the archonship of Callias,

just about a hundred years after the expulsion of the tyrants. The chief promoters of the revolution were Pisander, Antiphon, and Theramenes, all of them men of good birth and with high reputations for ability and judgement. When, however, this constitution had been established, the Five Thousand were only nominally selected, and the Four Hundred, together with the ten officers on whom full powers had been conferred, occupied the Council-house and really administered the government. They began by sending ambassadors to the Lacedaemonians proposing a cessation of the war on the basis of the existing position; but as the Lacedaemonians refused to listen to them unless they would also abandon the command of the sea, they broke off the negotiations.

33 • For about four months the constitution of the Four Hundred lasted, and Mnasilochus held office as Archon of their nomination for two months of the year of Theopompus, who was Archon for the remaining ten. On the loss of the naval battle of Eretria, however, and the revolt of the whole of Euboea except Oreum, the indignation of the people was greater than at any of the earlier disasters, since they drew far more supplies at this time from Euboea than from Attica itself. Accordingly they deposed the Four Hundred and committed the management of affairs to the Five Thousand, consisting of persons possessing a military equipment. At the same time they voted that pay should not be given for any public office. The persons chiefly responsible for the revolution were Aristocrates and Theramenes, who disapproved of the action of the Four Hundred in retaining the direction of affairs entirely in their own hands, and referring nothing to the Five Thousand. During this period the constitution of the state seems to have been admirable, since it was a time of war and the franchise was in the hands of those who possessed military equipment.

34 • The people, however, in a very short time deprived the Five Thousand of their monopoly of the government. Then, six years after the overthrow of the Four Hundred, in the ar-

chonship of Callias of Angele, the battle of Arginusae took place, of which the results were, first, that the ten generals who had gained the victory were all condemned by a single decision, owing to the people being led astray by persons who aroused their indignation; though, as a matter of fact, some of the generals had actually taken no part in the battle, and others were themselves picked up by other vessels. Secondly, when the Lacedaemonians proposed to evacuate Decelea and make peace on the basis of the existing position, although some of the Athenians supported this proposal, the majority refused to listen to them. In this they were led astray by Cleophon, who appeared in the Assembly drunk and wearing his breastplate, and prevented peace being made, declaring that he would never accept peace unless the Lacedaemonians abandoned their claims on all the cities allied with them. They mismanaged their opportunity then, and in a very short time they learnt their mistake. The next year, in the archonship of Alexias, they suffered the disaster of Aegospotami, the consequence of which was that Lysander became master of the city, and set up the Thirty in the following manner. One of the terms of peace stipulated that the state should be governed according to 'the ancient constitution'. Accordingly the popular party tried to preserve the democracy, while that part of the upper class which belonged to the political clubs, together with the exiles who had returned since the peace, aimed at an oligarchy, and those who were not members of any club, though in other respects they considered themselves as good as any other citizens, were anxious to restore the ancient constitution. The latter class included Archinus, Anytus, Cleitophon, Phormisius, and many others, but their most prominent leader was Theramenes. Lysander, however, threw his influence on the side of the oligarchical party, and the popular Assembly was compelled by sheer intimidation to pass a vote establishing the oligarchy. The motion to this effect was proposed by Dracontides of Aphidna.

35 • In this way were the Thirty established in power, in the archonship of Pythodorus. As soon, however, as they were

masters of the city, they ignored all the resolutions which had been passed relating to the organization of the constitution, but after appointing a Council of Five Hundred and the other magistrates out of a thousand selected candidates, and associating with themselves ten Archons in Piraeus, eleven superintendents of the prison, and three hundred 'lash-bearers' as attendants, they kept the city under their own control. At first, indeed, they behaved with moderation towards the citizens and pretended to administer the state according to the ancient constitution. They took down from the hill of Areopagus the laws of Ephialtes and Archestratus relating to the Areopagite Council; they also repealed such of the statutes of Solon as were obscure, and abolished the supreme power of the law-courts. In this they claimed to be restoring the constitution and freeing it from obscurities; as, for instance, by making the testator free once and for all to leave his property as he pleased, and abolishing the existing limitations in cases of insanity, old age, and undue female influence, in order that no opening might be left for professional accusers. In other matters also their conduct was similar. At first, then, they acted on these lines, and they destroyed the professional accusers and those mischievous and evil-minded persons who, to the great detriment of the democracy, had attached themselves to it in order to curry favour with it. With all of this the city was much pleased, and thought that the Thirty were doing it with the best of motives. But so soon as they had got a firmer hold on the city, they spared no class of citizens, but put to death any persons who were eminent for wealth or birth or character. Herein they aimed at removing all whom they had reason to fear, while they also wished to lay hands on their possessions; and in a short time they put to death not less than fifteen hundred persons.

36 • Theramenes, however, seeing the city thus falling into ruin, was displeased with their proceedings, and counselled them to cease such unprincipled conduct and let the better classes have a share in the government. At first they resisted

his advice, but when his proposals came to be known abroad, and the masses began to associate themselves with him, they were seized with alarm lest he should make himself the leader of the people and destroy their despotic power. Accordingly they drew up a list of three thousand citizens, to whom they announced that they would give a share in the constitution. Theramenes, however, criticized this scheme also, first on the ground that, while proposing to give all respectable citizens a share in the constitution, they were actually giving it only to three thousand persons, as though all merit were confined within that number; and secondly because they were doing two inconsistent things, since they made the government rest on the basis of force, and yet made the governors inferior in strength to the governed. However, they took no notice of his criticisms, and for a long time put off the publication of the list of the Three Thousand and kept to themselves the names of those who had been placed upon it; and every time they did decide to publish it they proceeded to strike out some of those who had been included in it, and insert others who had been omitted.

37 • Now when winter had set in, Thrasybulus and the exiles occupied Phyle, and the force which the Thirty led out to attack them met with a reverse. Thereupon the Thirty decided to disarm the bulk of the population and to get rid of Theramenes; which they did in the following way. They introduced two laws into the Council, which they commanded it to pass; the first of them gave the Thirty absolute power to put to death any citizen who was not included in the list of the Three Thousand, while the second disqualified all persons from participation in the franchise who should have assisted in the demolition of the fort of Eëtioneia, or have acted in any way against the Four Hundred who had organized the previous oligarchy. Theramenes had done both, and accordingly, when these laws were ratified, he became excluded from the franchise and the Thirty had full power to put him to death. Theramenes having been thus removed, they disarmed all the people except the

Three Thousand, and in every respect showed a great advance in cruelty and crime. They also sent ambassadors to Lacedaemon to blacken the character of Theramenes and to ask for help; and the Lacedaemonians, in answer to their appeal, sent Callibius as military governor with about seven hundred troops, who came and occupied the Acropolis.

38 • These events were followed by the occupation of Munichia by the exiles from Phyle, and their victory over the Thirty and their partisans. After the fight the party of the city retreated, and next day they held a meeting in the marketplace and deposed the Thirty, and elected ten citizens with full powers to bring the war to a termination. When, however, the Ten had taken over the government they did nothing toward the object for which they were elected, but sent envoys to Lacedaemon to ask for help and to borrow money. Further, finding that the citizens who possessed the franchise were displeased at their proceedings, they were afraid lest they should be deposed, and consequently, in order to strike terror into them (in which design they succeeded), they arrested Demaretus, one of the most eminent citizens, and put him to death. This gave them a firm hold on the government, and they also had the support of Callibius and his Peloponnesians, together with several of the Knights; for some of the members of this class were the most zealous among the citizens to prevent the return of the exiles from Phyle. When, however, the party in Piraeus and Munichia began to gain the upper hand in the war, through the defection of the whole populace to them, the party in the city deposed the original Ten, and elected another Ten, consisting of men of the highest repute. Under their administration, and with their active and zealous co-operation, the treaty of reconciliation was made and the populace returned to the city. The most prominent members of this board were Rhinon of Paeania and Phayllus of Acherdus, who, even before the arrival of Pausanias, opened negotiations with the party in Piraeus, and after his arrival seconded his efforts to bring about the return of the exiles. For it was Pausanias, the king of the Lacedaemonians,

who brought the peace and reconciliation to a fulfilment, in conjunction with the ten commissioners of arbitration who arrived later from Lacedaemon, at his own earnest request. Rhinon and his colleagues received a vote of thanks for the goodwill shown by them to the people, and though they received their charge under an oligarchy and handed in their accounts under a democracy, no one, either of the party that had stayed in the city or of the exiles that had returned from the Piraeus, brought any complaint against them. On the contrary, Rhinon was immediately elected general on account of his conduct in this office.

39 • This reconciliation was effected in the archonship of Eucleides, on the following terms. All persons who, having remained in the city during the troubles, were now anxious to leave it, were to be free to settle at Eleusis, retaining their civil rights and possessing full and independent powers of self-government, and with the free enjoyment of their own personal property. The temple at Eleusis should be common ground for both parties, and should be under the superintendence of the Ceryces and the Eumolpidae, according to ancient custom. The settlers at Eleusis should not be allowed to enter Athens, nor the people of Athens to enter Eleusis, except at the season of the mysteries. The secessionists should pay their share to the fund for the common defence out of their revenues, just like all the other Athenians. If any of the seceding party wished to take a house in Eleusis, the people would help them to obtain the consent of the owner; but if they could not come to terms, they should appoint three valuers on either side, and the owner should receive whatever price they should appoint. Of the inhabitants of Eleusis, those whom the secessionists wished to remain should be allowed to do so. The list of those who desired to secede should be made up within ten days after the taking of the oaths in the case of persons already in the country, and their actual departure should take place within twenty days; persons at present out of the country should have the same terms allowed to them after their return. No one who settled at Eleusis should

be capable of holding any office in Athens until he should again register himself on the roll as a resident in the city. Trials for homicide, in which one party had either killed or wounded another, should be conducted according to ancestral practice. There should be a general amnesty concerning past events towards all persons except the Thirty, the Ten, the Eleven, and the magistrates in Piraeus; and these too should be included if they should submit their accounts in the usual way. Such accounts should be given by the magistrates in Piraeus before a court of citizens in Piraeus, and by the magistrates in the city before a court of those rated.[3] On these terms those who wished to do so might secede. Each party was to repay separately the money which it had borrowed for the war.

40 • When the reconciliation had taken place on these terms, those who had fought on the side of the Thirty felt considerable apprehensions, and a large number intended to secede. But as they put off entering their names till the last moment, as people will do, Archinus, observing their numbers, and being anxious to retain them as citizens, cut off the remaining days during which the list should have remained open; and in this way many persons were compelled to remain, though they did so very unwillingly until they recovered confidence. This is one point in which Archinus appears to have acted in a most statesmanlike manner, and another was his subsequent prosecution of Thrasybulus on the charge of illegality, for a motion by which he proposed to confer the franchise on all who had taken part in the return from Piraeus, although some of them were notoriously slaves. And yet a third such action was when one of the returned exiles began to violate the amnesty, whereupon Archinus haled him to the Council and persuaded them to execute him without trial, telling them that now they would have to show whether they wished to preserve the democracy and abide by

---

[3] The text is uncertain.

the oaths they had taken; for if they let this man escape they would encourage others to imitate him, while if they executed him they would make an example for all to learn by. And this was exactly what happened; for after this man had been put to death no one ever again broke the amnesty. On the contrary, the Athenians seem, both in public and in private, to have behaved in the most unprecedentedly admirable and public-spirited way with reference to the preceding troubles. Not only did they blot out all memory of former offences, but they even repaid to the Lacedaemonians out of the public purse the money which the Thirty had borrowed for the war, although the treaty required each party, the party of the city and the party of Piraeus, to pay its own debts separately. This they did because they thought it was a necessary first step in the direction of restoring harmony; but in other states, so far from the democratic parties making advances from their own possessions, they are rather in the habit of making a general redistribution of the land. A reconciliation was made with the secessionists at Eleusis two years after the secession, in the archonship of Xenaenetus.

41 • This, however, took place at a later date; at the time of which we are speaking the people, having secured the control of the state, established the constitution which exists at the present day. Pythodorus was Archon at the time, but the democracy seems to have assumed the supreme power with perfect justice, since it had effected its own return by its own exertions.[4] This was the eleventh change which had taken place in the constitution of Athens. The first modification of the primaeval condition of things was when Ion and his companions brought the people together into a community, for then the people were first divided into the four tribes, and the tribe-kings were created. Next, and first after this, having now some semblance of a constitution, was that which took place in the reign of Theseus, consisting in a slight

[4] Kenyon obelizes this sentence.

deviation from absolute monarchy. After this came the constitution formed under Draco, when the first code of laws was drawn up. The third was that which followed the civil war, in the time of Solon; from this the democracy took its rise. The fourth was the tyranny of Pisistratus; the fifth the constitution of Cleisthenes, after the overthrow of the tyrants, of a more democratic character than that of Solon. The sixth was that which followed on the Persian wars, when the Council of Areopagus had the direction of the state. The seventh, succeeding this, was the constitution which Aristides sketched out, and which Ephialtes brought to completion by overthrowing the Areopagite Council; under this the nation, misled by the demagogues, made the most serious mistakes in the interest of its maritime empire. The eighth was the establishment of the Four Hundred, followed by the ninth, the restored democracy. The tenth was the tyranny of the Thirty and the Ten. The eleventh was that which followed the return from Phyle and Piraeus; and this has continued from that day to this, with continual accretions of power to the masses. The democracy has made itself master of everything and administers everything by its votes in the Assembly and by the law-courts, in which it holds the supreme power. Even the jurisdiction of the Council has passed into the hands of the people at large; and this appears to be a judicious change, since small bodies are more open to corruption, whether by actual money or influence, than large ones. At first they refused to allow payment for attendance at the Assembly; but the result was that people did not attend. Consequently, after the Prytanes had tried many devices in order to induce the populace to come and ratify the votes, Agyrrhius, in the first instance, made a provision of one obol a day, which Heracleides of Clazomenae, nicknamed 'the king', increased to two obols, and Agyrrhius again to three.

42 • The present state of the constitution is as follows. The franchise is open to all who are of citizen birth by both parents. They are enrolled among the demesmen at the age of eighteen. On the occasion of their enrolment the demes-

men give their votes on oath, first whether the candidates appear to be of the age prescribed by the law (if not, they are dismissed back into the ranks of the boys), and secondly whether the candidate is free born and of such parentage as the laws require. Then if they decide that he is not a free man, he appeals to the law-courts, and the demesmen appoint five of their own number to act as accusers; if the court decides that he has no right to be enrolled, he is sold by the state as a slave, but if he wins his case he has a right to be enrolled among the demesmen without further question. After this the Council examines those who have been enrolled, and if it comes to the conclusion that any of them is less than eighteen years of age, it fines the demesmen who enrolled him. When the youths [Ephebi] have passed this examination, their fathers meet by their tribes, and appoint on oath three of their fellow tribesmen, over forty years of age, who, in their opinion, are the best and most suitable persons to have charge of the youths; and of these the Assembly elects one from each tribe as guardian, together with a director, chosen from the general body of Athenians, to control them all. Under the charge of these persons the youths first of all make the circuit of the temples; then they proceed to Piraeus, and some of them garrison Munichia and some the south shore. The Assembly also elects two trainers, with subordinate instructors, who teach them to fight in heavy armour, to use the bow and javelin, and to discharge a catapult. The guardians receive from the state a drachma apiece for their keep, and the youths four obols apiece. Each guardian receives the allowance for all the members of his tribe and buys the necessary provisions for the common stock (they mess together by tribes), and generally superintends everything. In this way they spend the first year. The next year, after giving a public display of their military evolutions, on the occasion when the Assembly meets in the theatre, they receive a shield and spear from the state; after which they patrol the country and spend their time in the forts. For these two years they are on garrison duty, and wear the military cloak, and during this time they are exempt from all taxes. They also can neither bring an action at law, nor have one brought against them, in order that they may have no excuse for requiring leave of absence; though exception is made in cases of actions concerning inheritances and wards of state, or of any sacrificial ceremony connected with the family. When the two years have elapsed they thereupon take their position among the other citizens. Such is the manner of the enrolment of the citizens and the training of the youths.

43 • All the magistrates that are concerned with the ordinary routine of administration are elected by lot, except the Military Treasurer, the Commissioners of the Theoric fund, and the Superintendent of Springs. These are elected by vote, and hold office from one Panathenaic festival to the next. All military officers are also elected by vote.

The Council of Five Hundred is elected by lot, fifty from each tribe. Each tribe holds the office of Prytanes in turn, the order being determined by lot; the first four serve for thirty-six days each, the last six for thirty-five, since the reckoning is by lunar years. The Prytanes for the time being, in the first place, mess together in the Tholus and receive a sum of money from the state for their maintenance; and, secondly, they convene the meetings of the Council and the Assembly. The Council they convene every day, unless it is a holiday, the Assembly four times in each prytany. It is also their duty to draw up the programme of the business of the Council and to decide what subjects are to be dealt with on each particular day, and where the sitting is to be held. They also draw up the programme for the meetings of the Assembly. One of these in each prytany is called the 'sovereign' Assembly; in this the people have to ratify the continuance of the magistrates in office, if they are performing their duties properly, and to consider the supply of corn and the defence of the country. On this day, too, impeachments are introduced by those who wish to do so, the lists of property confiscated by the state are read, and also applications for inheritances and wards of state, so that nothing may pass unclaimed without the cognizance of any person concerned. In the sixth prytany, in addition to the business already stated, the question is put to the vote whether it is desirable to hold a vote of ostracism or not; and complaints against professional accusers, whether Athenian or aliens domiciled in Athens, are received, to the number of not more than three of either class, together with cases in which an individual has made some promise to the people and has not performed it. Another Assembly in each prytany is assigned to the hearing of petitions, and at this meeting any one is free, on depositing the petitioner's olive-branch, to speak to the people concerning any matter, public or private. The two remaining meetings are devoted to all other subjects, and the laws require them to deal with three questions connected with religion, three connected with heralds and embassies, and three on secular subjects. Sometimes questions are brought forward without a preliminary vote.

Heralds and envoys appear first before the Prytanes, and the bearers of dispatches also deliver them to the same officials.

44 • There is a single President of the Prytanes, elected by lot, who presides for a night and a day; he may not hold the office for more than that time, nor may the same individual hold it twice. He keeps the keys of the sanctuaries in which the treasures and public records of the state are preserved, and also the public seal; and he is bound to remain in the Tholus, together with one-third of the Prytanes, named by himself. Whenever the Prytanes convene a meeting of the Council or Assembly, he appoints by lot nine Proedri, one from each tribe except that which holds the office of Prytanes for the time being; and out of these nine he similarly appoints one as President, and hands over the programme for the meeting to them. They take it and see to the preservation of order, put forward the various subjects which are to be considered, decide the results of the votings, and direct the proceedings generally. They also have power to dismiss the meeting. No one may act as President more than once in the year, but he may be a Proedrus once in each prytany.

Elections to the offices of General and Hipparch and all other military commands are held in the Assembly, in such manner as the people decide; they are held after the sixth pry-tany by the first board of Prytanes in whose term of office the omens are favourable. There has, however, to be a prelimi-nary consideration by the Council in this case also.

45 • In former times the Council had full powers to inflict fines and imprisonment and death. When it had consigned Lysimachus to the executioner, and he was sitting in the im-mediate expectation of death, Eumelides of Alopece rescued him from its hands, maintaining that no citizen ought to be put to death except on the decision of a court of law. Accord-ingly a trial was held in a law-court, and Lysimachus was ac-quitted, receiving henceforth the nickname of 'the man from the drum-head'; and the people deprived the Council thence-forward of the power to inflict death or imprisonment or fine, passing a law that if the Council condemn any person for an offence or inflict a fine, the Thesmothetae shall bring the sen-tence or fine before the law-court, and the decision of the ju-rors shall be the final judgement in the matter.

The Council passes judgement on nearly all magistrates, especially those who have the control of money; its judge-ment, however, is not final, but is subject to an appeal to the law-courts. Private individuals, also, may lay an information against any magistrate they please for not obeying the laws, but here too there is an appeal to the law-courts if the Council declare the charge proved. The Council also examines those who are to be its members for the ensuing year, and likewise the nine Archons. Formerly the Council had full power to re-ject candidates for office as unsuitable, but now they have an appeal to the law-courts. In all these matters, therefore, the Council has no final jurisdiction. It takes, however, prelimi-nary cognizance of all matters brought before the Assembly, and the Assembly cannot vote on any question unless it has first been considered by the Council and placed on the pro-gramme by the Prytanes; since a person who carries a mo-tion in the Assembly is liable to an action for illegal proposal on these grounds.

46 • The Council also superintends the triremes that are already in existence, with their tackle and sheds, and builds new triremes or quadriremes, whichever the Assembly votes, with tackle and sheds to match. The Assembly appoints master-builders for the ships by vote; and if they do not hand them over completed to the next Council, they cannot receive the donation—that being normally given during the term of the following Council. For the building of the triremes it appoints ten commissioners, chosen from its own members. The Council also inspects all public buildings, and if it is of opinion that the state is being defrauded, it reports the culprit to the Assembly, and on condemnation hands him over to the law-courts.

47 • The Council also co-operates with the other magistrates in most of their duties. First there are the treasurers of Athena, ten in number, elected by lot, one from each tribe. According to the law of Solon—which is still in force—they must be Pentacosiomedimni, but in point of fact the person on whom the lot falls holds the office even though he be quite a poor man. These officers take over charge of the statue of Athena, the figures of Victory, and all the other ornaments of the temple, together with the money, in the presence of the Council. Then there are the Commissioners for Public Contracts [Poletae], ten in number, one chosen by lot from each tribe, who farm out all the public contracts. They lease the mines and taxes in conjunction with the Military Treasurer and the Commissioners of the Theoric fund, in the presence of the Council, and grant, to the persons indicated by the vote of the Council, the mines which are let out by the state, including both the workable ones, which are let for three years, and those which are let under special agreements for ten years. They also sell, in the presence of the Council, the property of those who have gone into exile from the court of the Areopagus, and of others whose goods have been confiscated, and the nine Archons ratify the contracts. They also hand over to the Council lists of the taxes which are farmed

out for the year, entering on whitened tablets the name of the lessee and the amount paid. They make separate lists, first of those who have to pay their instalments in each prytany, on ten several tablets, next of those who pay thrice in the year, with a separate tablet for each instalment, and finally of those who pay in the ninth prytany. They also draw up a list of farms and dwellings which have been confiscated and sold by order of the courts; for these too come within their province. In the case of dwellings the value must be paid up in five years, and in that of farms, in ten. The instalments are paid in the ninth prytany. Further, the King-archon brings before the Council the leases of the sacred enclosures written on whitened tablets. These too are leased for ten years, and the instalments are paid in the ninth prytany; consequently it is in this prytany that the greatest amount of money is collected. The tablets containing the lists of the instalments are carried into the Council, and the public clerk takes charge of them. Whenever a payment of instalments is to be made he takes from the pigeon-holes the precise list of the sums which are to be paid and struck off on that day, and delivers it to the Receivers-General. The rest are kept apart, in order that no sum may be struck off before it is paid.

48 • There are ten Receivers-General [Apodectae], elected by lot, one from each tribe. These officers receive the tablets, and strike off the instalments as they are paid, in the presence of the Council in the Council-chamber, and give the tablets back to the public clerk. If any one fails to pay his instalment, a note is made of it on the tablet; and he is bound to pay double the amount of the deficiency, or, in default, to be imprisoned. The Council has full power by the laws to exact these payments and to inflict this imprisonment. They receive all the instalments, therefore, on one day, and portion the money out among the magistrates; and on the next day they bring up the report of the apportionment, written on a wooden notice-board, and read it out in the Council-chamber, after which they ask publicly in the Council whether any one knows of any malpractice in reference to the apportionment, on the

part of either a magistrate or a private individual, and if any one is charged with malpractice they take a vote on it.

The Council also elects ten Auditors [Logistae] by lot from its own members, to audit the accounts of the magistrates for each prytany. They also elect one Examiner of Accounts [Euthunus] by lot from each tribe, with two assessors [Paredri] for each examiner, whose duty it is to sit at the ordinary market hours, each opposite the statue of the eponymous hero of his tribe; and if any one wishes to prefer a charge, on either public or private grounds, against any magistrate who has passed his audit before the law-courts, within three days of his having so passed, he enters on a whitened tablet his own name and that of the magistrate prosecuted, together with the malpractice that is alleged against him. He also appends his claim for a penalty of such amount as seems to him fitting, and gives in the record to the Examiner. The latter takes it, and if after reading it he considers it proved he hands it over, if a private case, to the local justices who introduce cases for the tribe concerned, while if it is a public case he enters it on the register of the Thesmothetae. Then, if the Thesmothetae accept it, they bring the accounts of this magistrate once more before the law-court, and the decision of the jury stands as the final judgement.

49 • The Council also inspects the horses belonging to the state. If a man who has a good horse is found to keep it in bad condition, he is mulcted in his allowance of corn; while those which cannot keep up or which shy and will not stand steady, it brands with a wheel on the jaw, and the horse so marked is disqualified for service. It also inspects those who appear to be fit for service as scouts, and any one whom it rejects is deprived of his horse. It also examines the infantry who serve among the cavalry, and any one whom it rejects ceases to receive his pay. The roll of the cavalry is drawn up by the Commissioners of Enrolment [Catalogeis], ten in number, elected by the Assembly by open vote. They hand over to the Hipparchs and Phylarchs the list of those whom they have enrolled, and these officers take it and bring it up before the Council, and there

open the tablet containing the names of the cavalry. If any of those who have been on the roll previously make affidavit that they are physically incapable of cavalry service, they strike them out; then they call up the persons enrolled, and if any one makes affidavit that he is either physically or pecuniarily incapable of cavalry service they dismiss him, but if no such affidavit is made the Council vote whether the individual in question is suitable for the purpose or not. If they vote in the affirmative his name is entered on the tablet; if not, he is dismissed with the others.

Formerly the Council used to decide on the plans for public buildings and the contract for making the robe of Athena; but now this is done by a jury in the law-courts appointed by lot, since the Council was considered to have shown favouritism in its decisions. The Council also shares with the Military Treasurer the superintendence of the manufacture of the images of Victory and the prizes at the Panathenaic festival.

The Council also examines infirm paupers; for there is a law which provides that persons possessing less than three minas, who are so crippled as to be unable to do any work, are, after examination by the Council, to receive two obols a day from the state for their support. A treasurer is appointed by lot to attend to them.

The Council also, speaking broadly, co-operates in most of the duties of all the other magistrates; and this ends the list of the functions of that body.

50 • There are ten Commissioners for Repairs of Temples elected by lot, who receive a sum of thirty minas from the Receivers-General, and therewith carry out the most necessary repairs in the temples.

There are also ten City Commissioners [Astynomi], of whom five hold office in Piraeus and five in the city. Their duty is to see that female flute- and harp- and lute-players are not hired at more than two drachmas, and if more than one person is anxious to hire the same girl, they cast lots and hire her out to the person to whom the lot falls. They also provide that no collector of sewage shall deposit any of his sewage within ten stadia of the walls; they prevent people from blocking up the streets by building, or stretching barriers across them, or making raised drain-pipes with a discharge into the street, or having doors which open outwards; they also remove the corpses of those who die in the streets for which purpose they have a body of state slaves assigned to them.

51 • Market Commissioners [Agoranomi] are elected by lot, five for Piraeus, five for the city. Their statutory duty is to see that all articles offered for sale in the market are pure and unadulterated.

Commissioners of Weights and Measures [Metronomi] are elected by lot, five for the city, and five for Piraeus. They see that sellers use fair weights and measures.

Formerly there were ten Corn Commissioners [Sitophy-laces], elected by lot, five for Piraeus, and five for the city; but now there are twenty for the city and fifteen for Piraeus. Their duties are, first, to see that the unprepared corn in the market is offered for sale at reasonable prices, and secondly, to see that the millers sell barley meal at a price proportionate to that of barley, and that the bakers sell their loaves at a price proportionate to that of wheat, and of such weight as the Commissioners may appoint; for the law requires them to fix the standard weight.

There are ten Superintendents of the Mart, elected by lot, whose duty is to superintend the Mart, and to compel merchants to bring up into the city two-thirds of the corn which is brought by sea to the Corn Mart.

52 • The Eleven also are appointed by lot to take care of the prisoners in the state gaol. Thieves, kidnappers, and pick-pockets are brought to them, and if they plead guilty they are executed, but if they deny the charge the Eleven bring the case before the law-courts; if the prisoners are acquitted, they release them, but if not, they then execute them. They also bring up before the law-courts the list of farms and houses claimed as state-property; and if it is decided that they are so, they deliver them to the Commissioners for Public

Contracts. The Eleven also bring up informations laid against magistrates alleged to be disqualified; this function comes within their province, but some such cases are brought up by the Thesmothetae.

There are also five Introducers of Cases [Eisagogeis], elected by lot, one for each pair of tribes, who bring up the one-month cases to the law-courts. The one-month cases are these: refusal to pay up a dowry where a party is bound to do so, refusal to pay interest on money borrowed at 12 per cent., or where a man desirous of setting up business in the market has borrowed from another man capital to start with; also cases of slander, cases arising out of friendly loans or partnerships, and cases concerned with slaves, cattle, and the office of trierarch, or with banks. These are brought up as one-month cases and are introduced by these officers; but the Receivers-General perform the same function in cases for or against the farmers of taxes. Those in which the sum concerned is not more than ten drachmas they can decide summarily, but all above that amount they bring into the law-courts as one-month cases.

53 • The Forty are also elected by lot, four from each tribe, before whom suitors bring all other cases. Formerly they were thirty in number, and they went on circuit through the demes to hear causes; but after the oligarchy of the Thirty they were increased to forty. They have full powers to decide cases in which the amount at issue does not exceed ten drachmas, but anything beyond that value they hand over to the Arbitrators. The Arbitrators take up the case, and, if they cannot bring the parties to an agreement, they give a decision. If their decision satisfies both parties, and they abide by it, the case is at an end; but if either of the parties appeals to the law-courts, the Arbitrators enclose the evidence, the pleadings, and the laws quoted in the case in two urns, those of the plaintiff in the one, and those of the defendant in the other. These they seal up and, having attached to them the decision of the arbitrator, written out on a tablet, place them

in the custody of the four justices whose function it is to introduce cases on behalf of the tribe of the defendant. These officers take them and bring up the case before the law-court, to a jury of two hundred and one members in cases up to the value of a thousand drachmas, or to one of four hundred and one in cases above that value. No laws or pleadings or evidence may be used except those which were adduced before the Arbitrator, and have been enclosed in the urns.

The Arbitrators are persons in the sixtieth year of their age; this appears from the schedule of the Archons and the Eponymi. There are two classes of Eponymi, the ten who give their names to the tribes, and the forty-two of the years of service. The youths, on being enrolled among the citizens, were formerly registered upon whitened tablets, and the names were appended by the Archon in whose year they were enrolled, and by the Eponymus who had been in course in the preceding year; at the present day they are written on a bronze pillar, which stands in front of the Council-chamber, near the Eponymi of the tribes. Then the Forty take the last of the Eponymi of the years of service, and assign the arbitrations to the persons belonging to that year, casting lots to determine which arbitrations each shall undertake; and every one is compelled to carry through the arbitrations which the lot assigns to him. The law enacts that any one who does not serve as Arbitrator when he has arrived at the necessary age shall lose his civil rights, unless he happens to be holding some other office during that year, or to be out of the country. These are the only persons who escape the duty. Any one who suffers injustice at the hands of the Arbitrator may appeal to the whole board of Arbitrators, and if they find the magistrate guilty the law enacts that he shall lose his civil rights. The persons thus condemned have, however, in their turn an appeal. The Eponymi are also used in reference to military expeditions; when the men of military age are despatched on service, a notice is put up stating that the men from such-and-such an Archon and Eponymus to such-and-such another Archon and Eponymus are to go on the expedition.

54 · The following magistrates also are elected by lot: Five Commissioners of Roads [Hodopoei], who, with an assigned body of public slaves, are required to keep the roads in order; and ten Auditors, with ten assistants, to whom all persons who have held any office must give in their accounts. These are the only officers who audit the accounts of those who are subject to examination, and who bring them up for examination before the law-courts. If they detect any magistrate in embezzlement, the jury condemn him for theft, and he is obliged to repay tenfold the sum he is declared to have misappropriated. If they charge a magistrate with accepting bribes and the jury convict him, they fine him for corruption, and this sum too is repaid tenfold. Or if they convict him of unfair dealing, he is fined on that charge, and the sum assessed is paid without increase, if payment is made before the ninth prytany, but otherwise it is doubled. A tenfold fine is not doubled.

The Clerk of the Prytany, as he is called, is also elected by lot. He has the charge of all public documents, and keeps the resolutions which are passed by the Assembly, and checks the transcripts of all other official papers and attends at the sessions of the Council. Formerly he was elected by vote, and the most distinguished and trustworthy persons were elected to the post, as is known from the fact that the name of this officer is appended on the pillars recording treaties of alliance and grants of consulship and citizenship. Now, however, he is elected by lot. There is, in addition, a Clerk of the Laws, elected by lot, who attends at the sessions of the Council; and he too checks all the transcripts. The Assembly also elects by open vote a clerk to read documents to it and to the Council; but he has no other duty except that of reading aloud.

The Assembly also elects by lot the Commissioners of Public Worship [Hieropoei], known as the Commissioners for Sacrifices, who offer the sacrifices appointed by oracle, and, in conjunction with the seers, take the auspices whenever there is occasion. It also elects by lot ten others, known as Annual Commissioners, who offer certain sacrifices and administer all the quadrennial festivals except the Panathenaea. There are the following quadrennial festivals: first that of Delos (where there is also a sexennial festival), secondly the Brauronia, thirdly the Heracleia, fourthly the Eleusinia, and fifthly the Panathenaea; and no two of these are celebrated in the same place. To these the Hephaestia has now been added, in the archonship of Cephisophon.

An Archon is also elected by lot for Salamis, and a Demarch for Piraeus. These officers celebrate the Dionysia in these two places, and appoint Choregi. In Salamis, moreover, the name of the Archon is publicly recorded.

55 • All the foregoing magistrates are elected by lot, and their powers are those which have been stated. To pass on to the nine Archons, as they are called, the manner of their first establishment has been described already. At the present day six Thesmothetae are elected by lot, together with their clerk, and in addition to these an Archon, a King, and a Polemarch. One is elected from each tribe. They are examined first of all by the Council of Five Hundred, with the exception of the clerk. The latter is examined only in the law-court, like other magistrates (for all magistrates, whether elected by lot or by open vote, are examined before entering on their offices); but the nine Archons are examined both in the Council and again in the law-court. Formerly no one could hold the office if the Council rejected him, but now there is an appeal to the law-court, which is the final authority in the matter of the examination. When they are examined, they are asked, first, 'Who is your father, and of what deme? who is your father's father? who is your mother? who is your mother's father, and of what deme?' Then the candidate is asked whether he possesses an ancestral Apollo and a household Zeus, and where their sanctuaries are; next if he possesses a family tomb, and where; then if he treats his parents well, and pays his taxes, and has served on the required military expeditions. When the examiner has put these questions, he proceeds, 'Call the witnesses to these facts'; and when the candidate has produced his witnesses, he next asks, 'Does any one wish to make any accusation against this man?' If an accuser appears, he

gives the parties an opportunity of making their accusation and defence, and then puts it to the Council to pass the candidate or not, and to the law-court to give the final vote. If no one wishes to make an accusation, he proceeds at once to the vote. Formerly a single individual gave the vote, but now all the members are obliged to vote on the candidates, so that if any unprincipled candidate has managed to get rid of his accusers, it may still be possible for him to be disqualified before the law-court. When the examination has been thus completed, they proceed to the stone on which are the pieces of the victims, and on which the Arbitrators take oath before declaring their decisions, and witnesses swear to their testimony. On this stone the Archons stand, and swear to execute their office uprightly and according to the laws, and not to receive presents in respect of the performance of their duties, or, if they do, to dedicate a golden statue. When they have taken this oath they proceed to the Acropolis, and there they repeat it; after this they enter upon their office.

56 • The Archon, the King, and the Polemarch have each two assessors, nominated by themselves. These officers are examined in the law-court before they begin to act, and give in accounts on each occasion of their acting.

As soon as the Archon enters office, he begins by issuing a proclamation that whatever any one possessed before he entered into office, that he shall possess and hold until the end of his term. Next he assigns Choregi to the tragic poets, choosing three of the richest persons out of the whole body of Athenians. Formerly he used also to assign five Choregi to the comic poets, but now the tribes provide the Choregi for them. Then he receives the Choregi who have been appointed by the tribes for the men's and boy's choruses and the comic poets at the Dionysia, and for the men's and boy's choruses at the Thargelia (at the Dionysia there is a chorus for each tribe, but at the Thargelia one between two tribes, each tribe taking its turn in providing it); he transacts the exchanges of properties for them, and reports any excuses that are tendered, if any one says that he has already performed this service, or that he is exempt because he has performed some other service and the period of his exemption has not yet expired, or that he is not of the required age; for the Choregus of a boys' chorus must be over forty years of age. He also appoints Choregi for the festival at Delos, and a chief of the mission for the thirty-oar boat which conveys the youths thither. He also superintends sacred processions, both that in honour of Asclepius, when the initiated keep house, and that of the great Dionysia—the latter in conjunction with the Superintendents of that festival. These officers, ten in number, were formerly elected by open vote in the Assembly, and used to provide for the expenses of the procession out of their private means; but now one is elected by lot from each tribe, and the state contributes a hundred minas for the expenses. The Archon also superintends the procession at the Thargelia, and that in honour of Zeus the Saviour. He also manages the contests at the Dionysia and the Thargelia.

These, then, are the festivals which he superintends. The suits and indictments which come before him, and which he, after a preliminary inquiry, brings up before the law-courts, are as follows: injury to parents (for bringing these actions the prosecutor cannot suffer any penalty); injury to orphans (these actions lie against their guardians); injury to a ward of state (these lie against their guardians or their husbands); injury to an orphan's estate (these too lie against the guardians); mental derangement, where a party charges another with destroying his own property through unsoundness of mind; for appointment of liquidators, where a party refuses to divide property in which others have a share; for constituting a wardship; for determining between rival claims to a wardship; for granting inspection of property to which another party lays claim; for appointing oneself as guardian; and for determining disputes as to inheritances and wards of state. The Archon also has the care of orphans and wards of state, and of women who, on the death of their husbands, declare themselves to be with child; and he has power to inflict a fine on those who offend against the persons under his charge, or to bring the case before the law-courts. He also leases the houses of orphans and wards of state until they reach the age of fourteen, and takes mortgages on them; and if the guardians fail to provide the necessary food for the children under their charge, he exacts it from them. Such are the duties of the Archon.

57 • The King in the first place superintends the mysteries, in conjunction with the Superintendents of Mysteries. The latter are elected in the Assembly by open vote, two from the general body of Athenians, one from the Eumolpidae, and one from the Ceryces. Next, he superintends the Lenaean Dionysia, which consists of a procession and a contest. The procession is ordered by the King and the Superintendents in conjunction; but the contest is managed by the King alone. He also manages all the contests of the torch-race; and to speak broadly, he administers all the ancestral sacrifices. Indictments for impiety come before him, or any disputes between parties concerning priestly rites; and he also determines all controversies concerning sacred rites for the ancient families and the priests. All actions for homicide come before him, and it is he that makes the proclamation requiring polluted persons to keep away from sacred ceremonies. Actions for homicide and wounding are heard, if the homicide or wounding is willful, in the Areopagus; so also in cases of killing by poison, and of arson. These are the only cases heard by that Council. Cases of unintentional homicide, or of intent to kill, or of killing a slave or a resident alien or a foreigner, are heard by the court of Palladium. When the homicide is acknowledged, but legal justification is pleaded, as when a man takes an adulterer in the act, or kills another by mistake in battle or in an athletic contest, the prisoner is tried in the court of Delphinium. If a man who is in banishment for a homicide which admits of reconciliation incurs a further charge of killing or wounding, he is tried in Phreatto, and he makes his defence from a boat moored near the shore. All these cases, except those which are heard in the Areopagus, are tried by the Ephetae on whom the

lot falls. The King introduces them, and the hearing is held within sacred precincts and in the open air. Whenever the King hears a case he takes off his crown. The person who is charged with homicide is at all other times excluded from the temples, nor is it even lawful for him to enter the market-place; but on the occasion of his trial he enters the temple and makes his defence. If the actual offender is unknown, the writ runs against 'the doer of the deed'. The King and the tribe-kings also hear the cases in which the guilt rests on inanimate objects and animals.

58 • The Polemarch performs the sacrifices to Artemis the huntress and to Enyalius, and arranges the contest at the funeral of those who have fallen in war, and makes offerings to the memory of Harmodius and Aristogeiton. Only private actions come before him, namely those in which resident aliens, both ordinary and privileged, and agents of foreign states are concerned. It is his duty to receive these cases and divide them into ten groups, and assign to each tribe the group which comes to it by lot; after which the magistrates who introduce cases for the tribe hand them over to the Arbitrators. The Polemarch, however, brings up in person cases in which an alien is charged with deserting his patron or neglecting to provide himself with one, and also of inheritances and wards of state where aliens are concerned; and in fact, generally, whatever the Archon does for citizens, the Polemarch does for aliens.

59 • The Thesmothetae in the first place have the power of prescribing on what days the law-courts are to sit, and next of assigning them to the several magistrates; for the latter must follow the arrangement which the Thesmothetae assign. Moreover they introduce impeachments before the Assembly, and bring up all votes for removal from office, challenges of a magistrate's conduct before the Assembly, indictments for illegal proposals or for proposing a law which is contrary to the interests of the state, complaints against Proedri or their president for their conduct in office, and the

accounts presented by the generals. All indictments also come before them in which a deposit has to be made by the prosecutor, namely, indictments for concealment of foreign origin, for corrupt evasion of foreign origin (when a man escapes the disqualification by bribery), for blackmailing accusations, bribery, false entry of another as a state debtor, false testimony to the service of a summons, conspiracy to enter a man as a state debtor, corrupt removal from the list of debtors; and adultery. They also bring up the examinations of all magistrates, and the rejections by the demes and the condemnations by the Council. Moreover they bring up certain private suits in cases of merchandise and mines, or where a slave has slandered a free man. It is they also who cast lots to assign the courts to the various magistrates, whether for private or public cases. They ratify commercial treaties, and bring up the cases which arise out of such treaties; and they also bring up cases of perjury from the Areopagus. The casting of lots for the jurors is conducted by all the nine Archons, with the clerk to the Thesmothetae as the tenth, each performing the duty for his own tribe. Such are the duties of the nine Archons.

60 • There are also ten Commissioners of Games [Athlothetae], elected by lot, one from each tribe. These officers, after passing an examination, serve for four years; and they manage the Panathenaic procession, the contest in music and that in gymnastics, and the horse-race; they also provide the robe of Athena and, in conjunction with the Council, the vases, and they present the oil to the athletes. This oil is collected from the sacred olives. The Archon requisitions it from the owners of the farms on which the sacred olives grow, at the rate of three-quarters of a pint from each plant. Formerly the state used to sell the fruit itself, and if any one dug up or broke down one of the sacred olives, he was tried by the Council of Areopagus, and if he was condemned, the penalty was death. Since, however, the oil has been paid by the owner of the farm, the procedure has lapsed, though the law remains; and the oil is a state charge upon the property

instead of being taken from the individual plants. When then, the Archon has collected the oil for his year of office, he hands it over to the Treasurers to preserve in the Acropolis, and he may not take his seat in the Areopagus until he has paid over to the Treasurers the full amount. The Treasurers keep it in the Acropolis until the Panathenaea, when they measure it out to the Commissioners of Games, and they again to the victorious competitors. The prizes for the victors in the musical contest consist of silver and gold, for the victors in manly vigour, of shields, and for the victors in the gymnastic contest and the horse-race, of oil.

61 • All officers connected with military service are elected by open vote. In the first place, ten Generals [Strategi], who were formerly elected one from each tribe, but now are chosen from the whole mass of citizens. Their duties are assigned to them by open vote; one is appointed to command the heavy infantry, and leads them if they go out to war; one to the defence of the country, who remains on the defensive, and fights if there is war within the borders of the country; two to Piraeus, one of whom is assigned to Munichia, and one to the south shore, and these have charge of the defence of the Piraeus; and one to superintend the symmories, who nominates the trierarchs and arranges exchanges of properties for them, and brings up actions to decide on rival claims in connexion with them. The rest are dispatched to whatever business may be on hand at the moment. The appointment of these officers is submitted for confirmation in each prytany, when the question is put whether they are considered to be doing their duty. If any officer is rejected on this vote, he is tried in the lawcourt, and if he is found guilty the people decide what punishment or fine shall be inflicted on him; but if he is acquitted he resumes his office. The Generals have full power, when on active service, to arrest any one for insubordination, or to cashier him publicly, or to inflict a fine; the latter is, however, unusual.

There are also ten Taxiarchs, one from each tribe, elected by open vote; and each commands his own tribesmen and appoints captains of companies [Lochagi]. There are also two Hipparchs, elected by open vote from the whole mass of the citizens, who command the cavalry, each taking five tribes. They have the same powers as the Generals have in respect of the infantry, and their appointments are also subject to confirmation. There are also ten Phylarchs, elected by open vote, one from each tribe, to command the cavalry, as the Taxiarchs do the infantry. There is also a Hipparch for Lemnos, elected by open vote, who has charge of the cavalry in Lemnos. There is also a treasurer of the Paralus, and another of the Ammonias, similarly elected.

62 • Of the magistrates elected by lot, in former times some, including the nine Archons, were elected out of the tribe as a whole, while others, namely those who are now elected in the Theseum, were apportioned among the demes; but since the demes used to sell the elections, these magistrates too are now elected from the whole tribe, except the members of the Council and the guards, who are still left to the demes.

Pay is received for the following services. First the members of the Assembly receive a drachma for the ordinary meetings, and nine obols for the 'sovereign' meeting. Then the jurors at the law-courts receive three obols; and the members of the Council five obols. The Prytanes receive an allowance of an obol for their maintenance. The nine Archons receive four obols apiece for maintenance, and also keep a herald and a flute-player; and the Archon for Salamis receives a drachma a day. The Commissioners for Games dine in the Prytaneum during the month of Hecatombaeon in which the Panathenaic festival takes place, from the fourteenth day onwards. The Amphictyonic deputies to Delos receive a drachma a day from the exchequer of Delos. Also all magistrates sent to Samos, Scyros, Lemnos, or Imbros receive an allowance for their maintenance. The military offices may be held any number of times, but none of the others more than once, except the membership of the Council, which may be held twice.

63 • The juries for the law-courts are chosen by lot by the nine Archons, each for their own tribe, and by the clerk to the Thesmothetae for the tenth. There are ten entrances into the courts, one for each tribe; twenty rooms in which the lots are drawn, two for each tribe; a hundred chests, ten for each tribe; other chests, in which are placed the tickets of the jurors on whom the lot falls; and two vases. Further, staves, equal in number to the jurors required, are placed by the side of each entrance; and counters are put into one vase, equal in number to the staves. These are inscribed with letters of the alphabet beginning with the eleventh *(lambda)*, equal in number to the courts which require to be filled. All persons above thirty years of age are qualified to serve as jurors, provided they are not debtors to the state and have not lost their civil rights. If any unqualified person serves as juror, an information is laid against him, and he is brought before the court: if he is convicted, the jurors assess the punishment or fine which they consider him to deserve. If he is condemned to a money fine, he must be imprisoned until he has paid up both the original debt, on account of which the information was laid against him, and also the fine which the court has imposed upon him. Each juror has his ticket of box-wood, on which is inscribed his name, with the name of his father and his deme, and one of the letters of the alphabet up to *kappa*; for the jurors in their several tribes are divided into ten sections, with approximately an equal number in each letter. When the Thesmothetes has decided by lot which letters are required to attend at the courts, the servant puts up above each court the letter which has been assigned to it by the lot.

64 • The ten chests are placed in front of the entrance used by each tribe, and are inscribed with the letters of the alphabet from *alpha* to *kappa*. The jurors cast in their tickets, each into the chest on which is inscribed the letter which is on his ticket; then the servant shakes them all up, and the Thesmothetes draws one ticket from each chest. The individual so selected is called the Ticket-hanger [Empectes], and his function is to hang up the tickets out of his chest on the

bar which bears the same letter as that on the chest. He is chosen by lot, lest, if the Ticket-hanger were always the same person, he might tamper with the results. There are five of these bars in each of the rooms assigned for the lot-drawing. Then the Archon casts in the dice and thereby chooses the jurors from each tribe, room by room. The dice are made of bronze, coloured black or white; and according to the number of jurors required, so many white dice are put in, one for each five tickets, while the remainder are black, in the same proportion. As the Archon draws out the dice, the crier calls out the names of the individuals chosen. The Ticket-hanger is included among those selected. Each juror, as he is chosen and answers to his name, draws a counter from the vase, and holding it out with the letter uppermost shows it first to the presiding archon; and he, when he has seen it, throws the ticket of the juror into the chest on which is inscribed the letter which is on the counter, so that the juror must go into the court assigned to him by lot, and not into one chosen by himself, and that it may be impossible for any one to collect the jurors of his choice into any particular court. For this purpose chests are placed near the Archon, as many in number as there are courts to be filled that day, bearing the letters of the courts on which the lot has fallen.

65 • The juror thereupon, after showing his counter again to the attendant, passes through the barrier into the court. The attendant gives him a staff of the same colour as the court bearing the letter which is on his counter, so as to ensure his going into the court assigned to him by lot; since, if he were to go into any other, he would be betrayed by the colour of his staff. Each court has a certain colour painted on the lintel of the entrance. Accordingly the juror, bearing his staff, enters the court which has the same colour as his staff, and the same letter as his counter. As he enters, he receives a voucher from the official to whom this duty has been assigned by lot. So with their counters and their staves the selected jurors take their seats in the court, having thus completed the process

of admission. The unsuccessful candidates receive back their tickets from the Ticket-hangers. The public servants carry the chests from each tribe, one to each court, containing the names of the members of the tribe who are in that court, and hand them over to the officials, five in number,[5] assigned to the duty of giving back their tickets to the jurors in each court, so that these officials may call them up by name and pay them their fee.

66 • When all the courts are full, two ballot boxes are placed in the first court, and a number of bronze dice, bearing the colours of the several courts, and other dice inscribed with the names of the presiding magistrates. Then two of the Thesmothetae, selected by lot, severally throw the dice with the colours into one box, and those with the magistrates' names into the other. The magistrate whose name is first drawn is thereupon proclaimed by the crier as assigned for duty in the court which is first drawn, and the second in the second, and similarly with the rest. The object of this procedure is that no one may know which court he will have, but that each may take the court assigned to him by lot.

When the jurors have come in, and have been assigned to their respective courts, the presiding magistrate in each court draws one ticket out of each chest (making ten in all, one out of each tribe), and throws them into another empty chest. He then draws out five of them, and assigns one to the superintendence of the water-clock, and the other four to the telling of the votes. This is to prevent any tampering beforehand with either the superintendent of the clock or the tellers of the votes, and to secure that there is no malpractice in these respects. The five who have not been selected for these duties receive from them a statement of the order in which the jurors shall receive their fees, and of the places where the several tribes shall respectively gather in the court for this purpose when their duties are completed; the object being

[5] Reading ἀριθμῷ πέντε.

that the jurors may be broken up into small groups for the reception of their pay, and not all crowd together and impede one another.

67 • These preliminaries being concluded, the cases are called on. If it is a day for private cases, the private litigants are called. Four cases are taken in each of the categories defined in the law, and the litigants swear to confine their speeches to the point at issue. If it is a day for public causes, the public litigants are called, and only one case is tried. Water-clocks are provided, having small supply-tubes, into which the water is poured by which the length of the pleadings is regulated. Ten gallons are allowed for a case in which an amount of more than five thousand drachmas is involved, and three for the second speech on each side. When the amount is between one and five thousand drachmas, seven gallons are allowed for the first speech and two for the second; when it is less than one thousand, five and two. Six gallons are allowed for arbitrations between rival claimants, in which there is no second speech. The official chosen by lot to superintend the water-clock places his hand on the supply-tube whenever the clerk is about to read a resolution or law or affidavit or treaty. When, however, a case is conducted according to a set measurement of the day, he does not stop the supply, but each party receives an equal allowance of water. The standard of measurement is the length of the days in the month Poseideon[6]. . . . The measured day is employed in cases when imprisonment, death, exile, loss of civil rights, or confiscation of goods is assigned as the penalty.

68 • Most of the courts consist of 500 members . . . ;[7] and when it is necessary to bring public cases before a jury of 1,000 members, two courts combine for the purpose,. . . .[8] The ballot balls are made of bronze with stems running through

[6] The next ten lines in the papyrus are mutilated.
[7] The papyrus is mutilated at this point.
[8] The papyrus is mutilated here.

the centre, half of them having the stem pierced and the other half solid. When the speeches are concluded, the officials assigned to the taking of the votes give each juror two ballot balls, one pierced and one solid. This is done in full view of the rival litigants, to secure that no one shall receive two pierced or two solid balls. Then the official designated for the purpose takes away the jurors' staves, in return for which each one as he records his vote receives a brass voucher marked with the numeral 3 (because he gets three obols when he gives it up). This is to ensure that all shall vote; for no one can get a voucher unless he votes. Two urns, one of bronze and the other of wood, stand in the court, in distinct spots so that no one may surreptitiously insert ballot balls; in these the jurors record their votes. The bronze urn is for effective votes, the wooden for unused votes; and the bronze urn has a lid pierced so as to take only one ballot ball, in order that no one may put in two at a time.

When the jurors are about to vote, the crier demands first whether the litigants enter a protest against any of the evidence; for no protest can be received after the voting has begun. Then he proclaims again, 'The pierced ballot for the plaintiff, the solid for the defendant'; and the juror, taking his two ballot balls from the stand, with his hand closed over the stem so as not to show either the pierced or the solid ballot to the litigants, casts the one which is to count into the bronze urn, and the other into the wooden urn.

69 • When all the jurors have voted, the attendants take the urn containing the effective votes and discharge them on to a reckoning board having as many cavities as there are ballot balls, so that the effective votes, whether pierced or solid, may be plainly displayed and easily counted. Then the officials assigned to the taking of the votes tell them off on the board, the solid in one place and the pierced in another, and the crier announces the numbers of the votes, the pierced ballots being for the prosecutor and the solid for the defendant. Whichever has the majority is victorious; but if the votes are equal the verdict is for the defendant. Then, if damages have

to be awarded, they vote again in the same way, first returning their pay-vouchers and receiving back their staves. Half a gallon of water is allowed to each party for the discussion of the damages. Finally, when all has been completed in accordance with the law, the jurors receive their pay in the order assigned by the lot.

INDEX OF NAMES

SUBJECT INDEX